LGBTQ LOBBYING IN THE UNITED STATES

LGBTQ Lobbying in the United States argues that the issues and tactics prioritized by the mainstream gay lobbying community fail to serve LGBTQ interests and are complicit in perpetuating heteronormative power dynamics and institutions that render queer and trans people vulnerable to structural oppression.

The book posits that there are different LGBTQ lobbying communities—a dominant gay mainstream lobbying category, whose work advances heteronormative ideals, and a second category of LGBTQ lobbying that is intersectional and challenges hegemonic heterosexual institutions. Analysis in the book builds on existing public policy literature and is aided by the author's practitioner experience in lobbying for LGBTQ issues in Washington, D.C. over the past 20 years.

This book is suitable as a textbook for students and researchers in LGBTQ studies, U.S. politics, and gender studies. The book will also appeal to activists and professionals in political lobbying.

Christopher L. Pepin-Neff is a Senior Lecturer in Public Policy at the University of Sydney. His research focuses on emotional policymaking and LGBTQ politics. He was the first full-time lobbyist for the repeal of "don't ask, don't tell" and founder of Q Street, the LGBTQ lobbying association of Washington, D.C. He lives and works in both Burlington, Vermont, and Sydney, Australia.

LGBTQ LOBBYING IN THE UNITED STATES

Christopher L. Pepin-Neff

Routledge
Taylor & Francis Group

LONDON AND NEW YORK

First published 2021
by Routledge
2 Park Square, Milton Park, Abingdon, Oxon OX14 4RN

and by Routledge
605 Third Avenue, New York, NY 10158

Routledge is an imprint of the Taylor & Francis Group, an informa business

British Library Cataloguing-in-Publication Data
A catalogue record for this book is available from the British Library

Library of Congress Cataloging-in-Publication Data
Names: Pepin-Neff, Christopher L., author.
Title: LGBTQ lobbying in the United States / Christopher L. Pepin-Neff.
Other titles: Lesbian, gay, bisexual, transgender, queer lobbying in the United States
Description: Milton Park, Abingdon, Oxon; New York, NY: Routledge, 2021.
Includes bibliographical references and index.
Identifiers: LCCN 2020055394 (print) | LCCN 2020055395 (ebook) |
Subjects: LCSH: Sexual minorities–Political activity–United States. |
Lobbying–United States.
Classification: LCC HQ73.73.U6 P47 2021 (print) |
LCC HQ73.73.U6 (ebook) | DDC 306.760973–dc23
LC record available at https://lccn.loc.gov/2020055394
LC ebook record available at https://lccn.loc.gov/2020055395

ISBN: 978-0-367-77223-9 (hbk)
ISBN: 978-0-367-77222-2 (pbk)
ISBN: 978-1-003-17033-4 (ebk)

Typeset in Bembo
by Newgen Publishing UK

For Larry Kramer
(1935–2020)

CONTENTS

ILLUSTRATIONS

Figures

Tables

PREFACE

The most consequential event in the history of LGBTQ lobbying is the Government assassination of hundreds of thousands of people who had HIV/AIDS in the 1980s and 1990s. This killing continues every day as Black MSM are denied access to affordable PrEP.

An engagement on the topic of LGBTQ lobbying in the United States must contend with the immovable tragedy that is HIV/AIDS. Lobbying by the LGBTQ community is more about the people who are not here, than the people who are here. Many of the best and brightest, many of the youngest, poorest, smartest, and most marginalized were left to die through Government and public indifference. Many Black and Brown activists. And students. And teenagers that were fighting for the chance to live. They all died.

Thus, the titanic toll on LGBTQ people and the debt owed to those who died building the advocacy community is unrepayable.

Specifically, the HIV/AIDS political assassinations, where LGBTQ lobbyists and activists were murdered by the affirmative and knowing neglect and negligence of the Reagan-Bush Governments and associated agencies, killing hundreds of thousands of people between the early 1980s and mid-1990s. This was violence. Judith Butler summaries violence this way:

> Michel Foucault distinguished between forms of sovereign violence, whereby a king, a monarch, or someone vested with a sovereign power, decides who should live and who should die. And there's a form of violence that he called biopolitical and that Cameroonian philosopher Achille Mbembe calls necropolitics: violence that leaves a set of people to die, abandons them to death, or refuses to offer the assistance that is necessary in order to save their lives.
>
> *(Terry & Butler, 2020)*

The AIDS political assassinations in the United States loom as an active and affirmative legacy over any discussion of the LGBTQ community. The mobilization of the LGBTQ community at both the state and federal level occurred due to the AIDS crisis (Gould, 2009), which killed 176,000 LGBTQ people between 1981 and 1995, just before the first antiretroviral drugs became available. This includes a long list of trailblazing LGBTQ lobbyists and activists. For instance, some of the best organizers the LGBTQ community has ever seen included Vietnam veteran Leonard Matlovich; Rodger McFarlane (the first paid executive director of Gay Men's Health Crisis); Steve Endean (the first paid executive director of what became the Human Rights Campaign); Spencer Cox from ACT UP New York; AIDS educator Pedro Zamora; and Simon Nkoli, who founded the first Black gay group in South Africa. All had AIDS and died before their time.

AIDS is an example where the LGBTQ community was thought so little of and demonized so greatly that their deaths raised little concern among the political class. To be clear, homophobia, sexism, racism, transphobia, ablism, and classism were weaponized by the U.S. Government to intentionally kill tens of thousands of people affected by AIDS. This included actions against HIV-positive communities that were Black, poor, female, transgender, nonbinary, and disabled. The fallout from murdering more than 100,000 trans and queer people at the foot of political fortresses that celebrate and invite LGBTQ assassination points to the desperate need for LGBTQ lobbying today. Because the murders and assassinations continue. For those trans women murdered and invisible, like Neulisa Luciano Ruiz in Puerto Rico. For the lesbians with cancer and no health insurance in Maryland. For the non-binary youth and adults, 42 percent of whom will attempt suicide. For those bisexual men caught in a police sting in Tampa. Police stings do not deter consensual sex, they criminalize gay sex in Florida in 2020 in order to destroy people's lives. It further penalizes HIV status because one of the penalties is HIV compulsory testing. Lobbying loses a lot. But there is fabulousness in trying. Once again, for all those lost to HIV/AIDS, RIP.

References

Butler, J., & Terry, B. M. (2020, January 7). The radical equity of lives. *Boston Review*. http://bostonreview.net/philosophy-religion/brandon-m-terry-judith-butler-radical-equality-lives

Gould, D.B. (2009). *Moving Politics: Emotion and ACT UP's Fight Against AIDS*. University of Chicago Press.

ACKNOWLEDGMENTS

I would first like to thank my family: my grandmother Virginia H. Pepin, my mother Barbara J. Pepin-Neff, and my twin brother David M. Neff. My work in LGBTQ rights and academia have only been possible because of them.

Next, this book is a tribute to the extraordinary bravery of AIDS activists.

I also owe a special debt to my friend and mentor Dr. Frank Kameny. I am also thankful for Kathi Westcott and Jeff Cleghorn who gave me my first shot at being an LGBTQ lobbyist. In addition, there are a great many friends and peers to thank for their support over the years. These include: Kristin Caporale, James Cox, Dr. Senthorun Raj, Alexander Sexton, Mary Langer, and Jamie Sheehan. I am also thankful for Dr. Stewart Jackson, Linda Neff, Timothy Moynagh, Dr. Christine Winter, Ian Palmquist, Eric Stern, Luke Edgell, Zachary Underwood, Alec Papazian, Danny Hammel, Paula Neira, Ken St. Pierre, Dr. Nathaniel Frank, Dave Noble, Kevin Cain, Toni Broadus, Kelly Young, Liz Hill, Ruby Hillsmith, Kathy Phillips, Kim King, Dr. Jen Hunt, Associate Professor Anika Gauja, Chris Pycroft, Professor Rodney Smith, Professor David Schlosberg, Professor Ariadne Vromen, Professor Allan McConnell, Professor Duncan Ivison, Professor Lisa Atkins, Professor Annamarie Jagose, Adam Myrick, John Geddes Lawrence, Tyron Garner, Elaine Nobel, James Dale, Larry Kramer, Michel Dubois, David Hall, Dan Choi, David Lett, Katie Miller, Lisa Mottet, Kasey Suffredini, Joanne Howes, Bridget Wilson, Sarah Wentz, Christian Berle, Damon Fitch, Jeffrey Guillot, Tim Lucason, Akira Yamaguchi, Scott Bonneau, Ben Abraham, Pat Monahan, Paige Burton, Scott Hendrichsen, Steven McDonnell, Alexander Johnston, Dr. Adam Grundt, Val Draper, Heather Robson, Kirsten Andrews, Dr. Eloise Brook, Clare Wood, Obie Wood-Brooks, Riki Wilchins, Gina Reiss, Chris Labonte, Kevin Ivers, Rich Tafel, Mick Everts, Matt McTighe, Pete Leon, Chris Hartmann, Lauren Briggerman, Sarah Wentz, Karen Armagost, Mieke Eoyang, Lucy Sunman, Professor Sarah Maddison, Hayley Comet, James Blackwell, Stephen Maoudis, Professor Gemma

Carey, Dr. David Shiffman, Sharon Alexander, Nadine Smith, Adam Marshand, Ryan Miller, Adam Smith, Norrie, John Marble, Eric Manke, Chris Geidner, Diane Mazur, Brad Luna, Shin Inouye, Heather Sheets, Clark Bucko, Jeff Trammell, Kevin Casey, Todd Houchins, Bryan Hughes, my Routledge Editor Alexandra McGregor, and Timothy Williams.

A longstanding thank you to Senator John Warner, Senator Ted Kennedy, Senator Harry Reid, Senator Daniel Akaka, Justice Anthony Kennedy, and the Notorious RBG. Also, the Department of Government and International Relations at the University of Sydney, The Bookshop Darlinghust, Lambda Rising, Servicemembers Legal Defense Network, Gay and Lesbian Activists Alliance, GenderPAC, Q Street, the Equality Federation, and Outright Vermont. Additionally, a very special thanks to my excellent research assistants Aaron Cohen and Alexander Webb. And finally, thank you to Jason Gonzalez and the staff and patrons of Onxy Tonics in Burlington, Vermont where many of these ideas were hashed out over hot chocolates.

I acknowledge that this book was written on the unceded land of the Abenaki people in Vermont and Gadigal people of the Eora Nation in Sydney who have cared for it for generations and continue to do so. I pay my respects to their Elders past and present.

1

LGBTQ LOBBYING

Introduction

Gay mainstream lobbying benefits heterosexual institutions *more* than it helps trans and queer people.

The central argument of this book is that mainstream gay lobbying in Washington, D.C. does not serve LGBTQ people. The white, gay, cis, English-speaking, Global North, male mainstream lobbying establishment in D.C. (and the broader mainstream gay movement) is complicit in perpetuating heteronormative power dynamics and institutions that render LGBTQ people vulnerable to structural oppression. Indeed, this is the story of a remarkable, once-in-a-generation political success for heterosexuality. The 20-year capitulation to heteronormative gay mainstream priorities and the demonization of LGBTQ lobbying and LGBTQ tactics has ushered in the fastest civil rights evolution in American history to the benefit of heterosexual institutions.

LGBTQ lobbying is a category of lobbying that is fundamentally different than gay mainstream lobbying.

LGBTQ lobbying is intersectional in nature and centers the marginalized. It challenges heterosexual institutions as well as mainstream gay lobbying and hegemonic organizations, which serve to advance heteronormative ideals. "Hegemony refers to the permeation of 'a way of life' or 'social organization' into every sphere of society and is a crucial mechanism by which the ruling power dominates" (Seybold, 1987: 176). In this case, we are talking about large organizations that dominate a policy area. This book argues that the gay mainstream lobbying has gained support from business and conservative sectors of the country by conforming to heterosexual institutions and thereby expanding hegemonic heterosexuality. While one is trying to sustain itself, the other is trying to put itself out of business. Therefore, the question that motivates this book addresses the tension about why advocacy on LGBTQ issues is not always designed to help LGBTQ people.

The question driving this book is: *Under what pressures and at what costs does LGBTQ lobbying occur?*

Pressure is about choice. The pressure on the type of lobbying people do to have access to power (McCann, 2011). This includes the influence on lobbyists to address or ignore certain issues and tactics. This impacts the agenda-setting process. In order to gain access to authority, lobbyists must make choices that return power to the powerful. For lobbyists who work on LGBTQ issues and tactics, this pressure comes in the form of heteronormative structures that encourage lobbyists to adopt more gay mainstream efforts and conform to the white, cis, male, English-speaking straight community, including those who do not have a disability. This political compromise gains gay mainstream lobbyists access to certain degrees of power. As a result, I argue in this book that LGBTQ lobbying has largely been a failure in the United States because the dominant focus is on benefiting heterosexual institutions.

Heteronormative power dynamics place extensive costs on lobbyists because LGBTQ issues and tactics are viewed as "loser issues" politically (Neff & Edgell, 2013: 235). For instance, there are political hurdles to engaging on issues related to trans sex work. Or poverty. Or homelessness. There may also be financial costs to changing a model of fundraising, or political costs to engaging in tactics that adversely disrupt the political system.

To distinguish between gay mainstream lobbying and LGBTQ lobbying, two different definitions are needed. For instance, they do not represent the same goals for power dynamics, and they have different relationships with the legislative and executive branches. To begin, I offer a unique definition of "lobbying." As a former lobbyist in Washington, D.C., I argue that lobbying is not about obtaining federal funding for a pet project, attaining a tax loophole, or keeping seals protected in the Atlantic. Lobbyists want to negotiate power. This book looks at the role of power in lobbying over the past 20 years.

I define lobbying as:

1. The negotiation of power in the executive and legislative branches in ways that return power to the powerful; and
2. The use of the "heterosexual ask" to prioritize or avoid certain issues, set limits on the degree of change, and contain discomfort to the powerful.

Importantly, this definition of lobbying preferences power and penalties above law and policy. The lobbyist's "ask" is an under-analyzed element of the agenda-setting process for the executive and legislative branches. The "ask" is the political action that is being requested by a lobbyist of the legislative and/or executive branches relative to the discomfort caused to an office or member. Shaw (2014: S44) states, "General principles around advocacy include a clear goal (the 'ask'), the rationale for why this issue is important, and a determination of what can be measured to determine success." Whereas Avner (2016: 404) argues that "Lobbying is the work that the organization does to prepare for the 'ask'—the request, for instance, to the head of the State House of Representative's Housing Committee to support a particular proposal."

An ask is the chief tactic of a lobbyist, after prioritizing an issue. It establishes if the marginalized stay marginalized, if the powerful keep power, and if difficulty will bring discomfort. Put another way, the "ask" is important because it is designed as a trade between a high proximity to power and a low proximity to penalty, which is why it returns power to power. Because power returning to power does not create distress for the powerful.

As a result, the "ask" is better construed as the "heterosexual ask," because the trade, the process, and the power in question is heteronormative.

The introduction of the "heterosexual ask" reveals that the agenda in agenda-setting is heterosexual. The issue in issue emergence is that the implementation of public policy is done in ways that advantage heterosexuality as a set of structures and institutions. This is the contribution that LGBTQ lobbying makes as a concept to both lobbying studies, LGBTQ studies, and public policy.

The "heterosexual ask" is most often recognized at the agenda-setting (identifying issues) stage of the policy process, while lobbyists act at every stage of the policy cycle. However, I argue that "the heterosexual ask" is common at the decision stage, which Howlett and Ramesh (2003) refer to as adoption. At this stage, there is close proximity to power. This period includes what is prioritized, the proposed solution, and the estimated political cost to take the action. This is a moment of recognizing where power is exchanged *before* policy action occurs. It might be in committee, a staff briefing, or Dear Colleague letter, but this request may be for action or stasis.

I define LGBTQ lobbying as:

1. The negotiation of power in the executive and legislative branches, in ways that disrupt the return of power to the powerful, from a position of disadvantage; and
2. The use of the "LGBTQ ask" to re-prioritize issues that center the marginalized and demand total equity, now.

LGBTQ lobbyists are resistance entrepreneurs: provocateurs and expert troublemakers to heterosexual dominance. The "LGBTQ ask" embraces an intersectional view of politics (Crenshaw, 1991). The "LGBTQ ask" stands out in the policy process for being important at both the decision-making stage of the policy cycle and the implementation stage. For marginalized groups, policy enactment, power redistribution, and stigma removal take more than a change in statute. Indeed, LGBTQ progress is not progress if the product of lobbying does not disrupt the benefits, rewards, and privileges that racism, sexism, homophobia, transphobia, and ableism confer on identities of whiteness, straightness, cisness, maleness, and ability.

The "LGBTQ ask" provides important insights about power in policymaking in the United States. It says that Congress and the White House are designed to be homophobic and transphobic. The policymaking process in the United States is homophobic and transphobic. As a result, LGBTQ lobbying must begin by addressing this power relationship, between the oppressed and an oppressor.

LGBTQ lobbyists face an adversarial political relationship in which the only true question is whether the lobbyist will serve the function of returning power to heteronormative policies and institutions that oppress them or whether the lobbyist will disrupt and challenge these systems and structures. This is important because a political system that is designed to return power back to the oppressors and to which we enthusiastically codify as lobbyists ensures second-class status for LGBTQ people. It is from this position of disadvantage and contestation with the policy process that the LGBTQ lobbyist works and asks for equity on behalf of all marginalized populations immediately, in total, and permanently. Thus, the implications of the "LGBTQ ask" is proposed as *equality permanence*. LGBTQ lobbying does not abandon one group, to provide shelter for another or afford those in power incremental discomfort.

Literature review

In this section, I build on the idea of "hegemonic heterosexuality" as a lobbying and public policy concept.

This book provides evidence to support the idea that hegemonic heterosexuality influences lobbying in ways that determine the power dynamics in the legislative and executive branches. This includes the way issues are prioritized or avoided in a lobbyist's "ask." Hegemonic heterosexuality is also a concept to be expounded upon in lobbying and policy studies. It has been reviewed in a number of contexts in the academic literature. Phillips (1991: 461) takes a sociological approach and notes that "the heterosexist hegemony presents the man–woman relationship as the standard for comparison." Bibbings (2009: 46) looks at the issue of the "heterostate" in a criminal justice context and argues that "beneath the supposedly calm waters of decriminalization, anti-discrimination, recognition and rights lies a hegemonic heterosexuality which still embraces very similar notions of acceptability to those of the 1970s." The regulation of lives is reviewed in a film studies analysis of the movie *Boys Don't Cry* where Brandon Teena is raped and murdered for being a man whose gender was assigned female at birth. Yamamoto (2017: 137) states, "Once they proved Brandon was biologically female, their idea of reinforcing gender binaries and hegemonic heterosexuality was through rape and violence."

The research in this area has been ground-breaking and includes hegemonic masculinity as a key concept. This has been noted by Noah Brand (2012), who says, "hegemonic heterosexuality is the model for straight relationships that carries as many damaging, ridiculous, impossible assumptions and requirements as does hegemonic masculinity." Raewyn Connell (2002) developed the concept of "hegemonic masculinity" and notes that it represents the unreachable idealized idea of masculinity. Connell and Messerschmidt (2005: 832) state that it is considered the "most honored way of being a man, it required all other men to position themselves in relation to it, and it ideologically legitimated the global subordination of women to men."

Hegemonic masculinity, hegemonic heterosexuality, and heteronormativity illustrate the way power dynamics (like jobs, housing, marriage, weddings, adoption, churches, medical visits, the military, police, and teaching) are all structurally privileged by society to reward heterosexuality as an institution. McCann (2011: 253) quotes Berlant and Warner's definition of heteronormativity as, "a constellation of practices that everywhere disperses heterosexual privilege as a tacit but central organizing index of social membership" (2002: 195). Thus, much like whiteness, heterosexuality remains an invisible, yet privileged center. It is everywhere and nowhere at the same time (see Nakayama & Krizek, 1995).

Hegemonic heterosexuality is important as a concept that is located in "lobbying studies" because it sets the terms of "the heterosexual ask" (Bird, 2014; Richardson & John, 2009). As noted, this "ask" is both more heterosexual and less LGBTQ at the same time.

The implication of the heterosexual ask is equality governance.

Equality governance is a lobbyist's or special interest group's request for limited equality relative to the discomfort of the powerful, from a position of advantage. Put another way, the lobbyist cares more about the discomfort of the powerful and cares less about the inequality of the LGBTQ population. Indeed, while disadvantage can mean an intersectional political approach, or a feminist approach, or embracing queerness and transness, lobbying from a position of advantage prioritizes whiteness, maleness, class, nation of origin, cisgender, people who do not have a disability, and heterosexuality.

In addition, hegemonic heterosexuality provides a critical lens with which to examine policies that are designed to marginalize non-heterosexual sexualities and identities. Much like the efforts of political scientists Anne Schneider and Helen Ingram (1993) in their social construction of target populations framework, the influence of hegemonic heterosexuality can be seen in examinations of categories of lobbying and types of tactics. In addition, as a concept within the policymaking process, I take hegemonic heterosexuality a step further and define it in three parts:

First, hegemonic heterosexuality gives more politically to lobbyists that honor it. For instance, "religious liberty" laws that are purported to protect the institution of marriage from homosexuals and transgender people are designed to return power to the overwhelmingly dominant norm of idealized white, male, cisgender, religious, heterosexuality (Garcia, 2009). This includes opposite sex attraction, opposite sex activity, and gender-appropriate performative relationships.

Hegemonic heterosexuality relies on the biases of political systems to maintain the rewards of sexuality and gender. As a default, the political process is heterosexual. In other words, the LGBTQ community members are guests of a heterosexual, cisgender, male, and white society. This is the dominant sexuality, and it commands the behavior of political institutions and lobbying structures. Alternatives to this are punished by systems and structures. Indeed, the effect of this is to enforce compulsory male-driven, white supremacist, religious heterosexuality on individuals in society. Heterosexuality is therefore seen as a site of policy power. Yet, it is more than the ultimate ideal to be obtained, but an institutional political structure that requires forms of performative heterosexuality as a gateway to citizenship and equal rights (work, accommodation, adoption).

The "heterosexual ask" demonstrates an anti-gay performative structure. The "ask" should not be too "feminist," too "queer," too "sexual," too "kinky," too "perverted." Also, not too "Black," too trans, too emotional, too uncomfortable, too disruptive, too demanding, too early, too late, or too far outside the congressperson or Senator's jurisdiction.

Second, hegemonic heterosexuality costs less politically. The "heterosexual ask" gets more and costs less. If a lobbyist is performing heterosexuality, returning power to heterosexual institutions then they are not perceived as disruptive to the established political system and therefore the cost for doing non-threatening business is low. However, structures and institutions also perform a function of complicity with oppression by continuing to establish queer sexualities as "the other."

Hegemonic heterosexuality creates a dominant narrative, discourse, and social policy that negates the personal existence of sexual minorities and those who are gender non-conforming. It invalidates the celebration of the sex they have and erases their relationships. In short, fucking and relationships are the property of the majority. The righteousness of heteronormativity is therefore enforced by institutional heterosexuality and the lobbying that returns heterosexual power back to the heterosexual powerful.

Third, hegemonic heterosexuality is influential at key points in the lobbying process in disrupting LGBTQ equality. Lobbying is the tip of the spear in being an accomplice to oppression, and complicit to inequality. It is an essential element of public policy distortion, to pervert equality. Put another way, lobbying on LGBTQ issues with a "heterosexual ask" demonstrates equality governance and together these are essential to maintaining the reproduction of marginalization of vulnerable LGBTQ communities. Lobbying's "heterosexual ask" for equality governance is essential to continued discrimination because it communicates the desire for inequality to those in power. It assures that those in power understand that we will ask for too little, demand too little, penalize too little, in order to achieve too little.

Importantly, this book also looks at the role of lobbying with social movements in the policy process.

I argue that there are two fundamentally different movements at work in the LGBTQ advocacy community. There are the gay mainstream movement and gay mainstream lobbying that has gained support from business and conservative sectors of the country by conforming to heterosexual institutions and thereby expanding hegemonic heterosexuality. And there is a second, radical queer movement with LGBTQ lobbying that challenges heterosexual institutions and mainstream LGBTQ hegemonic organizations, which serve to advance heteronormative ideals. While one is trying to sustain itself, the other is trying to put itself out of business.

The connection between these two elements of LGBTQ advocacy has not been fully explored. Brettschneider (2017: 11) notes that "relatively little scholarly attention has been paid to examining politics within a [sic] GLBT umbrella." Zein Murib in his 2017 book chapter, "Rethinking GLBT as a Political Category in U.S. Politics" states that there is "relatively little scholarly attention devoted to understanding the politics that occur *within* [sic] GLBT" (2017: 14). Moreover, Vaid (2012: 11) notes that when LGBTQ issues are raised, they are done so in specific ways: "Equality as it is currently articulated in the LGBT movement represents a politics of compliance with liberalism/capitalism rather than a critique of the exclusions these systems perpetuate."

In my analysis of "who" lobbies, the selection of the person is a tactic of lobbying, not an essential characteristic of lobbying. Volunteer lobbyists at the federal legislative and executive level count. It is also helpful to see that grassroots lobbying is acknowledged in the literature as a lobbying process within the policy process. Nownes (2006: 25) notes that "both Berry and Milbrath concluded that meeting personally with government officials (though neither specifies which government officials) and engaging in grassroots lobbying are particularly effective lobbying techniques."

There is also the question of where lobbying fits into social movement organizing. This is important because I am arguing not only that lobbying occurs in social movements, but that the differences in the types of lobbying in the LGBTQ advocacy community highlight the presence of two different social movements: the gay mainstream lobbying and radical queer movement. Essentially, I am arguing that there are many parts to social movements, and these include individuals and groups that lobby. As simple as this sounds, the literature paints a more restrictive picture that I am going to push back against. For instance, there are narrow views that separate lobbying from social movements, such as Diani (1992: 1), who argues that "social movements are defined as networks of informal interactions between a plurality of individuals, groups and/or organizations, engaged in political or cultural conflicts, on the basis of shared collective identities."

Diani adds "that the concept is sharp enough (a) to differentiate social movements from related concepts such as interest groups, political parties, protest events, and coalitions; (b) to identify a specific area of investigation and theorising for social movement research" (1992: 1). However, there are also those who do not see such a drastic distinction. Hrebenar and Morgan (2009: 10) note in their review that "some recent research has noted the difficulty in clearly separating interest groups from social movements."

Data

Problems with current definitions of lobbying

Queer and transgender (referred to as LGBTQ) lobbying in the lesbian, gay, bisexual, transgender, and queer community (also LGBTQ) is arguably protected by the U.S. Constitution. The Constitution states:

> Congress shall make no law respecting an establishment of religion, or prohibiting the free exercise thereof; or abridging the freedom of speech, or of the press; or the right of the people peaceably to assemble, and to petition the Government for a redress of grievances.

Importantly, while there is no specific Constitutional ruling protecting the right of lobbyists to "petition the government," LGBTQ lobbying has enjoyed the legal ambiguity of this issue. Indeed, in the face of federal and state governments assassinating LGBTQ Americans with HIV/AIDS, failing to represent LGBTQ Americans, and neglecting to deliver to them the rights enshrined in the Constitution, these events have historically eroded the relationship between LGBTQ people and the State.

Lobbying has been an important bridge between LGBTQ people and the fight against federally sanctioned political prejudice. Indeed, lobbyists on LGBTQ issues have endured—from marching in 1961 in front of the White House for federal equality; to the start of the longest continuous lobbying organization in 1971; the de-listing of homosexuality as a mental disorder in 1973; the 1991 Ryan White Care Act funding; 2009 Hate Crimes law; and 2010 "Don't Ask, Don't Tell" Repeal Act. There is a patchwork of lobbying in the LGBTQ community that has played key roles in the development of LGBTQ rights in the United States.[1]

The different types of LGBTQ victories highlight the mechanics of lobbying. There are registered lobbyists who are paid by an organization and file reports with the Secretary of the Senate. There are grassroots lobbyists who are unpaid volunteers and interns who march, meet with a member of congress, and/or write emails to the President. On these later tactics, you might hear them called "keyboard warriors."

Lobbying can be done alone or in groups—by those being paid, self-employed consultants, volunteers, and interns; by former Presidents, congresspeople, governors, or former staffers. Lobbying can be done by people working on one issue at an organization or many issues at a firm. It can also be divided into Republican and Democratic clients. There are silent lobbyists who go to meetings and are not authorized to speak.

The bridge between the State and the LGBTQ advocacy community also includes literature on the way lobbyists interact with social movements. For instance, the public policy and lobbying literature focuses on technical processes of lobbying (Godwin, Ainsworth, & Godwin, 2013; Richan, 2006; Scott, 2018), and the role of interest groups in lobbying (Cigler, Loomis, & Nownes, 2016; Hindman, 2019;

Hula, 1999; Strolovitch, 2007). Two others, Baumgartner, Berry, Hojnacki, Leech, & Kimball (2009) and Kingdon (1995) look at the role of lobbyists in agenda setting.

In LGBTQ literature, there are important reviews of LGBTQ social movements, history and politics; however, this does not include an examination of LGBTQ lobbying. An understanding of LGBTQ lobbying is not possible without noting the existing literature on LGBTQ studies. This work includes narratives on disability (Guter & Killacy, 2004; Luczak, 2015; McRuer, 2006), trans rights, (Currah, Juang, & Minter, 2006; Spade, 2009; Stryker, 2008; Wilchins, 2004), and intersex history (Harper, 2007). Indigenous experiences (Hodge, 2015), race (Johnson & Henderson, 2005; Quesada, Gomez, & Vidal-Ortiz, 2015), Radical Faeries (Thompson, 2011), and legal issues and activism (Barclay, Bernstein, & Marshall, 2009; Mezey, 2007; Mogul, Ritchie, & Whitlock, 2011; Raj, 2020). And political issues like non-profit management (Beam, 2018; Ward, 2008), the advancement of the movements (Adam, 1995; Armstrong, 2002; Bell, 2020; D'Emilio, Turner, & Vaid, 2000; Endean, 2006; Faderman, 2015; Rimmerman, 2015; Stewart-Winter, 2016; Stulberg, 2018; Vaid, 1995), marriage equality (Solomon, 2014), HIV/AIDS (Gould, 2009), marches (Ghaziani, 2008), and "don't ask, don't tell" (Haley, 1999).

There are several problems that challenge the current definition of lobbying: one is the emphasis on lobbying as the transaction taken to enact an issue into law, rather than the prioritization of an issue to distribute power, the cover-up of another issue, and the selection of an "ask" as a tactic that imposes a degree of discomfort on policy process. This is at odds with Baumgartner et al. (2009) who wrote a key text, "Lobbying and Policy Change." In it, they state "lobbying is about changing existing public policies" (Baumgartner et al., 2009: 19). This is supported by Avner (2016: 398) who looks specifically at non-profit lobbying and notes that, "Non-profit lobbying involves asking an elected official to take a particular position on a specific legislative proposal."

Under federal law and the Lobbying Disclosure Act, the United States Senate defines lobbying, stating:

> The term "lobbying activities" means lobbying contacts and efforts in support of such contacts, including preparation and planning activities, research and other background work that is intended, at the time it is performed, for use in contacts, and coordination with the lobbying activities of others.

However, I argue that lobbyists often (but not always) design their overall work to prioritize certain issues that return benefits to themselves by maintaining existing systems of power. Here, the "contacts" are the companies that hire them, but there is also an argument in the literature about the representative nature of lobbying. For instance, Berry (1977: 5) notes that "the act of lobbying is, in very general terms, an act of representation." This is not always true. Lobbyists may have more political capital than their organization or their membership. Therefore, there is no allegiance or direction to be taken except those that help the lobbyist. In addition, the issue of a constituency may be dubious. Special interests often boost their membership numbers to create the appearance of a larger constituency. Indeed, this argument about representation is often used to affirm the democratic nature of lobbying. While some would suggest that lobbying is unethical, others would say lobbyists work for under-represented groups to ensure they have a voice in the policy process. In truth, lobbyists work first for themselves. Follow the power, and you will find the lobbyist.

In addition, Baumgartner et al. (2009: 50) note that lobbying is about coalition building, rules, and attention. They state that lobbying is about, "how to get enough key players to pay attention, how to get enough support to move legislation forward, or how to mobilize enough participants to kill a bill." However, I argue that this is not always possible for LGBTQ issues because many of these issues come from a place of politically less power and because infighting means rallying other organizations to impose penalties is unworkable. Not all groups are trusted the same. I have been in coalition meetings in the Senate where the meeting was performative. After a key member left the room, the meeting was replayed with actual decisions made.

These are consistent with Scott (2018: 145) who combines several of the points. He argues that for lobbyists, "the primary relationship is with the client." Second is "lobbyists working together," and the third is the "politician and the lobbyist."

However, lobbying for a non-profit can be different than a business or trade association. There are handbooks for non-profit lobbying (Avner, Wise, Narabrook, Fox, & Brown, 2013) but little has been done specifically on lobbyist actions as opposed to interest group actions. Indeed, much of the literature points to lobbyists as an outside influence on the policy process, on the "outside looking in" (Baumgartner et al., 2009: 8). This is incorrect. Lobbyists are often more inside the system than the congressional staff or members themselves. In reality, lobbyists are frequently inside players. For instance, as a lobbyist, I was once asked by a congressional staff member to manage a speaker list on the floor of the House of Representatives. I watched on C-SPAN as members came to the floor. I sent staff their talking points, put all the members in order and watched them deliver my remarks.

And not all lobbyists are the same. Some are issue experts, from the biggest organization, in control of the most money. Some are from a key population, some are the closest to the office and have worked there, some have slept with the staff, and some used to be members themselves.

An important part of lobbying is what issues are not raised and what "asks" are not made. This issue requires more attention in lobbying studies. The idea of not choosing to ask for something has not been widely addressed by the lobbying literature. McConnell (2018: 1740) conducts important new work on "hidden agendas" in public policy and notes, "it is unsurprising that political scientists and policy analysts have steered clear of tackling such an elusive and grey phenomenon."

I would like to emphasize the independence of lobbyists. As an expert on both the issue and the legislative and executive process, lobbyists largely act at their discretion. The literature states, "lobbyists are not free to do as they please" (Baumgartner et al., 2009: 111). However, lobbyists decide what and when to make an "ask" and respond to shifting political winds. I have been in meetings getting shouted at and had to respond in kind, I've been told an issue is dead and had to bring it back to life. These were in-the-moment decisions independent of the groups for whom I worked.

There are two operational details that I would note. The first is recognizing how busy congressional staff and members are. Baumgartner et al. (2009) state that attention toward issues is scarce. It is important to consider when looking at lobbying meetings as a metric (for instance) that staff and members do not have time to meet, and the best lobbyists will recognize this and work around it. Second is the influence of family members. There are a number of issues where family members have made the difference, including Rob Portman, Dick Cheney, Doug Jones, and Matt Salmon on LGBTQ rights and Jeb Bush on immigration.

For example, I was working with a conservative Senator while the Federal Marriage Amendment to create a new amendment to the U.S. Constitution in order to ban same-sex marriage was under consideration. On the day of vote, he was visited by the Bishop of the local Diocese. The Bishop stayed in his office lobbying the Senator to vote in favor of the amendment until the floor vote. As the time arrived to go down to vote, the Senator called his daughter into his office and asked her what he thought of the amendment. In front of the Bishop, she said, "I just think it's wrong." The Senator walked out of the office and voted no. All the professional lobbying in the world, and the lobbying by the Bishop were unable to compete with the opinion and potential disappointment of his daughter.

Methodology

In this book, the research relies on participant-observation lobbying as a queer method. This is the real-life capturing of information by working in a community. It is an important way to gather data from hard-to-reach populations, especially when it has not been done before. The contribution of queerness is that it tells us that research methods that are outside the box are appropriate because existing methods are insufficient for reaching many marginalized groups. In particular, this case builds on traditional participant-observation by considering the role of lobbyists who are reflecting on their experience as a form of research.

Directing this methodology is the research question, "under what pressures and at what costs does LGBTQ lobbying occur?" To collect data on this population requires information about them and their work environment. For instance, this means specifically knowing how someone identifies sexually, knowing their gender identity, knowing the portfolio of issues they work on, the organizations they work with, the sexuality and gender identity of allies, the portfolio of those allies, how the target group and allies work together on issues, and that they are all federal lobbyists. This is a complex set of variables.

Therefore, the most important factor in participant-observer lobbying is the unique way this queer method collects narrative information on the costs and pressures that motivate LGBTQ lobbying in the legislative and executive branches. Being in the room when political decisions are made and providing feedback on the research implications of this conduct (as experienced by the participant-observer lobbyist) opens up research possibilities which are (again) important for target populations where traditional collection methods simply do not work.

LGBTQ lobbyists are a small population, within a small population. In a study by Pepin-Neff and Wynter (2020), they look at the macro data by surveying activists in the United States to see if they identify as LGBTQ and if they are lobbying on LGBTQ issues. Of the 240 respondents, 91% identify as queer or trans (Pepin-Neff & Wynter, 2020). Within this group, 13% identified as paid staff and 5% identified explicitly as lobbyists who work on LGBTQ issues. This identification of LGBTQ lobbyists was consistent across the other countries that were surveyed by Pepin-Neff and Wynter (2020) with Australia (4%), United Kingdom (5%) and South Africa (7%).

This section will move forward by noting the way the participant-observer lobbying is built around existing methodological frameworks and serves as the best option for attempting to answer the research question. This is consistent with the important work by Gary Andres and Paul Hernnson in their 2009 book *Lobbying Reconsidered*. Andres and Hernnson (2009: 16) noted that their work as corporate lobbyists was part of the foundation for their research on lobbying. They note that this is, "the byproduct of over 20 years of serving as a participant and observer in the fields of lobbying and public policy." Andres adds that "in addition to scholarly literature and my personal experiences and observations, I draw on information and anecdotes" (2009: 16). In short, participant-observer lobbying is the best queer method for gathering data, addressing a hard population to study, and considering limitations.

The methodology for this book builds on queer methods with an autoethnography (participant-observer) and retrospective study. Jones and Adams (2010) discuss the importance of queer methods for autoethnography because data collection is hard. In this research, ethnography with data generated through participant-observation was used to gather information because it is a search for "as accurate an account of that reality as possible." Ethnographic research is an iterative process. The other LGBTQ actors are participants in the research, positioning the researcher in long-term contact with participants. There is also a discourse analysis of documents and public records.

In a similar case, Ward (2008: 24) examined LGBTQ non-profits by working for them and notes, "this kind of queer research produces firsthand knowledge about gendered and sexual practices, subculture formations, and the maintenance of sex and gender taboos, and it could not be accomplished without fully entering queer worlds."

The way issues are prioritized are analyzed through narratives in this book serves as a way to collect information. Finding the method for collecting data from the LGBTQ lobbying population is difficult. To gather this data on LGBTQ lobbying and understand the pressures and costs that influence LGBTQ lobbying,

I reconciled that I would use my experiences as an LGBTQ lobbyist as data to be collected and scrutinized. I was familiar with people who were LGBTQ, worked on LGBTQ issues at the federal level, and served as lobbyists. I could account for my own pressures and costs and reflect on those for the advocacy community.

In my experience, I collected data about the following:

1.   Working as a participant-observer lobbyist;
2.   The power dynamics of the legislative and executive branches;
3.   The way LGBTQ issues are prioritized by lobbyists; and
4.   Experience working with multiple LGBTQ organizations.

Fourth, participant-observer lobbying relies on experience interacting with the legislative and executive branches. My experiences include the following: professionally, I have been a registered Republican and registered Democrat. I have been a lower-level staffer and a non-profit Executive Director. For instance, I worked as a part-time door knocker one summer for PIRG's environmental causes in 1997. I was a junior aide in the U.S. Senate for Senator John Warner (R-VA) for a short time in 1999. I was then an administrative assistant for Log Cabin Republicans in 2000 for three months until they endorsed George W. Bush for President. I did small contract work with GenderPAC to help them with direct mail. I then switched political parties and spent a year in the office of Senator Harry Reid (D-NV), starting at the very bottom and doing administrative work.

In 2001, I started working for Servicemembers Legal Defense Network (SLDN) as a development associate doing their direct mail until 2002, when I was promoted to the first full-time lobbyist for the repeal of "don't ask, don't tell" (DADT) in the U.S., from 2002 to 2005. I then continued as Political Director and Deputy Executive Director working on DADT repeal for a think tank from 2006 to 2011. Also, in 2007, I became the Executive Director of the state-wide queer and trans youth center Outright Vermont. In January 2010, I returned to work on DADT repeal. In 2012, I began work on Capitol Hill regarding openly transgender military service, from 2012 to 2018.

I was also involved in politics as a volunteer. I worked for the Bob Dole (R-KS) Presidential campaign in 1996 and the John McCain (R-AZ) Presidential campaign in 2000. In 2003–2004, I was President of the Gay and Lesbian Activists Alliance (GLAA) in D.C., the oldest LGBTQ organization in the United States. In 2004, I worked on the John Kerry (D-MA) Presidential campaign, dealing with LGBTQ issues. I was also an incorporating director of the Equality Federation, the national umbrella organization for state-wide LGBTQ organizations. In 2005, I founded Q Street, Washington, D.C.'s LGBTQ lobbyist and government affairs association. Lastly, I was on the Board of the Vermont Pride Center in 2020.

In addition, I review the tactics of these groups from both an academic and a practitioner's perspective. In this book, data collection under these methods relies, in part, on anecdotes and critical narratives. I understand why some statements may be seen as polemic or controversial. This book makes an evidence-based argument.

It illustrates a critical narrative that breaks new ground by identifying LGBTQ lobbying and interest group activity within public policy research. This book can be seen as critical of D.C. culture, special interest groups, such as the Human Rights Campaign, and others. However, the goal is to follow the data and answer the research question.

The presentation of data (stories, narratives, primary documents) reflects a more casual narrative structure, and some does break new ground and add to the analysis of LGBTQ lobbying: (1) in the greater lobbying world; and (2) the LGBTQ community. The use of narratives in a reflective autoethnography embraces queer methods. This is less constrained by style but still guided by rigor. I have noted that the type of information being collected, and the analysis are also queer methods.

This information has also provided practical applications. Three elements that I use to approach lobbying as a practitioner, include:

1. Know your facts. There is no amount of money that you can give as a donor that will be more valuable than the penalty for being wrong about something. Giving bad information is more costly than any donation. It can end careers;
2. Know your strengths. What is the product that you provide? Is it your analytical ability, computer-savvy, social media skills? Whatever it is, you want to specialize, specialize, specialize. There are two ways that the world works: you need your job more than your job needs you, and the other way around. Information is worth more than money; anyone can get money. If you can bring value-added to every meeting you are in while every meeting without you is a loss to those working on an issue, then you can dictate the terms of your employment; and
3. Know your audience. Your job is to make this the most important meeting that they have had all day. You are doing them a favor by walking in and telling them this critically important information.

In addition, there is also a gap in the literature around LGBTQ public policy. There have been important contributions from research in sociology that has looked at the role of non-governmental organizations (NGOs) outside of D.C. (e.g. Chicago, New York City, or San Francisco) or social movement organizing around LGBTQ issues, but this book will look at tactics used in federal lobbying in D.C., for both the gay mainstream lobbying and LGBTQ lobbying.

Critical reviews of lobbying in the LGBTQ movements have not kept up with the rapid advancement of LGBTQ issues in the United States. Given that my work has covered the periods of President George W. Bush, President Barack Obama, and former President Donald Trump, this research provides a contemporary analysis of the evolution of LGBTQ and LGBTQ lobbying for nearly 20 years and how it has changed.

Lastly, there are significant limitations that should be acknowledged in this study. First is the heavy reliance on participant observation as a data collection tool.

This is a biased form of data gathering. Negative events are over-represented, and important details are forgotten. One of the methodological concerns that has been noted about this text is its tendency to lean into polemic style. I accept this point. Parker (2018: 158) echoes this concern noting,

> if participant observers seek too much publicity and spend too much time in the world of journalism or the world of practical politics, our work would be seen as damaged goods by the referees we value the most: our political science colleagues.

Additional limitations include that this research cannot be extrapolated. Also, key target populations are under-represented. Lesbians are under-represented in the narrative data as are Black people, bisexuality, and pansexuality. Lastly, I experienced a limited perspective on the relationship between groups. There were doubtless emails and meetings that I missed or was not included in.

Is this research? Yes. There has been thorough research conducted with a mixed-methods approach, a detailed review of the literature in both public policy and LGBTQ studies, and the presentation of conclusions, relative to a considered judgement of their potential impact. In keeping with concerns regarding ethics, Chapter 7 was reviewed by a defamation lawyer twice who cleared the chapter for publication. Moreover, in political science, it is not good enough to discount the lived experience of every political operative who moves into academia and wishes to critically reflect on those experiences within a research context.

Lobbying on LGBTQ issues starts from a baseline

To begin, it is useful to set a baseline for gay mainstream lobbying in the United States. This will be considered again in the LGBTQ context at the end of the book. There are useful heuristics (mental shortcut) for looking at the baseline for the priority's lobbyists give to certain issues and not others as well as their tactics. One heuristic is Harold Lasswell's (1936) policy question, "who, gets, what, when, and how." This is a useful way to think about the practical application of lobbying. I will reflect on this at the beginning and end of the book. To begin, I argue the following:

Who? On whose behalf is the lobbying being done? All LGBTQ Americans, some LGBTQ Americans? Two-spirit Native Americans? Usually, the beneficiaries are able-bodied, middle-class, cisgender, white, male, gays with organizations that are tailored to that population. Let me be clear from the beginning of this book that I argue that we (gay, white, cisgender, English-Speaking, Global North, males) are a racist, sexist, transphobic, ableist, HIV-phobic, classist, and usually homophobic community. Problems such as poverty and homelessness plague the LGBTQ community but are not priorities for many of the leading organizations. Poverty, in particular, has been erased from the modern LGBTQ identity and replaced with a consumer-driven alternative that presumes a certain type of class status with a certain amount of money.

Gets? What is the "getting process" in the lobbying world? When we fight for something, usually white people "get" things through laws or regulations. People of color "fight" for things in which changing a law may or may not be enough to deal with institutional racism. For example, people living with HIV fight for the availability and access to PrEP but still may not be able to afford it or may have to deal with anti-HIV stigma. In Black male communities, 26% have access to PrEP, while among white males, the number is double that at 52%. So, there is a difference in what getting something means, depending on who is reaching for it.

What? What are we lobbying for? This is a fundamental question of the LGBTQ advocacy community and the community as a whole. Are we working toward equality? To be treated the "same" as heterosexuals? To start with, let's acknowledge that this isn't quite right, that we will never be treated the "same" because the LGBTQ community did not design the rules that we are asking to be a part of. Other people made the rules, and built the institutions, in many cases to specifically exclude LGBTQ people. So just flipping a switch to include the LGBTQ population in a system that for 243 years was made to discriminate against LGBTQ people doesn't produce automatic sameness. It produces the appearance of sameness for select issues based on a definition and implementation of "equality" that operates within the systems of the oppressor. So, equality, even if we wanted that to be our goal, would be a functional fallacy. However, equality has become the dominant narrative of LGBTQ advocacy in the United States. Equality is the discourse of how the powerful set the bar to maintain power. It focuses on outputs, not systems or structures that include what inputs can result in changes to equity.

When? Let's keep this all together. Who (white gays), gets (receives through law), what (equality on issues), when (when they are perceived as respectable)? So, "when" do white people get their equality? The heteronormative answer is usually when they want it. But this is more complicated for the LGBTQ community. As a group that is marginalized, this is where the fight occurs. If the issue is an acquiescing to a process of assimilation by heteronormative power brokers, this is determined by oppressors for the oppressed.

In the case of LGBTQ politics there are penalties, like public support for marriage equality. However, support was not enough to gain political action. There also needed to be a signal that the institution of marriage would be respected, thereby legitimizing the action. Marriage was seen to be about love or hospital visitation rather than recreational sex. So same-sex marriage fit into a heteronormative structure that allowed it to be accepted by the public. Therefore, we are looking at a given amount of pressure relative to a given amount of perceived respectability.

This was epitomized in Supreme Court Justice Anthony Kennedy's comment justifying the constitutionality of same-sex marriage in the *Obergefell* case. He wrote:

> As some of the petitioners in these cases demonstrate, marriage embodies a love that may endure even past death. It would misunderstand these men and women to say they disrespect the idea of marriage. Their plea is that they do respect it, respect it so deeply that they seek to find its fulfillment for themselves.

In short, Justice Kennedy was stating that gay and lesbian people were being granted access to the stately tradition of heterosexual marriage: not radical and perverted queer marriage. Access to the constitutional right of heterosexual marriage was based on the way LGBTQ people were seen to be respectful.

Whereas once LGBTQ people were outsiders, now we were guests. It is not, therefore, the institution of marriage that has changed in this equation but LGBTQ people's perceived actions. As a result, systems of power around marriage remain straight and unchanged.

One more note is about the concept of penalties. I argue that policy change is governed by political penalties (Neff, 2016). Political penalty is defined as pressures "that may reduce their [political actors'] ability to hold onto their office or further their ambitions" (Neff, 2016: 142). Specifically, policy change is "based on the degree of political damage an individual actor or collective institution is willing to assume for the benefit of inaction" (Pepin-Neff, 2019: 51). We see this play out in other policy heuristic, high-emotion, low-policy threshold (HELP) events where there are acute penalties. Terrorist attacks, extreme weather events, and even shark bites lead to the distribution of penalties that damage political actors, whether that is bad and repetitive news coverage, Twitter outrage, or criticism from within a political party. These factors can lead to action.

And how? This sounds like where the actual lobbying comes in. How do white, gay men receive things under the law, at a time that their oppressors agree on, relative to the LGBTQ community's respectability and the redistribution of power back to the oppressor? That is really what is being asked in the current state of LGBTQ affairs. The answer to "how" is power negotiated and, if I may, by whom, are the last questions. These negotiations are determined by those in power, for the purpose of those in power, to remain in power. What comes out of this negotiation is often a form of delegated hetero-patriarchal recognition—symbolic recognition rather than actual power redistribution, for the most part.

We are allowed to be assimilated into their system so long as we do not disrupt the underlying structures of power and privilege. But how exactly is this symbolic recognition negotiated? One way this happens is through social movement organizations and interest groups that work with Congress, the President, and the courts to change the behavior of the State toward LGBTQ people. However, I argue that this is more about changing the behavior of LGBTQ people toward the State. The changes that are looked for are directed at more respectability, more assimilation, and more deference and complicity to heteronormative norms and rules of action.

Conclusion

There are a number of conclusions to draw from Chapter 1. The most important is that this book will make an argument. The way hegemonic heterosexuality influences lobbyists to make the "heterosexual ask" which leads to equality governance means that not all lobbying on LGBTQ issues is LGBTQ lobbying. In fact, LGBTQ rights work is designed to return power to the powerful and oppressors so the real victor in the LGBTQ rights movement is heterosexuality.

In addition, participant-observer lobbying was the right method to answer this book's research question given the complexity of the data collection. This methodology relies on an important queer methods approach. This includes the use of anecdotes which are used throughout the book. Jones and Adams (2010: 197) note that autoethnography as a queer method "satisfies the call and need to provide a pragmatic, accessible way of representing research, a way that devotes itself with 'grounded, everyday life.'"

The last part of this chapter looks at the outline for the rest of this book. This includes a way to situate LGBTQ lobbying in public policy; lobbying tactics, LGBTQ lobbying with regard to the White House and Congress, as well as sex and LGBTQ lobbying, which will look at heteronormative pressures; a review of the largest organization working on LGBTQ rights, the Human Rights Campaign; and closing thoughts on the future of LGBTQ lobbying.

Each chapter is divided into seven parts: Introduction; Literature review; Methods; Data; Discussion; Conclusion; and References. This has two goals: to provide a more unified voice given the different narratives, and to illustrate how stories and narratives can be viewed as data.

Discussion—outline and summaries

LGBTQ lobbying

Chapter 1 has five main roles. The first is to identify the research question, which directs the narrative around the pressures and costs that make LGBTQ lobbying occur. The second is to define lobbying and LGBTQ lobbying by highlighting differences in their relationship with power dynamics, which will be used throughout the book. I define lobbying as, "the negotiation of power in the executive and legislative branches in ways that returns power to the powerful; and the use of 'the ask' to prioritize or avoid certain issues, set limits on the degree of change, and contain discomfort caused to the powerful." And LGBTQ lobbying is defined as the negotiation of power in the executive and legislative branches, in ways that disrupt the return of power to the powerful, from a position of disadvantage and the use of 'the LGBTQ ask' to re- prioritize issues that center the marginalized and demand total equity, now.

The third is to look at the role of the "heterosexual ask" and "LGBTQ ask" as key features of lobbying and power. For LGBTQ issues, the "ask" can determine whether it is an example of "equality permanence" in which there is total discomfort and power disruption to the powerful in exchange for an intersectional approach to permanent equality legislation.

Alternatively, there is the compromise of "equality governance" where there is a proportionate request for equality relative to the discomfort of the powerful. The prioritization of more heteronormative issues lessens the distress. Lastly is the methodology of the book and chapter outlines. The methodology in Chapter 1 is the longest of the book and gives the overall picture of the methods used to answer the research question. The outlines provide snapshots of the book to come.

LGBTQ lobbying framework

Chapter 2 helps answer the research question by looking at the elements that contribute to LGBTQ lobbying, and other types of lobbying. It follows up on the definition of LGBTQ lobbying and is a theory-building exercise that proposes a framework for considering four different types of lobbying. These include: LGBTQ lobbying; conformist lobbying; non-conformist lobbying; and assimilation lobbying. These categories are designed around two variables: the prioritization of LGBTQ issues, and use of LGBTQ tactics. This chapter looks at the pressure and costs that come from the heteronormative political environment that considers certain types of LGBTQ issues and tactics "loser issues." The impact of loser issues on lobbying pushes the "heterosexual ask" as a tactic of lobbying. Loser issues impose a political burden on lobbyists for raising the issue and working on the issue and therefore may act as an agenda-setting tool to keep things off the itinerary.

LGBTQ lobbying tactics

The LGBTQ advocacy community includes two different lobbying categories: gay mainstream lobbying and LGBTQ lobbying, which are in competition with one another. This chapter reviews the tactics that gay mainstream lobbyists and their special interest hegemons use to control or advantage themselves over LGBTQ lobbyists. To do this, I review how LGBTQ lobbyists in each movement use key tactics employed in the United States. These policy tools, lobbying strategies, and social movement activities stand out for the unique way they highlight these different approaches to LGBTQ equality and coalition interaction. LGBTQ policy tools are different for several reasons. First, the context of the political environment is contentious. This facilitates a tension where presumed allies are often more dangerous to an organization's success than their anti-LGBTQ opponents. Second, LGBTQ issues have been considered a "loser issue" at the federal political level, until very recently. This affects the way groups organize themselves and are able to mobilize or fail to assemble support. Third, the roles of an organizational hegemon in representing the LGBTQ community is analyzed to show how control is often centralized.

The White House and LGBTQ lobbying

LGBTQ lobbying is defined as the prioritization of LGBTQ issues with LGBTQ tactics. In this chapter, LGBTQ lobbying in the White House is examined though the lens of the "White House ask." Three asks are looked at, including a request to sign an executive order to stop the discharge of LGBTQ troops; to include repeal in a "base" bill; and to lift the ban on transgender service. Here, we see the emotional connection between the issues and the President. There is also a consideration of the role of the White House and the Pentagon. In all, I note that this type of lobbying considers the degree of power present in the lobbying process. Narratives around "don't ask, don't tell" help motivate this analysis. We find that saying no to "asks" can be better than a poor yes.

The Congress and LGBTQ lobbying

Lobbyists can legislate. This chapter looks at the environment surrounding LGBTQ lobbying in Washington, D.C.. I argue that real and fictional portrayals of lobbying in D.C. contribute to a perspective that paints lobbyists as corrupt. In addition, I place lobbying in a framework around the concept of lobbyist-legislator, where the degree of disruption to power and the level of capacity to achieve the take provide a way to understand lobbying and the role of LGBTQ lobbying in Congress. In short, LGBTQ lobbying in Congress can write laws and place holds on Senate actions. What is required is an expertise on the process and issues as well as the right timing to make it possible.

Sex and LGBTQ lobbying

This chapter looks at the ways in which the hierarchy of sexuality and gender identity impact lobbying on LGBTQ issues. This hierarchy has implications for lobbying on LGBTQ issues because it reinforces the underlying power dynamics of racism and sexism that privilege heteronormative life. The result ultimately damages lobbying on LGBTQ issues. Things that mark the damage to lobbying in the LGBTQ advocacy community are: (1) the staffing within the movements has been uneven through the HIV/AIDS political assassinations of the Reagan-Bush years, followed by low levels of funding and high burnout rates; and (2) the difficulty of being a lobbyist within a heteronormative sexual hierarchy. There is a reliance on a particular sexual hierarchy in gay mainstream lobbying that preferences gay, white, young, masculine, English-speaking, cisgender male bodies based on conventional sexual attractiveness that work as organizational staff to satisfy the male gaze of donors and to other target audiences (Capitol Hill, coalition stakeholders). This means increased structural levels of racism, sexism, transphobia, and ableism within movements; (3) the literature on "impossible people" advanced by Dean Spade (2015) helps articulate the difficulty, particularly for trans and non-binary identities; and (4) burnout where most staff in LGBTQ organizations are often transitory which makes planning and strategy more short-term in terms of focus in the face of long-term, systemic oppression. Part of this is also related to the nature of the non-profit industrial complex.

The Human Rights Campaign and LGBTQ lobbying

This chapter looks at the largest LGBTQ lobbying organization in the United States, the Human Rights Campaign (HRC). The Human Rights Campaign is a hegemonic organization within the LGBTQ advocacy community. Hegemons often function to manage advocacy coalitions. This includes encouraging actors that support their strategies and punishing those that oppose them. This chapter argues that the Human Rights Campaign engages in gay mainstream lobbying, which advances a heteronormative model of organizing and fundraising. This includes the expansion of respectability politics as a norm-setting function within the community, and the perpetuation of certain sexual hierarchies that appeal to cis, white, gay, male, English-speaking constituencies from the Global North. Ultimately, I argue that the Human Rights Campaigns furthers hegemonic heterosexuality by gaining access to power by advancing heterosexual models and issues. For instance, this model reproduces systems of oppression including racism, sexism, ableism, classism, homophobia, and transphobia. As a result, this stifles progress in LGBTQ advocacy. Importantly, the Human Rights Campaign's actions are consistent with other hegemons in various movements. In this case, a review of the LGBTQ advocacy community highlights the tensions around "don't ask, don't tell," the starting of Q Street (the LGBTQ lobbyist association), and the ways the Human Right's Campaign's fundraising model can promote a commercial identity of gayness as a consumable product that often privileges white, cis, English-speaking men and cis, English-speaking, women from the middle and upper class.

Conclusion: the future of LGBTQ lobbying

The future of LGBTQ lobbying is transgender. This book concludes by looking at the future of LGBTQ public policy by reviewing transgender lobbying and its potential. It looks at the role of new organizations to address the marginalized, including Q Street, the LGBTQ lobbying association. This chapter also reflects on the definition of lobbying that is put forward, the idea that lobbying is about choices and power more than policy. Finally, marginalized lobbying is looked at as the umbrella for LGBTQ lobbying, and the way Pride informs the LGBTQ community and the direction of public advocacy is examined.

Note

1 This book approaches lobbying from the author's position as a privileged white, queer, cis, English-speaking male, from the Global North with a disability. It is therefore limited in how it can or should speak about trans lobbying, or race, or sex.

References

Adam, B.D. (1995). *The Rise of a Gay and Lesbian Movement* (Rev. Ed.). Twayne Publishers.

Andres, G.J., & Hernnson, P. (2009). *Lobbying Reconsidered: Under the Influence*. Pearson Education.

Armstrong, E.A. (2002). *Forging Gay Identities: Organizing Sexuality in San Francisco, 1950–1994*. University of Chicago Press.

Avner, M.A. (2016). Advocacy, lobbying, and social change. In D.O. Renz & Associates (Eds.), *The Jossey-Bass Handbook of Nonprofit Leadership and Management* (4th ed., pp. 396–426). Jossey-Bass.

Avner, M., Wise, J., Narabrook, J., Fox, J., & Brown, S. (2013). *The Lobbying and Advocacy Handbook for Non-Profit Organizations: Shaping Public Policy at the State and Local Level* (2nd ed.). Fieldstone Alliance.

Barclay, S., Bernstein, M., & Marshall, A.-M. (Eds.). (2009). *Queer Mobilizations: GLBT Activists Confront the Law*. New York University Press.

Baumgartner, F.R., Berry, J.M., Hojnacki, M., Leech, B.L., & Kimball, D.C. (2009). *Lobbying and Policy Change: Who Wins, Who Loses, and Why*. University of Chicago Press. https://doi.org/10.7208/chicago/9780226039466.001.0001

Beam, M. (2018). *Gay, Inc.: The Non-Profitization of Queer Politics*. University of Minnesota Press.

Bell, J. (2020). (Ed.). *Beyond the Politics of the Closet: Gay Rights and the American State Since the 1970s*. University of Pennsylvania Press.

Berlant, L., & Warner, M. (2002). Sex in public. In M. Warner (Ed.), *Publics and Counterpublics* (pp. 187–208). Zone Books.

Berry, J.M. (1977). *Lobbying for the People: The Political Behavior of Public Interest Groups*. Princeton University Press.

Bibbings, L.S. (2009). The heterostate: Hegemonic heterosexuality and state power. In R. Coleman, J. Sim, S. Tombs, & D. Whyte (Eds.), *State Power Crime* (pp. 35–48). SAGE Publications. https://doi.org/10.4135/9781446269527

Bird, N. (2014). *Fair Share: Climate Finance to Vulnerable Countries*. ODI. www.odi.org/sites/odi.org.uk/files/odi-assets/publications-opinion-files/9164.pdf

Brand, N. (2012, March 13). *Hegemonic heterosexuality*. The Good Men Project. https://goodmenproject.com/sex-relationships/hegemonic-heterosexuality

Brettschneider, N. (2017). Part 1: Building LGBTQ movements. In M. Brettschneider, S. Burgess, & C. Keating (Eds.), *LGBTQ Politics: A Critical Reader* (pp. 11–14). New York University Press.

Cigler, A.J., Loomis, B.A., & Nownes, A.J. (Eds.). (2016). *Interest Group Politics* (9th ed.). CQ Press.

Connell, R.W. (2002). On hegemonic masculinity and violence: Response to Jefferson and Hall. *Theoretical Criminology*, *6*(1), 89–99. https://doi.org/10.1177%2F136248060200600104

Connell, R.W., & Messerschmidt, J.W. (2005). Hegemonic masculinity: Rethinking the concept. *Gender and Society*, *19*(6), 829–859. https://doi.org/10.1177/0891243205278639

Crenshaw, K. (1991). Mapping the margins: Intersectionality, identity politics, and violence against women of color. *Stanford Law Review*, *43*(6), 1241–1299. https://doi.org/10.2307/1229039

Currah, P., Juang, R.M., & Minter, S.P. (Eds.). (2006). *Transgender Rights*. University of Minnesota Press.

D'Emilio, J., Turner, W.B., & Vaid, U. (Eds.). (2000). *Creating Change: Sexuality, Public Policy, and Civil Rights*. St. Martin's Press.

Diani, M. (1992). The concept of social movement. *Sociological Review*, *40*(1), 1–25. https://doi.org/10.1111/j.1467-954X.1992.tb02943.x

Endean, S. (2006). *Bringing Lesbian and Gay Rights into the Mainstream: Twenty Years of Progress*. Harrington Park Press.

Faderman, L. (2015). *The Gay Revolution: The Story of the Struggle*. Simon & Schuster.

Garcia, L. (2009). "Now why do you want to know about that?" Heteronormativity, sexism, and racism in the sexual (mis)education of Latina youth. *Gender & Society*, *23*(4), 520–541. https://doi.org/10.1177%2F0891243209339498

Ghaziani, A. (2008). *The Dividends of Dissent: How Conflict and Culture Work in Lesbian and Gay Marches on Washington*. University of Chicago Press.

Godwin, K., Ainsworth, S.H., & Godwin, E. (2013). *Lobbying and Policymaking: The Public Pursuit of Private Interests*. CQ Press. https://doi.org/10.4135/9781483349336

Gould, D.B. (2009). *Moving Politics: Emotion and ACT UP's Fight against AIDS*. University of Chicago Press.

Guter, B., & Killacky, J.R. (Eds.). (2004). *Queer Crips: Disabled Gay Men and their Stories*. Harrington Park Press.

Haley, J.E. (1999). *Don't: A Reader's Guide to the Military's Anti-Gay Policy*. Duke University Press.

Harper, C. (2007). *Intersex*. Berg.

Hindman, M.D. (2019). Promiscuity of the past: Neoliberalism and gay sexuality pre- and post-AIDS. *Politics, Groups, and Identities*, *7*(1), 52–70. https://doi.org/10.1080/21565503.2017.1310117

Hodge, P. (2015). A grievable life? The criminalisation and securing of asylum seeker bodies in the 'violent frames' of Australia's *Operation Sovereign Borders*. *Geoforum*, *58*, 122–131. https://doi.org/10.1016/j.geoforum.2014.11.006

Howlett, M., & Ramesh, M. (2003). *Studying Public Policy: Policy Cycles and Policy Subsystems* (2nd ed.). Oxford University Press.

Hrebenar, R.J., & Morgan, B.B. (2009). *Lobbying in America: A Reference Handbook*. ABC-Clio.

Hula, K.W. (1999). *Lobbying Together: Interest Group Coalitions in Legislative Politics*. Georgetown University Press.

Johnson, E.P., & Henderson, M.G. (Eds.). (2005). *Black Queer Studies: A Critical Anthology*. Duke University Press.

Jones, S.H., & Adams, T.E. (2010). Autoethnography is a queer method. In K. Browne & C.J. Nash (Ed.), *Queer Methods and Methodologies: Intersecting Queer Theories and Social Science Research* (pp. 195–214). Taylor & Francis.

Kingdon, J.W. (1995). *Agendas, Alternatives, and Public Policies* (2nd ed.). Harper Collins.

Lasswell, H.D. (1936). *Politics: Who Gets What, When, How*. Whittlesey House.

Lobbying Disclosure Act, 2 U.S.C. § 1602 (1995). https://lobbyingdisclosure.house.gov/lda.html

Luczak, R. (Ed.). (2015). *QDA: A Queer Disability Anthology*. Squares & Rebels.

McCann, B.J. (2011). Queering expertise: Counterpublics, social change, and the corporeal dilemmas of LGBTQ equality. *Social Epistemology: A Journal of Knowledge, Culture and Policy*, *25*(3), 249–262. https://doi.org/10.1080/02691728.2011.578302

McConnell, A. (2018). Hidden agendas: Shining a light on the dark side of public policy. *Journal of European Public Policy*, *25*(12), 1739–1758. https://doi.org/10.1080/13501763.2017.1382555

McRuer, R. (2006). *Crip Theory*. New York University Press.

Mezey, S.G. (2007). *Queers in Court: Gay Rights Law and Public Policy*. Rowan & Littlefield.

Mogul, J., Ritchie, A., & Whitlock, K. (2011). *Queer (In)justice: The Criminalization of LGBT People in the United States.* Beacon Press.

Murib, Z. (2017). Rethinking GLBT as a political category in U.S. politics. In M. Brettschneider, S. Burgess, & C. Keating (Eds.), *LGBTQ Politics: A Critical Reader* (pp. 14–33). New York University Press.

Nakayama, T.K., & Krizek, R.L. (1995). Whiteness: A strategic rhetoric. *Quarterly Journal of Speech, 81*(3), 291–309. https://doi.org/10.1080/00335639509384117

Neff, C. (2016). The performance of roll call votes as political cover in the U.S. Senate: Using C-SPAN to analyze the vote to repeal "Don't Ask, Don't Tell." In R.X. Browning (Ed.), *Exploring the C-SPAN Archives: Advancing the Research Agenda* (pp. 191–212). Purdue University Press. https://doi.org/10.2307/j.ctv15wxr41.13

Neff, C.L., & Edgell, L.R. (2013). The rise of repeal: Policy entrepreneurship and Don't Ask, Don't Tell. *Journal of Homosexuality, 60*(2–3), 232–249. https://doi.org/10.1080/00918369.2013.744669

Nownes, A.J. (2006). *Total Lobbying: What Lobbyists Want (and How They Try to Get It).* Cambridge University Press.

Parker, D.C.W. (2018). Following Fenno: Learning from senate candidates in the age of social media and party polarization. *The Forum, 16*(2), 145–170. https://doi.org/10.1515/for-2018-0017

Pepin-Neff, C. (2019). *Flaws: Shark Bites and Emotional Public Policymaking.* Palgrave Macmillan. https://doi.org/10.1007/978-3-030-10976-9

Pepin-Neff, C., & Wynter, T. (2020). The costs of pride: Survey results from LGBTQI activists in the United States, United Kingdom, South Africa, and Australia. *Politics & Gender, 16*(2), 1–27. https://doi.org/10.1017/S1743923X19000205

Phillips, S.R. (1991). The hegemony of heterosexuality: A study of introductory texts. *Teaching Sociology, 19*(4), 454–463. https://doi.org/10.2307/1317887

Quesada, U., Gomez, L., & Vidal-Ortiz, S. (Eds.). (2015). *Queer Brown Voices: Personal Narratives of Latina/o LGBT Activism.* University of Texas Press.

Raj, S. (2020). Contested feelings: Mapping emotional journeys of LGBTI rights and reforms. *Alternative Law Journal, 45*(2), 125–130. https://doi.org/10.1177%2F1037969X20927500

Richan, W. (2006). *Lobbying for Social Change* (3rd ed.) The Hawthorne Press.

Richardson, L., & John, P. (2009). Is lobbying really effective? A field experiment of local interest group tactics to influence elected representatives in the UK. Paper presented at the European Consortium for Political Research Joint Sessions, Lisbon, Portugal, April. https://ecpr.eu/Events/Event/PaperDetails/11091

Rimmerman, C.A. (2015). *The Gay and Lesbian Movements: Assimilation or Liberation?* (2nd ed.). Westview Press.

Schneider, A., & Ingram, H. (1993). Social construction of target populations: Implications for politics and policy. *American Political Science Review, 87*(2), 334–347. https://doi.org/10.2307/2939044

Scott, J.C. (2018). *Lobbying and Society: A Political Sociology of Interest Groups.* Polity Press.

Seybold, P. (1987). Behind the veil of neutrality. In R.F. Levine & J. Lembcke (Eds.), *Recapturing Marxism: An Appraisal of Recent Trends in Sociological Theory* (pp. 175–193). Praeger.

Shaw, D. (2014). Advocacy: The role of health professional associations. *International Journal of Gynecology & Obstetrics, 127*(S1), S43–S48. https://doi.org/10.1016/j.ijgo.2014.08.002

Solomon, M. (2014). *Winning Marriage: The Inside Story of How Same-Sex Couples Took on the Politicians and Pundits—and Won.* University Press of New England/ForeEdge.

Spade, D. (2009). Trans politics on a neoliberal landscape. *Temple Political & Civil Rights Law Review, 18*(2), 353–373. https://digitalcommons.law.seattleu.edu/faculty/161

Spade, D. (2015). *Normal Life: Administrative Violence, Critical Trans Politics, and the Limits of the Law.* Duke University Press.

Stewart-Winter, T. (2016). *Queer Clout: Chicago and the Rise of Gay Politics.* University of Pennsylvania Press.

Strolovitch, D.Z. (2007). *Affirmative Advocacy: Race, Class, and Gender in Interest Group Politics.* University of Chicago Press.

Stryker, S. (2008). *Transgender History.* Seal Press.

Stulberg, L. (2018). *LGBTQ Social Movements.* John Wiley.

Thompson, M. (2011). *The Fire in Moonlight: Stories from the Radical Faeries 1971–2010.* White Crane Books.

U.S. Const. amend. I.

Vaid, U. (1995). *Virtual Equality: The Mainstreaming of Gay and Lesbian Liberation.* Anchor Books.

Vaid, U. (2012). *Irresistible Revolution: Confronting Race, Class and the Assumptions of Lesbian, Gay, Bisexual, and Transgender Politics.* Magnus Books.

Ward, J. (2008). *Respectably Queer: Diversity Culture in LGBT Activist Organizations.* Vanderbilt University Press.

Wilchins, R. (2004). *Queer Theory, Gender Theory: An Instant Primer.* Read How You Want.

Yamamoto, S. (2017). Hegemonic heterosexuality in the film Boys Don't Cry. *Horizons, 2*(1), 135–138. https://kahualike.manoa.hawaii.edu/horizons/vol2/iss1/24

2

LGBTQ LOBBYING FRAMEWORK

Introduction

This book provides a step forward in lobbying studies. In this chapter, I propose a framework to identify LGBTQ lobbying. I argue that LGBTQ organizations who return power to heteronormative institutions are not engaged in LGBTQ lobbying. The issues and tactics prioritized by the mainstream gay lobbying in D.C. are not designed to serve LGBTQ interests. The adoption of heteronormative principles illustrates the victory of institutions and structures of heterosexuality.

In this chapter, LGBTQ lobbying is distinguished by its focus on the disruption to power brought by advocating for LGBTQ issues using LGBTQ methods. Critically:

> LGBTQ lobbying is not the issue, itself. Lobbying is the act of the choice regarding which issue to advocate and which issue not to advocate for in the legislative and executive branches in order to challenge or appease power; and the use of tactics (the "ask") to disrupt and redirect power.

This analysis highlights the competitive environment that advantages certain types of lobbying over others and provides a heuristic categorization of conformist lobbying that bends to heteronormative institutions before non-conformist and LGBTQ lobbying, which do not. Lobbyists must tackle more conservative hegemonic organizations, a rule-based emotional habitus, and LGBTQ social hierarchy that advantage specific LGBTQ issues and ascribe punishments to unwelcome LGBTQ methods. What is at stake is the way underlying power dynamic that can either empower or erase non-conforming LGBTQ identities.

This section is a theory-building exercise. From this understanding, politicians and their staff most often choose a decision because it is the right thing to do—they do it because the penalty for not doing it is too great. In this way, lobbying exists in the social world and is not restricted to legislative, legal, or executive domains. Influencing the agenda by choosing to prioritize issues that reproduce or resist the systematic, structural, social, and political oppression that individuals or groups face is lobbying. This conception of lobbying is important because it connects policy dynamics and power by validating the way actors bring light or dark to an issue. Here we see how lobbyists identify that a policy area has been made invisible through overt power (Dahl, 1957), hierarchically diminished by covert power (Bachrach & Baratz, 1962), or manipulated the target population through latent power (Lukes, 1974).

As noted, public policy can be situated in the State and includes what governments choose to do and not to do (Dye, 1979), or the strategic selection of personnel (Davis, 2009). Policy can also be made by governments in ways that are distributive to target populations (Schneider & Ingram, 1993) or by street-level bureaucrats in the implementation and delivery of programs (Lipsky, 1980).

Policy can be made outside of government and include private governance (Pattberg, 2005) by businesses and non-governmental organizations, by individuals, and norm co-production (Brandsen & Pestoff, 2006) or "governmentality" (Foucault, 1991) where people self-police themselves to create the implementation of policy. One example is the way we sit at red lights late at night when no cars are coming. It is mildly preposterous behavior and yet many of us do it to conform to the law by self-policing ourselves. Policy may be made when the emotions around an issue create both our understanding of the issue and set our political limits for engaging with the issue. In sociology, this is called an "emotional habitus" (Gould, 2009) for an issue. This can change over time to produce a mobilization among activists, the public, or policy entrepreneurs (Pepin-Neff & Caporale, 2018). In this situation of change, not only is there a rupture in the constellation of actors who are involved in an issue but a shift in the political horizon or trajectory of an issue. Gould's example is the issue of HIV/AIDS and how the emotional sentiment around this issue changed as the outrage grew and this translated into more radical political action. As a result, the varying forms of policy production impacts how we look at lobbying.

Gamson (1961: 374) notes that "power is the currency of politics." How power can be wielded to influence policy has also been viewed in different ways. The structures of resistance or incentives that are used by a lobbyist to lobby include evidence, votes, causal stories, money, protests, phone calls, emotionality, manipulation, lies, and illusion, just to name a few. Resistance to a dominance of an existing policy issues prioritization on the agenda or in a program is lobbying because it can create a new emotional habitus, norms, or rules that govern an issue subsystem.

This point about penalties is crucial because lobbying as a choice of issues (what) includes venues (where) and intensity (how much/how hard), as well as a question of on what timeline, in what order, and with what degree of discomfort and potential penalty to existing issue stakeholders.

This chapter moves forward in three sections. First, I review the background and literature on lobbying and special interest group coalitions. Second, I examine how LGBTQ lobbying can be identified, including how the kinds of issues that are addressed and the tactics used to address them create distinguishing categories for analysis, including mainstream lobbying, conformist lobbying, non-conformist lobbying, and LGBTQ lobbying. Third, I consider the conditions under which LGBTQ lobbying is its own type of lobbying. By this I mean that lobbying can be "queered" in a public policy sense. However, what is required is for patriarchal heteronormative institutions and queer homonormative institutions to allow space for LGBTQ lobbying.

Literature review

This book highlights how lobbying is personal. It also raises several academic questions that should be noted. A key question that this book asks is, what is queer? Queer is the "Q" in LGBTQ and the two are interchangeable for the purposes of this book. To begin, I would note that the word *queer* is a reclaimed word, which originally meant odd, different, or a bit off. Keisling (2017: 3) notes that queer was

> a derogatory term for homosexuals in the beginning, queer has later been reclaimed by HIV/AIDS activists and is currently used as an umbrella term for LGBT, a term for non-heterosexual or gender non-conforming practices, or as a radically non-identitarian, contradicting, and politically challenging term with a keen sense of positionality.

However, it is also important to remember that reclaiming "queer" as a community is a process. Muñoz (2009: 1) notes that "we have never been queer, yet queerness exists for us as an ideality that can be distilled from the past and used to imagine a future. The future is queerness's domain." This is a future that prioritizes the value of difference, centers the marginalized on the political agenda, and owns its own identity.

I define queer as the disruption of normal. It is the celebration of difference and pushes back against assimilating into heteronormative systems. It embraces racial justice, feminism, non-binary identity, diverse languages, indigeneity, disability, and marginalized identities. It offers a counterculture, revolutionary approach that locates those who are most marginalized at the center of their work. Queer undermines systems of oppression that erase identity by offering an intersectional attitude that highlights the hierarchical nature of identity and norms. In addition, what makes something queer is the way the action produces a non-normative effect. It is the collection of these non-normative effects that strike down discrimination and cultural bias. In short, queer is the process and the action. The action is those things that stand on their own to undermine normality.

For instance, Audre Lorde (1984: 102) says, "For the master's tools will never dismantle the master's house. They may allow us temporarily to beat him at his own game, but they will never enable us to bring about genuine change." In this case, we are using different tools. We are taking down the master's heteronormative house, using queer, non-normative tools.

> *Therefore, this definition of queer is based on celebrating difference, centering marginalized identities; and undermining perceived normativity.*

There are a number of different approaches and definitions of "queer" that can be seen in the LGBTQI advocacy community. For instance, Lauren Berlant (1997: 148) looks at Queer Nation's tactics and approach to activism: "Queer Nation's tactics of invention appropriate for gay politics both grassroots and mass-mediated forms of countercultural resistance from left, feminist, and civil-rights movements of the sixties—the ones that insisted that the personal is political, engaging the complex relation between local and national practices." She adds, for Queer Nation,

> Being queer is not about a right to privacy: it is about the freedom to be public …. It's not about the mainstream, profit-margins, patriotism, patri-archy or being assimilated …. Being queer is grass roots because we know that everyone of us, every body, every cunt, every heart and ass and dick is a world or pleasure waiting to be explored. Everyone one of us in an infinite possibility.
>
> *(Berlant 1997: 154)*

This highlights the celebration of difference.

Radical queer sexuality and gender diversity are important forces in the queer advocacy community and the broader community. Sex unites communities. And non-reproductive sexuality is a threat to patriarchal systems of oppression that use sex as a way to control women, heterosexual dominance, and masculine norms (Bronski, 1998).

Huffington Post contributor Nadia Cho (2016) addresses the definition of queer in a longer essay, which (in part) states,

> Being queer means constantly questioning what's considered "normal" and why that norm gets privileged over other ways of being. It means criticizing who sets these norms and recognizing the privilege that comes with being able to identify as "normal." Being queer means confronting all forms of oppression and bringing as many unheard, minority experiences and stories to light. Being queer means addressing and understanding the intersectionality between race, gender, sexuality and class and how it affects each person's experience and identity differently.

Cho highlights that the queer approach takes sides. It is progressive, outrageous, and defends difference. This includes fighting anti-LGBTQ work, but it also includes work against sexism, racism, classism, ableism, and other forms of oppression and discrimination.

> *Queer is a critical lens that looks at the way "normality" is weaponized by institutions in society to erase identities and create a hierarchy of norms that control who has power and who does not.*

In addition, there remains tension between the way queer can act as an overarching umbrella term and the possibility that in being inclusive of multiple identities it actually excludes some. Megarry, Tyler, Farhall, and Weiss (2018: 2) note that there are "tensions around the use of 'queer,' particularly for lesbian women" because "some lesbian women feel excluded from notions of queerness and, in a material sense, do not feel that spaces and events branded as 'queer' are necessarily welcoming of lesbian women."

To say that queer is an approach is controversial. It sounds dramatic, and it is. It means fundamentally challenging the premise that power returns power to the powerful. Instead, it means power returns power to the powerless. To say that it can be employed everywhere is also contested. Indeed, some would argue, "Why would you want to queer lobbying? Isn't that assimilating to a heteronormative set of institutions?" Ball (2016: 165) introduces the queer critique of same-sex marriage to note

> that critique is based on the view that the pursuit of marriage rights for same-sex couples is ultimately an assimilationist effort that prioritizes access to an intrinsically hierarchical and patriarchal institution, precluding or displacing more radical and transformative changes in legal and social policies in matters related to families and relationship recognition.

It is fair to note that there are hierarchies of political issues that leave some in and push some out. Attention on marriage did block out the political sun for more than a decade and our community was ill-equipped to deal with the financial impact of this on different issues and smaller LGBTQ groups. The argument can also be made that marriage is a luxury item preferred by a section of the community that is mostly white, affluent, and gay.

This fight within the theoretical and practitioner wings of the LGBTQ advocacy community highlights why it is important to look at policy entrepreneurs and consider participant–observer methodologies. There are individuals using queer methods that may not be visible or captured from an organization-wide perspective.

Indeed, these fights define equality, define identity, and define the parameters of the fight. Again, to fight for true liberation asks if an individual, organization, or group of people are willing to sacrifice everything. To leverage every network. To burn every bridge. To donate every resource. To commit every dollar money, whatever the cost, for the equity of the poor. The migrant. The homeless youth. The trans sex worker. The senior facing elder abuse. Black HIV rates. Intersectional racism. Ableism and homophobia for Black bipolar lesbians. To break the silence that erases bisexuality and asexuality. That shuns open discussions of sexual violence. And mental illness. Of suicide as more than a word but a systematic persecution belittling the queer soul. An act that steals the last bit of hope from the hopeless. An epidemic of thievery that steals our children. Are we willing to sacrifice everything at the cost of everything? And from this position, to exact a price from those in power for homophobia, transphobia, ableism, and serophobia. That is the measure of liberation in the LGBTQ lobbying context. It is neither lofty nor humble; it is simply the difference between the fight for all people or some people.

Coalition management

Gamson (1961: 374) defines coalitions by stating,

> coalitions are temporary, means oriented, alliances among individuals or groups which differ in goals. There is generally little value consensus in a coalition and the stability of a coalition requires tacit neutrality of the coalition on matters which go beyond the immediate prerogatives.

I disagree strongly on this later point but will pass for now. Kirsch (2006: 40) adds that "the ability to create a true political movement assumes identification with the struggles and projected outcomes of that movement while recognizing the differences between members that need to be accommodated." Temporary accommodation is certainly part of any coalition; however, this also includes ways to deal with competition, opposition, and larger, more dominant hegemonic organizations.

In public policy literature, the Advocacy Coalition Framework (ACF) provides a number of useful concepts for examining LGBTQ lobbying (Sabatier & Jenkins-Smith, 1993). The first is identifying the political players by considering how groups operate around issues and geographic jurisdictions. The way groups organize around a policy issue for a certain location or jurisdiction, is referred to as a "policy sub-system." Other researchers call this an issue domain (Moser, 2006) or policy community (Wright, 1988). For our purposes, I would define the subsystem to include all of the groups working for or against federal LGBTQ legislation and policy. This includes LGBTQ groups working on federal issues, Congress, the White House, administration agencies, conservative groups, government departments, and think tanks. This is intentionally broad because what happens at one federal agency regarding transgender access to Medicare, for instance, can influence congressional backlash regarding oversight and funding of LGBTQ youth centers.

In addition, there are new coalitions of networked lobbyists that work apart from coalitions of organizations. Lobbyists who are members of associations, political parties, or university alumni groups may coordinate activity. One example of this is Florida House on Capitol Hill (2020), where receptions are held for lobbyists and legislators from the state of Florida. Another example is Q Street, the lobbyist association for lesbian, gay, bisexual, transgender, and LGBTQ government relations professionals (Q Street, 2020). I founded this group in 2004–2005. McAdam (1982) notes that one of the advantages of diverse coalitions is that they can pressure governments from all sides, so these developments are particularly useful for multi-issue coalitions.

However, different groups may have different approaches for a number of reasons. For example, one group may be nascent and another one mature, because of the different demands of their members or as a means of mediating differences within one organization's membership. The fact that nascent lobbying also means a nascent donor class is key. Money is often seen as a finite resource. The "slices of pie" model is frequently used in conversations, and one additional slice for one group is interpreted to mean one less slice for another. However, Nadine Smith, Executive Director of Equality Florida, in the state-wide movement of LGBTQ organizations, has encouraged the "build a bigger pie" model (Sprayregen, 2020). Goals may also be tied to donations from fundraising more broadly on a popular issue. The gift of a single or group of donors may encourage or influence an organization's direction and policy goals. This might include ear-marked funds for a particular project, research, or staff member.

Schattschneider (1960) was concerned about the role that interest groups would play in the policy process. He noted that "the flaw in the pluralist heaven is that the heavenly chorus sings with a strong upper-class accent." This is borne out by much of the research because, structurally, the organizations are designed to be top-down and also because policymakers are closest to upper-class donors and organizers (so-called "grass-tops") rather than their grassroots organizers (Mitchell, 1998). Influencing these members then concedes this power dynamic and class bias, where proximity to power comes from being near the top, not the bottom. The motivation to be near the powerful is an important variable in lobbying.

There may be other motivations affecting lobbyists as well. Holyoke (2009: 362) states that "lobbyists do *not* always advocate for policies strictly reflecting their members' interests" because they have multiple audiences and want to keep other people happy. This may include members in a coalition, or members of Congress. However, Holyoke (2009) argues that there is a degree of ambiguity around lobbyists' flexibility to compromise against a membership's wishes, which extends to all the groups in a coalition. An individual organizational lobbyist is driven by an attempt to win on the issue, relative to how much they care about the issue, whom they need in the future, and the levels of dissatisfaction from members, congressional contacts, and other organizations. The larger the portfolio, the more difficult and more meaningful the network, which means the riskier it is for them professionally and personally to go against a White House or member of Congress.

The material benefit in joining a coalition is to acquire information at a low cost (Hula, 1999). There are also professional benefits, including networking and career advancement, and social benefits from working with a group of colleagues from a similar social group. In addition, there are political benefits for a lobbyist or organization to join a coalition because legislators or power brokers (i.e. lobbying firms, advocacy organizations, and the White House) like harmony, and they also prefer certain groups over others. They may like a group because they are friends with the executive director, because their tone and actions are seen as moderate, because they have a political action committee that donates to a legislator's re-election campaign, or because the lobbyist used to be on the legislator's staff. As a result, having that link within a coalition through a trusted organization is valuable for members of Congress. This trust can be returned in the form of political capital for that organization to help secure its goals in the future. However, there is not always trust or friendship within LGBTQ coalitions.

Frenemies

In many political scenarios, your friends are adversarial allies who will delay on an issue that penalizes those working on it. LGBTQ activist Steve Endean's title for chapter 4 of his book is "We've met the enemy … and the enemy is us: internal conflicts can be far more painful than fighting homophobes." Jeff Levi, executive director of National Gay and Lesbian Task Force (NGLTF), stated, "We're more willing to attack one another than go after our common enemy." In short, engaging on these issues can drag an organization down. This often means that allies don't want your loser issue to win because it will come at the cost of their perceived "winning" issues. In addition, there is a tangible effect, as loser issues can lead to higher burnout rates for staff and less financial support.

The issues that are worked on may be less appealing to a mainstream audience, making it harder to succeed. As a result, people may pick political issues to work on and tactics to employ that will incur less personal cost (i.e. emotional taxation). The result is that loser issues shape the type of coalitions that form, and what types of engagement organizations conduct.

In short, your allies and friends are your biggest opponents. They don't want your loser issue to win. This highlights an unspoken truth in progressive organizing that one of the chief problems to winning is the falsity of coalitions. Very few colleagues are eager to help you. They have their own priorities and you are alone in getting on the agenda. The issue is a loser issue, so your friends will not want to be dragged down by it or see it as a priority, so you will have to force the issue onto the agenda. As a result, at some point your friends will be your problem, and you will need to inoculate them from the process of opposing you. You might join forces with another hegemon like People for the American Way to protect yourself or launch a media campaign.

The make-up of a loser issue coalition is essential. Loser issues cannot win without an exceptional team that sticks together. The types of people it takes to withstand the long hours, little pay, and an uphill fight (with no recognition) are different, and the time it takes to see an issue evolve is different. Policy entrepreneurship and people matter. Staying together matters. The people who sign up to work on loser issues are willing to stay with the issue longer. Loser issue groups that win know how to put a team together that can last a long time.

On most loser issues, a chief reason for failure is burnout. This means the right skills, allegiances, and minimal burnout are essential for a team to survive. Importantly, this is not a group of workers; this is a team of policy entrepreneurs based around an individual or a dyad that produce lasting energy, innovation, and strategy for change. Winning is rare. So, the team and the effort need to be exceptional as well.

We see adversarial opponents who will overreach. The incumbent powerful cannot resist exploiting the people they see as losers. They see weakness and political opportunity. In the case of DADT, President Bush, the House Republicans, and the Senate Republicans played essential roles in advancing the repeal of DADT through their animosity against LGBTQ troops. Their provocations to oppress LGBTQ people caused a counter mobilization that organized activists and step by step, oppressive resistance by oppressive resistance built the self-esteem and resilience of actors who would see repeal as within reach and inevitable. History should record that they did as much as anyone to advance the repeal of "Don't Ask, Don't Tell."

This is a key concept of policy change under the social construction of target populations conceived by political scientists Anne Schneider and Helen Ingram. Under this theory, there are four groups of people based on being positively perceived. The backlash against negatively perceived people is a key reason why policy change occurs. The crackdown on the LGBTQ community in New York that led to the Stonewall Riots is an excellent example.

This helps reframe a loser issue and redirects the community against a recognized enemy. This devil shift is effective. In this case, the groups essentially show up the LGBTQ groups that are not being supportive in order to get them to align under the devil-shift model. This is, therefore, not a simple process.

In LGBTQ lobbying, I have noted that it is wise to "keep your enemies close and your friends as far away as possible." This is important because adversarial allies or frenemies in a coalition can be worse than an organization's formal opponents. This chapter argues that political organizations in a coalition may be members of a different social movement and compete with groups from another movement, which can impose greater penalties on each other because what appears to be one united movement with common goals is really two different movements, with different goals.

In certain circumstances, not working with coalition groups may present the best chance for an organization to succeed on its issue. This is consistent with Audre Lorde's analysis of emergent racial movements:

> In the 1960s, the awakened anger of the Black community was often expressed, not vertically against the corruption of power and true sources of control over our lives, but horizontally toward those closest to us who mirrored our own importance.
>
> *(Lorde, 1984: 127–128)*

She adds,

> We are poised for attack, not always in the most effective places. When we disagreed with one another about the solution to a particular problem, we are

often far more vicious to each other than to the originators of our common problem.

(Lorde, 1984: 128)

Fights within movements were also on display with the Lavender Menace in the women's movement, where there was concern that the women's movement was being taken over by lesbians. Meyer and Imig (1993), in Hathaway and Meyer (1993: 161), are also consistent in noting that "the most critical decisions a group makes involve its relations with potential allies/competitors: those organizations which share the same basic concerns and work on the same sets of issues." Key questions are: what are the rules, how big is the tolerated deviation for certain groups relative to contextual factors, and how big is the punishment relative to the political capital of the group? In these situations, what matters is not specifically the size of the group or how much funding they might have, but how the group and its target population are regarded. For instance, there may be a smaller organization that has few resources but still carries socio-political clout on the basis of their membership.

Actual organizational or issue enemies are often easier to defend against than adversarial allies. Real enemies are predictable, provide counter mobilizing opportunities, and reverse staff burnout. Frenemies are harder to mobilize against, poach staff, and fight for resources. For instance, Rahm Emmanuel was an opponent of action on gay rights in the first term of the Clinton Administration, as was Pat Buchanan. The difference was that Rahm Emmanuel was inside the White House and was a more formidable foe. As a result, LGBTQ groups are often more grateful for their enemies than for their friends because the damage that can be done by internal forces exceeds that of external forces.

Ward (2008) notes that there are also conflicts in the way LGBTQ groups distinguish themselves. For instance, "Queer activists use diversity rhetoric to compete with nonprofit groups to garner corporate funding and mainstream legitimacy, enhance their public reputation or moral standing, establish their diversity-related competence or expertise, and accrue 'liberal capital'" (Ward, 2008: 6). In addition, Ward (2008) says that organizations highlight threatening "risk-based" issues to appeal to supporters. These actions invest the organization in a model where profitability is based on a marketized and normalized definition of harms toward queerness and diversity.

Diversity in this analysis is more than a valuable asset to inter-organizational development; it is a discursive language that is used to locate lobbyists on the side of a particular kind of inclusion. Indeed "diversity" is a way to gain resources against other similar organizations and accrue funds. Therefore, diversity and queerness is shaped into "homonormativity" (Duggan, 2002) to appeal to LGBTQ consumers and funders, who are often white, cisgender, English-speaking, male, and middle-class from the Global North. Most national organizations therefore work with corporate businesses who adopt equality stances that misrepresent and reimagine what it means to be LGBTQ. The result is a situation where "capital is shaping national lesbian and gay politics" (Ward, 2008: 13). As a result, when these selective issues (such as same-sex marriage or military service) are victorious, the business model often disintegrates, and the organizations go out of business.

In all, there is a cost to the group in having a competing organization that desires a different policy involved in an issue. The hegemon's "capacity to persuade is thus diminished by the amount of resources the competitor wields because not only must legislators be persuaded to change their positions, but the competitor's efforts at persuasion must now be overcome as well" (Holyoke, 2009: 364). The groups may also not be able to provide any material benefit. The hegemon may already have the brand, contacts, access, and key proximity to power. McCann (2011: 250): "members of the mainstream LGBTQ rights movement privilege proximity to electoral power and upward economic mobility as preferred avenues for winning rights." All that forming a coalition achieves is showing unity and keeping potential problems under control; however, if the group becomes a bigger problem and is not containable or controllable, it may be better to make clear that they are unaffiliated with the hegemon's work so that it doesn't tarnish their reputation and access to contacts.

In 2009, then co-chair of the Congressional LGBT Equality Caucus, Rep. Barney Frank (D-Mass.), in the process of passing a hate crimes bill and in advocating for a more expansive employment non-discrimination bill that would cover transgender people, noted that, "They [Q Street] are very helpful because they help strategize and may be people who know other Members of Congress" (Palmer, 2009).

Formalizing is one way to erase the past, assume control, and claim credit. The harder work was building it from nothing, paying the cost, developing the network with few Democrats, during a scary time to be out.

Hegemons and coalition management

The fight for access and proximity to power is complex. Organizations are most likely to seek access by hiring lobbyists who have worked for key members on related jurisdictions. Holyoke (2014: 97) notes that overall 80 percent of lobbyists in Washington has worked for the government. In the George W. Bush White House, Heritage associates included Labor Secretary Elaine Chao, who was a Distinguished Fellow; Interior Secretary Gale Norton, who was the founder of the National Chair of the Council of Republicans for Environmental Advocacy; and Kay Cole James, Director of the Office and Personnel Management (OPM), having previously worked as Heritage's Citizenship Project Director. In the Obama Administration, Center for American Progress (CAP) Founder John Podesta served as Counselor to President Obama; CAP President Neera Tanden formerly worked with the Department of Health and Human Services (HHS); former White House Chief of Staff Denis McDonough served as a CAP Senior Fellow; and former Communications Director Jennifer Palmieri had worked for CAP's Action Fund.

Organizations assume a hierarchy that is uniquely social and political. One comparison might be "high society," where elite manners and etiquette are designated by hegemonic groups that set the norms. Wouters (2012) notes that the arrangements of norms within a community include the way problems are identified. This can contain individuals or groups that are seen as a problem. Wouters (2012) also notes the way historic discipline has given way to self-regulation and to an "emancipation of emotions" that involves additional control. However, Ghaziani (2008: 5) says that competition can be good, stating "infighting can be generative by allowing activists to muse on what I call the state of the movement." Infighting gives voice to "cultural concerns, it also serves as a guide to future organizing" (Ghaziani, 2008: 6).

At stake in the competitions between groups is the goal of access and proximity to power. However, this comes with an asymmetrical price because relevant access can be taken away by lawmakers or their congressional staff. Interest groups face pressure from congressional offices, political parties, and White House administrations to pick an ideological side on their issue, "with their access ... [being] ... threatened ... if they do not" (Holyoke, 2014: 99). As a result, LGBTQ groups are incentivized to have a similar model of discipline for how they cooperate and collaborate with groups, in order to maintain trust, access, and proximity to powerful players.

One of the factors that set an organization apart as a hegemon within an issue network is its actual or perceived ability to speak for the community in question. The commodity then is unity—to be seen to be representative of the broader community, to keep other organizations in line and thereby be able to speak for them, mobilize them in favor of a political candidate or position, control the discourse, and influence the media around that issue, limiting the amount of bad press after a decision is made. Hathaway and Meyer (1993: 164) note that authenticity refers to how "political organizations seek recognition from both the government and the public as the institutional voice of a larger public concern or political movement." Grassroots groups are seen to lack credibility on the Hill because their goals are considered extreme or politically impractical. Moderation is typically rewarded and viewed as a more credible partner for government officials (Hathaway & Meyer, 1993: 164).

Importantly, Ward (2008) notes that a diverse number of groups makes a positive contribution to the LGBTQ movement because they provide different ways for different people to participate. However, Ward (2008: 36) also states that coalitions are not equal partnerships: "When it comes time for convergence, privileged groups may still attempt to control, lead, or otherwise take ownership of a given political struggle, particularly when they have greater access to traditional political power."

Legislators look to hegemons to help find their position on an issue where they might have looked previously to senior members within their own party or committee members in Congress, or even the White House. This relationship works both ways. Lobbyists need to support legislators in order to further their organizational goals outside the individual issue (Hirschman, 1971, Holyoke, 2009).

With so much at stake, hegemons will impose political penalties as a chief way to achieve their goals of unity and coalition management for the sake of their access to Congress. Issue groups need to be seen to be working together or risk fracturing support for the hegemon with congressional offices. As a result, a hegemonic organization may isolate selectively, and directly punish only those groups that it can live without (Hula, 1999).

In addition, hegemonic organizations may see other smaller groups as essentially members of a club that it controls. As a result, the hegemon may act in keeping with Hirschman's (1971) prediction and "likely try to punish the lobbyist by 'exiting' the organization, stripping it of resources and even legitimacy, or use 'voice' by trying to have the lobbyist fired" (Holyoke, 2009: 363). Hathaway and Meyer (1993: 157) look at the inner workings of long-term lobbying coalitions and note

> activist choices about how to organize a movement, specifically cooperation and competition among potential allies, dramatically influence a movement's emergence, development, demise, and ultimately its impact. The generally untold story of a movement is about the political and tactical decisions groups make about the extent and content of their cooperation with each other.

This last point is a key feature of this book: two competing movements with one large hegemon to contend with.

Methods

Analytically, how do we identify LGBTQ lobbying?

Policy subsystems function within a set of norms that designate a hierarchy of identities, politically acceptable issues for those identities, and appropriate methods for dealing with those issues. LGBTQ-ness changes the way we think about lobbying because it centers the marginalized and its tactics do not seek to return power to the powerful. This upends lobbying because rather than it being a process where someone is trying to convince a politician to do something that will ultimately benefit the politician, it disrupts this system and offers an alternative where the target populations promise nothing and the benefits of the politician are removed from the equation. The direction of benefit has changed, and the tactic is about redistributing power to those who are marginalized and invisible. Figure 2.1 considers the main elements of LGBTQ lobbying: the advocacy or absence of certain issues and tactics which ask for degrees of change.

LGBTQ lobbying addresses the way issues are prioritized and the "ask" is made. LGBTQ issues are queer issues. LGBTQ lobbying issues center the marginalized and these lobbyists are authorized to operate by and with the groups they represent. The priorities given to the issues they choose, and the employment of LGBTQ tactics destabilizes the power and comfort around these political topics. The lobbyist's goal is to generate total, immediate, and permanent discomfort to those in power by disrupting heteronormative power dynamics and redistributing power to marginalized populations.

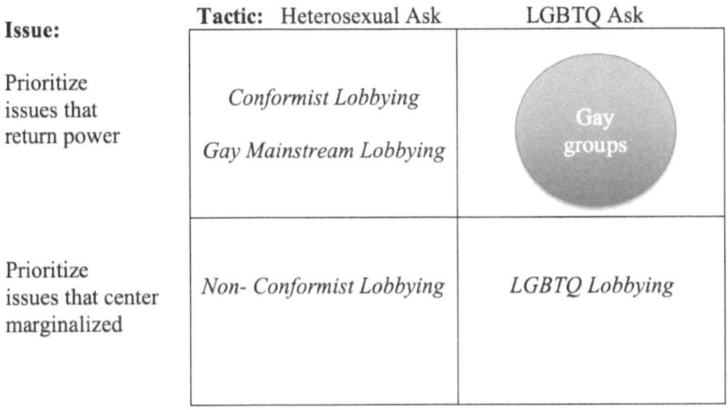

Issue:	Tactic: Heterosexual Ask	LGBTQ Ask
Prioritize issues that return power	*Conformist Lobbying* *Gay Mainstream Lobbying*	Gay groups
Prioritize issues that center marginalized	*Non- Conformist Lobbying*	*LGBTQ Lobbying*

FIGURE 2.1 Categories of lobbying

Issues: The prioritization of some issues and not others as the designation of hierarchical political agenda items that generate different levels of discomfort for those in power and negotiate the return of power.

Tactics: The selection of the target for "the ask," which prioritizes one target over another. Like issues, this produces political distress for those in power and influences the way in which power is returned to the powerful or disrupted.

LGBTQ issues are intersectional. These include progressive issues like women's rights, environmental justice, pro-Black agendas, sexual liberation, immigrant rights, disability rights, female genital mutilation, HIV decriminalization, abolishing prisons, universal healthcare, livable wage reform, and indigenous rights. They also include issues like: free healthcare, ending police brutality, legalizing sex work, anti-bullying education in schools, ending sexism, and ensuring all public accommodation is accessible to those with a disability.

LGBTQ tactics and the "LGBTQ ask" are queer tactics. One of the most powerful LGBTQ tactics is having LGBTQ-identified people selecting the priority of issues to be lobbied on and making the "LGBTQ ask" themselves. They are best understood as the target of the "LGBTQ ask." While there are tactics that lobbyists use that are transactional and they give something back, such as information, research, and labor, that is not the focus. Here, we look at the tools used by lobbyists to generate total, immediate, and permanent discomfort to those in power by disrupting heteronormative power dynamics and redistributing power to marginalized populations. The tactic is a non-conformist tactic where the target is placed in maximum political distress to enable the maximum disruption to power dynamics for the benefit of a reconstituted system that structures the negotiation of power as equity. This is equality permanence.

Gay mainstream lobbying is, first, highlighting some issues over others in ways that reward the powerful and are not consistent with intersectionality. These are usually LGBTQ issues that return power to the State. This may also be the way mainstream business models influence mainstream lobbying by returning power to the powerful. Second, the "ask" is consistent with equality governance, to ask for a relative degree of equality based on the level of comfort for the powerful. I argue that this is the most common form of lobbying in the LGBTQ advocacy community. I have noted in the circle in Figure 2.1 that there are perceptions for different groups under different boxes (or interpretations). In this case, "Gay groups" are seen to be making an "ask" based on the interests of the LGBTQ community. I have argued this is not the case. Instead, discomfort to those in power is carefully calibrated and power is returned to oppressors. Gay mainstream tactics are heteronormative tactics.

For instance, gay mainstream lobbying is designed to benefit heterosexuals over the queer and trans community in a number of ways. This can be seen in mainstream lobbying and "asks" for employment discrimination (capitalism as the solution), immigration (some people are illegal), hate crimes legislation (prisons, executions and tough on crime), and marriage equality (monogamy, children). The repeal of "don't ask, don't tell" could fit here as an attempt to further the military-industrial complex.

Non-conformist lobbying centers the marginalized and addresses power by working within the system. Under this model, environmental reform, ocean rights, and animal protection are still heteronormative institutions from a lobbying point of view. Forests are saved, but still not accessible to many with a physical disability.

Conformist lobbying has an agenda of non-LGBTQ issues and non-LGBTQ tactics. This includes most corporations who will always have both access and more access. It is for the marginalized populations that lobbying is so important. For these groups, their votes do not translate into representation. They are deviants and queers in a system based around white, male, cisgender, English-speaking masculine, heterosexual, Christian, middle-class, able-bodied people from the Global North. This category advances heteronormative topics using heteronormative tactics. This is the most common category for toxically masculine, hegemonically heterosexual anti-LGBTQ lobbying.

Here, we literally see the opposite of LGBTQ lobbying and the way this system of lobbying is designed to do more than return power to power but build on the existing dominance of underlying power dynamics. The goal of the conformist lobbyist is to take power away from those at the bottom and redistribute it to those at the top. A lobbyist's selection of each type of lobbying is a process of choosing which issues to prioritize, influenced by the political calculation of an issue, consideration of political capital, or status as a loser issue.

Loser issues

Guiding the lobbyist's prioritization of one style of lobbying and one issue over another is the concept of "loser issues." This book is about the factors that go into influencing lobbying choices.

The political penalties associated with "loser issues" push lobbyists toward mainstream lobbying, the "heterosexual ask," and "equality governance."

Loser issues in the political context play a key role in this process and are defined by seven factors. First, loser issues play an influential role of what issues are made visible and invisible relative to power. Second, a loser issue affects an already marginalized or deviant group of people. This means the group has a hard time fighting back against this marginalization and there is a political cost for politicians in trying to solve their problem. Third, loser issues are issues for which there is a policy monopoly, organizational structure, and resources in favor of the status quo. Fourth, raising the issue promotes a counter-mobilization of discourse, groups, media, and validators against change. And fifth, associating yourself with a loser issue places additional burdens (such as emotional taxation) for rejecting norms and tackling these types of issues. Loser issues are more prone to backlash. Working on a loser issue means understanding that you are virtually alone because your friends and allies would confront some form of harm by the majority for taking on the issue.

Sixth, these issues are associated with negative timing elements. This may include a cluster of negative events, one large negative indicator, or the historic first of an issue. Seventh, and lastly, it is important to recognize that for the elements noted above, these are mainstream issues. Mainstream issues are loser issues because they fall into existing systems where LGBTQ issues (for instance) are already marginalized. Operating within this system is to guarantee overwhelming losses to the issue being addressed.

Twenty years in politics has taught me that not all groups of people and not all political issues are created equal. Some problems happen to convenient populations that are marginalized by society and the political system. Baumgartner, Berry, Hojnacki, Leech, and Kimball (2009: 77) note that political "issues may be linked to stigmatized or otherwise unpopular target populations whose interests, for whatever reason, are rather easy (and politically acceptable) to ignore." LGBTQ issues have historically been loser issues.

Loser status for the LGBTQ community could also be seen on other political issues. For instance, myself and co-author Luke Edgell note in a journal article in the *Journal of Homosexuality* that "the issue of gays in the military became legislatively radioactive as the painful political process of what became known as the 'Don't Ask, Don't Tell' policy took shape" (Neff & Edgell, 2013: 235). Indeed, there has been a great deal of opportunistic political capital in attacking lesbian, gay, bisexual, and transgender issues. From Pat Buchanan to former President Donald Trump, the impact of being seen as a loser issue is that it can make congressional staff/allies less receptive to action. There are particular loser issues within LGBTQ rights that come with a higher cost for the community than others, either because of little public support, public education, and under-funding, or because it presents an easy target for right-wing backlash or anti-gay laws. For example, in 2004, 11 anti-marriage amendments were passed in one day. In addition, the plight of transgender asylum seekers and refugees has long been overlooked by the LGBTQ community because of the combination of latent racism and a lack of political will.

In addition, some social issues impose greater burdens on lobbyists than others. This can be an emotional burden or a structural burden that is reflected in the way political capital as a concept (i.e. organizing capacity or coalition value) is looked at in Washington. Therefore, knowing the dynamics of loser issues is important, particularly for LGBTQ lobbyists who work on more of them. Being able to diagnose your strategy as a loser or your issue as "radioactive" is the first step in being able to re-prioritize an issue from loser status. This is important because the lower an issue is ranked, the further it has to go. This is critically important.

Aligning with a loser issue is a political penalty for most groups and politicians. The first task for a lobbyist is to transition from being an issue for which people feel a penalty for getting next to, to an issue that is capable of being seen as positive enough to inflict a political penalty on opponents. This process is crucial, strategic, and lengthy.

The loser issue concept is also important because it introduces the importance of hegemonic organizations. Hegemonic organizations are the largest and often the most powerful members of a coalition. In this book, the Human Rights Campaign is identified as a hegemonic organization. In addition, hegemons are designed to disrupt the ability of loser issues to gain traction. The issue hegemon wants to keep its members happy and also has to keep key issue stakeholders happy in order to maintain its level of access. These stakeholders include important actors like the White House and congressional leaders but also other issue or ideological hegemons who are gatekeepers of access, such as the Heritage Foundation and National Rifle Association on the right, and the Center for American Progress (CAP), and National Association for the Advancement of Colored People (NAACP) on the left. These groups serve key conduit functions as go-to organizations on issues that matter to political constituencies. They are the largest member organizations of a target group, and sometimes function as a shadow White House through which former White House or congressional staffs rotate. In all, hegemons want to be seen as chief representatives for their identity group or constituency.

For hegemonic organizations and lobbyists to navigate political issues, particularly loser issues, they must keep strategic track of their wins and losses. Hegemons and lobbyists may need a certain percentage of wins on the board to satisfy their supervisor, Board of Directors, or major donors. This is not about the pure number of wins, but rather the relative ratio of wins to losses and losses to losses. For instance, a lobbyist cannot lose too many efforts in a row. This may turn a winning issue into a loser issue. And the hegemon may have spent years carefully curating and fundraising off public perceptions of certain issues or social problems. To mitigate this, a lobbyist or organization may: (1) compromise on issues to increase the number of wins on the board; (2) reduce the number of legislative efforts on issues so only winning opportunities are considered; (3) venue shop to other avenues or issues (impact litigation, trans, trans, trans) in order to increase the number of wins; (4) wait for a better Congress or President, chairman of a committee, or ranking member; (5) coordinate with a political party to create a coalition style effort for their legislative plans; and (6) coordinate with party leaders to manufacture wins, such as announcements at major donor fundraising events and galas.

Also, loser issues may only be losers at certain times. Lobbyists understand that loser issues are a political phenomenon that are generated by more than the toxic nature of an issue (Pepin-Neff, 2019). Sometimes there is a loser environment. The media can be fickle to designate an issue as a problem when it has been around for years, decades. Here, salience is the indicator. Salience is more than the relative frequency, relative nascency or maturity of exposure to an issue. It is also the degree to which the public has the capacity to deal with the frequency, exposure, and emotionality of the issue. Put another way, loser issues rise on the political agenda within the LGBTQ community as a product of how often they occur, how important the issue is, and what else is going on in the news.

There are also clusters of losses, even small losses that create concern in a community. This may occur from different venues, including district courts, federal agencies, and state legislatures. Loser issues can be constructed based on the accumulation of multiple losses or one big loss that puts pressure on the type of lobbying lobbyists do.

A key point of this book is about the strategy for lobbyists that work primarily on loser issues. I suggest using and embracing queerness and transness as a tactic to refute oppression. But it is also about the way heteronormative oppression structurally exerts power to make some issues losers, and others winners in the political arena. As a result, there are advantages for organizations (i.e. mainstream groups) that defer to the consumer model and those types of hegemonically heterosexual issues. In response, groups in the radical movement must maneuver for a win on their issues by inflicting penalties on their friends.

> *Loser issues are managed through the choice of lobbying style (heterosexual ask) and redistribution of power to the oppressor (equality governance).*

Flipping the loser issue idea

Consider for a moment the opposite. That the real loser issues in the LGBTQ community are the mainstream issues. That those issues that are most likely to end up on the heterosexual agenda are those that abide by the "heterosexual ask," and "equality governance." The welcome that these issues receive is predicated on their allegiance to a political system that will render them vulnerable and return power to itself. For instance, in 30 years there have only been two major pieces of affirmatively LGBTQ federal legislation: The Hate Crimes Bill, and repeal of "Don't Ask, Don't Tell." This is the legislative revolution? This is a shift in acceptance?

As I write this book, President Biden is on the verge of taking office. However, in the past four years President Trump tried to undo many of the regulatory protections for transgender Americans. Clearly, the war on trans people will continue in the courts and regulatory solutions, while important in addressing immediate discrimination, are not the long-term solution. Moreover, the coming shift to the right of the Supreme Court will have catastrophic impacts for LGBTQ rights, again particularly trans people.

As a result, lobbying is the hope for LGBTQ rights in the next 20 years. The focus will shift from the courts to the states and federal government. And because the federal courts will change state laws, the most likely remedy is federal legislation like the Equality Act. Therefore, LGBTQ issues may all face a perilous future but those radical issues outside the system may be even more likely than mainstream issues.

Data

There have been several important developments to the lobbying environment since the 1990s, and each has increased the importance of hegemonic lobbying organizations. The first was the cutting of congressional staff in 1994 (Jacobson, 1996) as part of the Contract with America, which left staff in Congress to rely more on lobbyists for assistance. The second was the rise of shadow-administration advocacy organizations, like the Center for American Progress and the Heritage Foundation (Brodwin, 2013). These shadow branches are used by the White House of different parties to vet and lobby on issues. The third is the increased role of lobbying firms like Holland and Knight and the Podesta Group (The Hill Staff, 2016) in managing coalitions and issue campaigns. Firms serve the role of further tightening the management of coalitions. The fourth is the integration of campaign-related staff into lobbying organizations such as Dean for America into Democracy for America (McNutt, 2008) and Obama for America into Organizing for America (Burge & Lewis, 2010). Here, a White House can invent a non-governmental organization (NGO) and establish itself as the hegemon of an issue campaign that influences the issues chosen to act upon and the methods employed.

Emotional habitus

There has been an evolution in the emotional habitus of the LGBTQ movement. First, the Mattachine Society, then Daughters of Bilitis, GAA/GLAA, NGLTF, HRCF, and ACT UP were founded to provide private representation for the LGBTQ community before the State because the government and public institutions were not representative of the community. However, it is important to note that even ACT UP was rightly criticized for its focus on the white, cisgender, male experience of AIDS. In addition, the government rendered many of these early groups illegal and subject to harassment and criminal prosecution. Eggan (2008: 17) notes that it was AIDS that moved the LGBTQ community past representation in some ways and "stretched our vision of liberation to include fighting for medical treatment and sometimes a renewed struggle against race, gender, and economic discrimination." The alternative is erasure, to erase from existence an LGBTQ voice to keep a straight or closeted leader happy. We see this all the time, as oppressors (i.e.

politicians) are appeased on LGBTQ issues at the expense of the LGBTQ community. Indeed, it should be noted that LGBTQ electoral politics today is still mostly about trying to help straight people get re-elected to political office.

Building off this, Deborah Gould (2009) argues that the emotional habitus of the LGBTQ movement changed after the court case *Bowers v. Hardwick*, toward more acceptance of direct action and ACT UP. The *Bowers v. Hardwick* ruling took citizenship away from queer Americans. It stated that there was no constitutional right to sex between people of the same gender. Queer relationships were not valid and sex in that relationship was illegal. In the face of this loss and the political assassinations of the AIDS catastrophe, the community saw little option but to revolt. This shook the emotions of lobbyists and with it the radical queer movement. The stability of the emotional habitus and LGBTQ rules of engagement were broken again after *Lawrence v. Texas*. Gould notes that:

> *Hardwick* magnified and bolstered an emergent new constellation of affects and emotions, effectively authorizing sentiments and expressions of gay rage and indignation and directing them toward the government, the pharmaceutical industry, the scientific-medical establishment, the corporate media, and other institutions seen as contributing to the AIDS crisis. These new emotional practices and new sentiments about gay selves and about dominant society created a new, counterhegemonic emotional habitus and challenged the limits of the previous political horizon, offering new attitudes about what was politically possible, desirable, and necessary in the fight against AIDS, and thereby creating fertile ground for the emergence and development of confrontational direct-action AIDS activism.
>
> *(Gould, 2009: 134)*

There is also a counter-frame that challenged this habitus. Eggan (2008: 17) adds that

> those who witnessed the deaths of hundreds of friends and lovers understandably want to protect themselves. What is sad is survivors of the epidemic started thinking that if we were only more normal—reproducing and marrying like straight people—we'd be protected.

The shifting LGBTQ movement's emotional habitus also runs up against the much more conservative emotional habitus in Congress, where the expression of emotion is looked down upon. Professionalism means stripping the emotion from political conflict. It is not a question of no emotion but referencing one emotion (suppression or happiness) over another (anger and frustration). This is one way that professionals also see themselves as a distinct class from others. It might be hard-nosed to be thrown under a bus, but you are expected to smile and say thank you on the way under. This runs in the face of David Ehrstein's estimation that, "the essence of gay liberation is politics you can dance to" (Schwarz, 2011). Indeed, lobbying town halls, local government, or federal bodies can be a fabulously LGBTQ affair. Even sexual. There are reports of cruising at ACT UP meetings, in the halls of Congress, and at federal agencies. One of the worst-kept secrets of Washington, D.C., is that it is run by queers and trans folk. Yet, work on LGBTQ issues (aside from queer methods) can impose an emotional tax on those involved (Neff, 2016). Emotional taxation is defined by Neff (2016) as:

> The emotional cost, intentional or not, that a policy, program, or scheme places on an individual or group for entering into the political process or addressing a political issue. The impact of this emotional tax (the level of taxation) to enter the policy process is relative to an individual or groups political power (i.e. degree of stigma), capacity to pay the cost, and collective support. As a result, there would be one kind of emotional cost for someone entering a political process as a positively constructed identity (race, color, religion, gender, sexual orientation, gender identity, ability) and a potentially higher emotional tax to enter the process from a marginalized community.

There is also a structural element to congressional conservatism in lobbying. One of the questions that influences the hierarchy of issues that are chosen is whether people are motivated to act more on issues that have less emotional taxation than issues with higher emotional taxation, either because they are easier to mobilize on or easier to raise money for. It may be that some people pick the habitus, the political issue to work on, that will incur less cost, emotional or otherwise, while others pick more difficult circumstances. Or not. The implication of this affects the issues selected and the type of political engagement that follows. In addition, there are added penalties for these issues. Emotional taxation may make it more burdensome to continue to enter the political process with fewer and fewer resources. Such a taxing environment may also attract those who want a more aggressive approach to equality or liberation. Overall, while there is tension with congressional practices, the rules of engagement for these LGBTQ issues are designed by the LGBTQ community in most cases. Ostrom (1998: 8) notes, "the particular rules adopted by participants vary radically to reflect local circumstances and the cultural repertoire of acceptable and known rules used generally in a region."

Pushing back against this conservative habitus are concerns that corporate LGBTQ-ness packages issue campaigns in ways that can be sold to high-dollar donors to keep an organization alive. More attractive issues like youth homelessness are invested with resources more than trans sex worker rights or elder care. Ward (2008) warns that capital is shaping LGBTQ politics based on access to LGBTQ consumers and that the picture of the LGBTQ consumer that businesses want to buy is being reimagined in the way groups and leaders choose and frame issues to present the picture of LGBTQ discrimination in the community. What it means to be queer is defined under this analysis by the consumer market. It is a market identity and as a result discrimination is market related as well. This may mean being denied employment, or equal pay, or both. As a result, LGBTQ lobbying is influenced by the way hegemonic forces influence the types of issues and tactics used to make an issue or group appealing to this market and these market forces are reinforced or challenged by the emotional habitus, emotional taxation, and the dire state of outside events.

Discussion

Can you "queer" lobbying?

The domains for lobbying in this book include the House of Representatives, the United States Senate, the White House and the nature of lobbying organizations themselves. To conduct LGBTQ lobbying means to engage with these institutions in ways that disrupt highly conservative and heteronormative traditions. In many cases, this includes a perspective that emphasizes perceptions of heterosexuality and of a gender binary.

Under the right circumstances, you can "queer" lobbying. Queering lobbying means redirecting the benefits from the politician or the lobbyist to the marginalized population. However, there are systematic and structural reasons; this is difficult.

One particular example highlights how difficult it is to disrupt heteronormative structures: congressional staff. Even if an LGBTQ lobbyist works for an LGBTQ organization and they are lobbying a progressive politician they must still deal with the staff who truly run Congress. Among the most rigid forces on Capitol Hill are the closeted staff or openly gay staff, who must survive in a heteronormative environment. The maintenance of this heteronormative atmosphere is one way that staff often protect themselves. As a result, it may be that the least likely actor to change the environment from heteronormative to LGBTQ may be the LGBTQ staffers of the time because the combination of LGBTQ issues and LGBTQ tactics that are addressed openly may put them in a vulnerable position.

As a result, hegemonic heterosexuality wins. Congress as an institution of white, male, cisgender English-speaking heterosexuality is provided protection from one of the least likely sources, LGBTQ staff. Disruption of the systems that force LGBTQ staff into this position is needed. This can occur by centering the marginalized and using queerness as a solution to the issue, rather than a problem.

Conclusion

This chapter was a theory-building exercise that looked at the issue of LGBTQ lobbying in the LGBTQ advocacy community. There were four key questions: what does queer mean? What is lobbying? What is LGBTQ lobbying? And can lobbying be queer? I argue that queer is best thought of as celebrating difference, centering marginalized identities, and disrupting or undermining perceptions of normativity. As a result, LGBTQ lobbying can be very powerful when it advocates on behalf of marginalized groups.

To understand LGBTQ lobbying, I divide lobbying up into four categories: mainstream lobbying; conformist lobbying; non-conformist lobbying; and LGBTQ lobbying. Each of these is distinguished by whether they work on LGBTQ issues (such as transgender sex worker rights) and whether they use LGBTQ tactics (such as glitter-bombing police stations). Looking at lobbying through these categories and elements allows for an analysis of the types of activities and targets that make up the mainstream gay movement and the radical queer movement.

Other factors that help govern the nature of lobbying are the presence of an emotional habitus to set emotional norms around an issue and the emotional cost or taxation that an issue or tactic imposes. Issues with more rigid emotional norms or that produce greater taxation for dealing with them would be more difficult to change. This difficulty makes the question of queering lobbying a challenge. I argue that the answer is that it is possible to queer lobbying but that this is unlikely given the structures and systems opposing it. LGBTQ lobbying redirects the benefits back to the marginalized and this is something that requires a major change to the policy process. This book acknowledges the way the forces of heteronormativity function to stymie LGBTQ lobbying and the conditions where this can be overcome.

References

Bachrach, P., & Baratz, M.S. (1962). Two faces of power. *American Political Science Review*, 56(4), 947–952. https://doi.org/10.2307/1952796

Ball, C.A. (2016). *After Marriage Equality: The Future of LGBT Rights*. New York University Press.

Baumgartner, F.R., Berry, J.M., Hojnacki, M., Leech, B.L., & Kimball, D.C. (2009). *Lobbying and Policy Change: Who Wins, Who Loses, and Why*. University of Chicago Press. https://doi.org/10.7208/chicago/9780226039466.001.0001

Berlant, L.G. (1997). *The Queen of America Goes to Washington City: Essays on Sex and Citizenship*. Duke University Press.

Brandsen, T., & Pestoff, V. (2006). Co-production, the third sector and the delivery of public services: An introduction. *Public Management Review*, 8(4), 493–501. https://doi.org/10.1080/14719030601022874

Brodwin, D. (2013, August 30). Americans lose when think tanks become lobbyists. *US News*. www.usnews.com/opinion/blogs/economic-intelligence/2013/08/30/heritage-foundation-center-for-american-progress-and-think-tanks-as-lobbyists

Bronski, M. (1998). *The Pleasure Principle: Sex, Backlash, and the Struggle for Gay Freedom*. St. Martin's Press.

Burge, C.D., & Lewis, D.E. (2010). Campaigning for a job: Obama for America, patronage, and presidential appointments. Paper presented at the 2010 Midwest Political Science Association annual conference, Chicago, IL. https://my.vanderbilt.edu/davidlewis/files/2011/12/burge-lewis-wisconsin.pdf

Cho, N. (2016, February 2). Being queer means…. *Huffington Post*. www.huffpost.com/entry/being-queer-means_b_3510828

Dahl, R.A. (1957). The concept of power. *Behavioral Science*, 2(3), 201–215. https://doi.org/10.1002/bs.3830020303

Davis, G.B. (2009). Personnel is policy: Schools, student groups, and the right to discriminate. *Washington and Lee Law Review*, 66(4), 1793–1830.

Duggan, L. (2002). The new homonormativity: The sexual politics of neoliberalism. In R. Castronovo & D.D. Nelson (Eds.), *Materializing Democracy: Toward a Revitalized Cultural Politics* (pp. 175–194). Duke University Press. https://doi.org/10.1215/9780822383901

Dye, T.R. (1979). *Who's Running America? The Carter Years.* Prentice-Hall.

Eggan, F. (2008). Dykes and fags want everything: Dreaming with the Gay Liberation Front. In M.B. Sycamore (Ed.), *That's Revolting! LGBTQ Strategies for Resisting Assimilation* (pp. 11–18). Soft Skull Press.

Florida House on Capitol Hill (2020). *Our mission.* https://floridahousedc.org/mission

Foucault, M. (1991). *The Foucault Effect: Studies in Governmentality.* University of Chicago Press.

Gamson, W.A. (1961). A theory of coalition formation. *American Sociological Review, 26*(2), 373–382. https://doi.org/10.2307/2090664

Ghaziani, A. (2008). *The Dividends of Dissent: How Conflict and Culture Work in Lesbian and Gay Marches on Washington.* University of Chicago Press.

Gould, D.B. (2009). *Moving Politics: Emotion and ACT UP's Fight Against AIDS.* University of Chicago Press.

Hathaway, W., & Meyer, D.S. (1993). Competition and cooperation in social movement coalitions: Lobbying for peace in the 1980s. *Berkeley Journal of Sociology, 38*, 157–183. www.jstor.org/stable/41035469

The Hill Staff (2016, October 26). *Top lobbyists 2016: Hired guns.* https://thehill.com/business-a-lobbying/top-lobbyists/302777-top-lobbyists-2016-hired-guns

Hirschman, A. (1971). *Exit, Voice, and Loyalty.* Harvard University Press.

Holyoke, T. (2009). Interest group competition and coalition formation. *American Journal of Political Science, 53*(2), 360–375. https://doi.org/10.1111/j.1540-5907.2009.00375.x

Holyoke, T.T. (2014). *Interest Groups and Lobbying: Pursuing Political Interests in America.* Westview Press.

Hula, K.W. (1999). *Lobbying Together: Interest Group Coalitions in Legislative Politics.* Georgetown University Press.

Jacobson, G.C. (1996). The 1994 House elections in perspective. *Political Science Quarterly, 111*(2), 203–223. https://doi.org/10.2307/2152319

Keisling, E. (2017). The missing colors of the rainbow: Black queer resistance. *European Journal of American Studies, 11*(3), 1–21. https://doi.org/10.4000/ejas.11830

Kirsch, M. (2006). Queer theory, late capitalism, and internalized homophobia. *Journal of Homosexuality, 52*(1–2), 19–45. https://doi.org/10.1300/J082v52n01_02

Lipsky, M. (1980). *Street-Level Bureaucracy: Dilemmas of the Individual in Public Services.* Russell Sage Foundation.

Lorde, A. (1984). *Sister Outsider: Essays and Speeches.* Crossing Press.

Lukes, S. (1974). *Power: A Radical View.* Macmillan Press.

McAdam, D. (1982). *Political Process and the Development of Black Insurgency, 1930–1970.* University of Chicago Press.

McCann, B.J. (2011). Queering expertise: Counterpublics, social change, and the corporeal dilemmas of LGBTQ equality. *Social Epistemology: A Journal of Knowledge, Culture and Policy, 25*(3), 249–262. https://doi.org/10.1080/02691728.2011.578302

McNutt, J.G. (2008). Web 2.0 tools for policy research and advocacy. *Journal of Policy Practice, 7*(1), 81–85. https://doi.org/10.1080/15588740801909994

Megarry, J., Tyler, M., Farhall, K., & Weiss, C. (2018). *Queer inclusion or lesbian exclusion?* www.academia.edu/37906812/Queer_Inclusion_or_Lesbian_Exclusion_Project_Update_Nov_2018_

Meyer, D.S., & Imig, D. (1993). Political opportunity structure and the rise and decline of interest group sectors. *Social Science Journal, 30*(3), 253–270. https://doi.org/10.1016/0362-3319(93)90021-M

Mitchell, A. (1998, September 30). A new form of lobbying puts public face on private interest. *New York Times.* www.nytimes.com/1998/09/30/us/a-new-form-of-lobbying-puts-public-face-on-private-interest.html

Moser, S.C. (2006). Climate change and sea-level rise in Maine and Hawai'i: The changing tides of an issue domain. In R.B. Mitchell, W.C. Clark, D.W. Cash, & N.M. Dickson (Eds.), *Global Environmental Assessments: Information and Influence* (pp. 201–240). MIT Press.

Muñoz, J.E. (2009). *Cruising Utopia: The Then and There of Queer Futurity.* New York University Press.

Neff, C. (2016). Emotional taxation lecture [Blackboard slides]. University of Sydney GOVT 6159 Emotions, Agendas and Public Policy. www.blackboardconnect.com

Neff, C.L., & Edgell, L.R. (2013). The rise of repeal: Policy entrepreneurship and Don't Ask, Don't Tell. *Journal of Homosexuality, 60*(2–3), 232–249. https://doi.org/10.1080/00918369.2013.744669

Ostrom, E. (1998). A behavioral approach to the rational choice theory of collective action: Presidential address, American Political Science Association, 1997. *American Political Science Review, 92*(1), 1–22. https://doi.org/10.2307/2585925

Palmer, A. (2009, March 10). *Q Street on K Street: New group lobbies for LGBT interests.* Roll Call. www.rollcall.com/2009/03/10/q-street-on-k-street

Pattberg, P. (2005). The institutionalization of private governance: How business and non-profit organizations agree on transnational rules. *Governance, 18*(4), 589–610. https://doi.org/10.1111/j.1468-0491.2005.00293.x

Pepin-Neff, C.L. (2019). *Flaws: Shark Bites and Emotional Public Policymaking.* Palgrave Macmillan.

Pepin-Neff, C.L., & Caporale, K. (2018). Funny evidence: Female comics are the new policy entrepreneurs. *Australian Journal of Public Administration, 77*(4), 554–567. https://doi.org/10.1111/1467-8500.12280

Q Street (2020). *About us.* www.q-street.org/about-q-street-2/

Sabatier, P.A., & Jenkins-Smith, H.C. (Eds.) (1993). *Policy Change and Learning: An Advocacy Coalition Approach.* Westview Press.

Schattschneider, E.E. (1960). *The Semisovereign People: A Realist's View of Democracy in America.* Holt, Rinehart, and Winston.

Schneider, A., & Ingram, H. (1993). Social construction of target populations: Implications for politics and policy. *American Political Science Review, 87*(2), 334–347. https://doi.org/10.2307/2939044

Schwarz, J. (Director). (2011). *Vito* [Film]. Automat Pictures.

Sprayregen, M. (2020, June 11). Activist Nadine Smith on centering racial justice in the fight for LGBTQ equality. *Forbes.* www.forbes.com/sites/mollysprayregen/2020/06/11/activist-nadine-smith-on-centering-racial-justice-in-the-fight-for-lgbtq-equality/

Ward, J. (2008). *Respectably Queer: Diversity Culture in LGBT Activist Organizations.* Vanderbilt University Press.

Wouters, C. (2012). The slippery slope and the emancipation of emotions. In S. Thompson & P. Hoggett (Eds.), *Politics and the Emotions: The Affective Turn in Contemporary Political Studies* (pp. 199–216). Continuum.

Wright, M. (1988). Policy community, policy network and comparative industrial policies. *Political Studies, 36*(4), 593–612. https://doi.org/10.1111/j.1467-9248.1988.tb00251.x

3

LGBTQ LOBBYING TACTICS

Introduction

This chapter reviews the tactics that gay mainstream lobbyists and hegemons use to control or advantage themselves in the LGBTQ community. A large part of this is analyzing the types of lobbying that occur in the two different movements. The two movements are: the radical queer movement, which includes LGBTQ lobbying; and the gay mainstream, which appropriately includes gay mainstream lobbying. These movements are examined because they influence the pressure and costs that impact the types of lobbying that occur. Importantly, the movements also include activists, grassroots lobbyists, and organizations. Together, the tactics that are employed are designed to compete with one another.

These tactics matter because they show how hegemons preference assimilation over revolution in the LGBTQ advocacy community. These policy tools, lobbying strategies, and social movement activities stand out for the unique way they highlight different approaches to LGBTQ equality and coalition interaction. Public policy is often defined as "anything a government chooses to do or not to do" (Dye, 1972: 2).

> *I believe that lobbying tactics are what lobbyists choose to ask for or choose not to ask for.*

Lobbying and greater movement tools in the LGBTQ community are different for several reasons. The context of the political environment is contentious. This facilitates the development of "frenemies" and a tension where presumed allies are often more politically dangerous to an organization's success than anti-LGBTQ opponents. In addition, I analyze the roles of an organizational hegemon in representing the LGBTQ community to show how one movement supplants another.

Tactics are one way that lobbyists privilege one category of issues over another. Glitter bombs and kiss-ins are seen as more radical and board meetings between lobbyists are seen as more mainstream. Through the gay mainstream movement, we acquiesce to assimilation. In short, the tactics of the gay mainstream movement are the tactics that cause limited discomfort to the powerful. And when the mainstream movement wins, they do so as part of a respectability politics that yields to a heteronormative worldview. Heteronormativity wins. What looks like winning is actually losing.

"My sometimes friends" is a quote from the late drag-queen Lee Brewster as she was heckled off the stage for calling attention to gender-diverse issues such as prison accommodation at the 1973 lesbian, gay, bisexual, transgender, and queer (LGBTQ) Pride rally in Washington Square Park in New York City (Stryker, 2008). This conflict between the portrait of a united LGBTQ "movement" and the reality of a contentious divide is the lens for this chapter. The research question driving this chapter is how do hegemonic organizations control coalitions to politically advantage one type of movement over another? On the left, hegemonic organizations include the LGBTQ organization the Human Rights Campaign, the Democratic National Committee (DNC), and the Center for American Progress (CAP). Herrmann (2017: 1093) defines hegemony by noting that

> according to Gramsci, hegemony is created when the Weltanschauung, or worldview, of the ruling class is consented to as the cultural norm for society. Hegemony occurs when the leadership class accomplishes its goal of presenting its understandings of society for the whole society, reifying the status quo.

This can include hegemonic nations, organizations, narratives, and in this case, LGBTQ groups.

Let's be clear from the very start: there are not two movements by accident. The most politically defining moment in our history, Stonewall, was led by non-normative queer and trans folk, and they were rewarded with abuse. The gay mainstream lobbying followed this up by kicking people off stage and reproducing oppressions that pushed the radical queer movement to the fringes. This was not a polite disagreement. It wasn't polite in 1973 during the Washington Square Park march, and it's not civil now. For the life of the struggle for queer and trans rights, there have been queers and transgender people pushing and pulling. Radical identities were ignored for the benefit of those in power. So, the poor and the powerless organized, like the Street Transvestite Action Revolutionaries (STAR). That is the genesis of the two movements, and tension exists to this day.

Literature review

As an academic housekeeping matter, I would note that social movement is defined by Touraine (1981: 32–33) as "collective organized action through which a class actor battles for the social control historicity in a given and identifiable historical context." Social movement theory research has taken a number of different forms. Diani (1992: 8) notes that "to be considered a social movement, an interacting collectivity requires a shared set of beliefs and a sense of belongingness." Jenkins (1983: 528) further states, "Traditionally the central problem in the field had been explaining individual participation in social movements." Diani (1992: 7) adds that there are

> at least four aspects of social movement dynamics: a) networks of informal interaction; b) shared beliefs and solidarity; c) collective action on conflictual issues; d) action which displays largely outside the institutional sphere and the routine procedures of social life.

In addition, David Aberle (1966) describes four types of social movements including: alterative, redemptive, reformative, and revolutionary. He argues that each category is based upon two characteristics: (1) who the movement is looking to change and (2) how much change is being promoted. Aberle (1966) then identifies four categories:

A. Alternative social movements are looking at a selective part of the population, and the amount of change is limited due to this. Planned Parenthood is an example of this, because it is directed toward people of childbearing age to teach about the consequences of sex.
B. Redemptive social movements also look at a selective part of the population, but they seek a radical change. Some religious sects fit here, especially the ones that recruit members to be "reborn."
C. Reformative social movements are looking at everyone, but they seek a limited change. The environmental movement fits here, because they try to address everyone to help the environment in their lives (like recycling).
D. Revolutionary social movements want to change all of society. The Communist Party is an example of wanting to radically change social institutions.

Activism on LGBTQ issues, more formally, began with Harry Hay, and then with the homophile movement in the 1950s, which later staged marches in formal dress clothes as early as 1965 with Barbara Gittings and Frank Kameny to push a narrative that normalized gay life and assimilated into the heterosexual lifestyle. The energy of the movement then shifted to gay liberation with the 1969 Stonewall riots, which was ignited by transgender liberation activists Marsha P. Johnson and Sylvia Riveria, gay activists, and radical queer revolutionaries. In the 1980s, Larry Kramer, Peter Staley, and others took on the HIV/AIDS assassinations while the gay mainstream lobbying was born out of corporatization of the LGBTQ community in the 1990s.

Importantly, the LGBTQ community has relied on organizations, especially dominant hegemonic groups, to gain representation in public life. For most of the post-Second World War twentieth century, queer lives were considered illegal, sex was illegal, adoption was illegal, transgender transitioning was ridiculed, and being in personal relationships were not acknowledged by the State. Simply put, queerness was a disqualifying feature of U.S. citizenship until 2003 and the *Lawrence* decision (Carpenter, 2012). Queer rights were not recognized under the U.S. Constitution, and as a result, gay people lived in an underground private existence where their bars and their partnerships were often kept in the closet.

Moreover, "As late as 1971, police arrested an average of 2,800 gay men a year on public sex charges in San Francisco, in contrast to only sixty-three such arrests during that year in New York City" (Foss, 1994: 27). So, there was little reliance on the State to provide for LGBTQ people. As a result, parts of the LGBTQ community's identity came from their affiliation with representative non-profit organizations. Groups like the Mattachine Society and the Gay Activist Alliance (GAA) in New York provided enormous support and advocacy to the community. One part of this was a dance hall where queers and trans people could connect, the Daughters of Bilitis put out written materials and provided a support group for lesbians, and the Radical Faeries offered alternative spaces and a style of communal living.

The 1980s saw the movement divided, with white, gay, English-speaking, cisgender men pooling resources into a more reserved and mainstream nature and the adoption of a capitalistic, mainstream gay movement. Importantly, this neoliberal approach included the development of a hegemon, the Human Rights Campaign Fund, in 1980. This did not occur in the radical wing, where groups like the Gay Men's Health Crisis, the National LGBTQ Task Force, and the AIDS Coalition to Unleash Power (ACT UP) were activist-service organizations that divided into other affinity groups in the late 1980s and early 1990s.

Between the movements, there are different pictures of liberation. Lobbying seeks to change the underlying power dynamics of society and politics for marginalized populations like the LGBTQ community, whereas the gay mainstream movement is attempting to change things for select groups within the LGBTQ community and on select equality issues. Heroes are subjective but I argue these are figures who move the LGBTQ community forward through their actions or inspiration. Frenemies prioritize their LGBTQ issues alone to the exclusion of other rights. They are not movement building; they are issue or self-interest building. In all, mainstream groups focus on building heteronormative institutions and homonormative institutions, whereas radical groups are interested in disrupting unequal norms and upending institutions.

In this model of two lobbying categories for LGBTQ issues, there are two different ideological goals. The gay mainstream goal seeks to protect themselves and their interests before the full equality of LGBTQ peoples. This advantages heterosexuality. They offer equality governance as a principle advocacy model, again, which is a form of non-state private governance where lobbyists and non-profits create a distributive formula for the delivery of equal rights to certain groups proportionally based on the discomfort of those in power.

Equality governance has several elements: the lobbyist prioritization of issues that return power to the powerful, the way the hegemon helps determine the segmentation of equality, which includes what issues are advocated for, in what order, and at what cost. The third element, is that equality victories present a paradox that will, once achieved, put them out of business. As a result, equality governance is the business model that limits community success, sustains corporate groups' existences, and preserves inequality.

This analysis is important to the study of interest groups and coalition organizing because there are theoretically important considerations: a coalition organization's biggest opponent to achieving policy goals may be organizational friends, not an opponent because allied organizations know your weaknesses, and they often have more opportunities to engage in ways that are damaging. The goal is to seize the political agenda at a moment of opportunity for the LGBTQ community.

The split has meant that different lobbying categories serve different groups. The radical queer movement has adopted an intersectional approach (Crenshaw, 1991) to movement building that came out of Stonewall. Indeed, rather than embracing the diversity of the grassroots movement, the assimilationist community erases some identities and appropriates others. Within the neoliberal mainstream LGBTQ social movement, bisexuals are still often ignored, as are intersex people, and until more recently, transgender rights. This friction between radical queer and mainstream movements has been a mainstay of the community. It was on full display at the 1965 march around the White House, where queer hippies and more conservatively dressed activists participated. In short, the LGBTQ movements reproduce systems of oppression against one another. Even when we know better. Audre Lorde (1984: 130) notes, "There is no such thing as a single-issue struggle because we do not live single-issue lives." She adds, "We are not perfect, but we are stronger and wiser than the sum of our errors" (Lorde, 1984: 130).

Methods

This section puts forward a set of four categories of lobbying tactics. The four categories are non-conformist, LGBTQ tactics, gay mainstream, and conformist tactics (Table 3.1). The elements to be considered are the degree to which a lobbyist returns power to the powerful or disrupts the return of power to the powerful and the level of political discomfort the tactic is designed to inflict. Baumgartner, Berry, Hojnacki, Leech, and Kimball (2009) divide lobbying tactics into three categories: inside, outside, and grassroots. These are useful divisions for lobbying tactics that look at objective data to divide analysis. Another typology is based on the target: staffer, member, and coalition. The benefit of the framework that I have proposed is that it examines the negotiation of power and considers the role of penalties.

Inside the box for each category is a number of political issues which correspond to help look at the category critically. In addition, following the description of each category of tactics there are several examples of tactics that fall under that label.

TABLE 3.1 Categories of lobbying tactics

	Power returned	*Power disrupted*
Political discomfort high	*Non-conformist tactics*	*LGBTQ tactics*
	Guns	*Racism*
	Abortion	*Sexism*
	Immigration	*Disability justice*
	Environmental reg.	*Trans rights*
	Health care	*Homophobia*
Political discomfort low	*Gay mainstream tactics*	*Conformist tactics*
	Tax bills	*War*
	Shipping contracts	*International Relations*
	Privatization	*NATO/UN*
	LGB employment	*States lobbying*
	Gay marriage	*FEMA*

These are subjective elements based on how I would deploy the tactics and where I believe you would see this most often, when the moment of opportunity arises.

It is important to remember that when putting together an "ask" you are targeting both the staffer in the congressional personal office and the more formal minority or majority committee staff. In the executive branch this is more complicated. In short, you want to have a contact in the White House to "ask" if possible. There is lobbying with no ask. Those are referred to as "cultivation meetings." But that is not what this book is looking at. Instead this book is looking at LGBTQ lobbying as a broader form of "marginalized lobbying" for intersectionally oppressed populations. And marginalized groups rely on "asks," and should not be missing valuable opportunities to request support for their cause. The "ask" exemplifies that proximity to power is everything in Washington, D.C. In addition to a White House staffer a lobbyist would target one or two agency contacts who work on the issue to move things forward.

LGBTQ tactics

High disruption to the return of power to the powerful and high level of political discomfort in achieving the policy. This is the most politically uncomfortable category of tactics. This category both disrupts power and makes completing the policy goal deeply politically unpleasant at the end. In short, to get at an issue on the agenda disrupts power and reaching the goal disrupts power. For example, federal sex work decriminalization would represent a perceived moral evolution for the nation *and* then sex work would become more visible in hundreds of cities, where it is already occurring around the country. Other issues that would fall into this category are systemic and structural, including racism, sexism, disability justice, trans rights, classism, and homophobia. Other issues include eliminating poverty, homelessness, and incarceration reform. These goals would return power to these populations.

Under the LGBTQ tactics category, it is useful to note that these are often controversial, loser issues with a dispersed constituency and no hegemon. It is hard to find a hegemon for racism, or sexism. The tactics I have employed include supplying strategy and expert information. Because this issue is asking for disruption, money will not solve the problem. Information is just as valuable.

Staffing staff. Anyone who has worked on Capitol Hill will know what this means. Beyond information, this LGBTQ tactic is to be valuable to key offices. You are asking them to be difficult in a world of risk aversion. The only real way to be valuable is to be an expert who makes staff look good. As a result, staffing staff means doing the work of the congressional staffer for them. Drafting speeches, coming up with ideas for amendments, drafting the legislative language for amendments and bills, collecting co-sponsors for amendments and bills, and writing the one-pagers that explain the issue to other congressional offices, including the legislative process and the political liabilities or challenges.

In addition, LGBTQ tactics include organizing meetings with emotionally salient constituents (families, linguists, cancer victims and elite and front-line validators like generals, soldiers, doctors, nurses, and teachers). One part of the staff management process is to get them and the member (congressperson, President) emotionally invested in the issue. On "don't ask, don't tell" there were several key stories that influenced Congress. The first was General Keith Kerr, Virgil Richard, and Admiral Al Steinman coming out as the highest-ranking gay officers in U.S. history. They came out in *People* magazine on December 11, 2003. That day they met with Congressman Marty Meehan who became the lead member of the House of Representatives on the issue. Senator Ted Kennedy was the lead in the Senate.

Issues involved in LGBTQ tactics also need inside validators. In 2004, I made requests for data on "don't ask, don't tell" to the General Accountability Office (GAO) and Congressional Research Service (CRS) to gain more data on "don't ask, don't tell." Another form of inside validation is a "Dear Colleague letter" or DC. Dear Colleague letters are letters that inform members about an issue and look for co-signers to show it is an emerging issue. From a DC, the lobbyist will know who to target for co-sponsors and a path to gaining bipartisan co-sponsors. For instance, I worked with a Democratic member who had introduced different legislation with a Republican member. Knowing this relationship, we asked the Democrat to reach out to the Republican. They did and the Republican came onboard our legislation. With one Republican, we were able to get four more. This illustrates the point that lobbying is not chess, as many think. Lobbying is dominoes. It is about making big things fall, to make other big things fall.

Gay mainstream tactics

Low disruption to the return of power to the powerful and low level of political discomfort in achieving the policy. These are issues that demand the least and cost the least politically. Here you might see Presidential proclamations, the introduction of statement legislation that is going nowhere. Appointments for Ambassador, federal executive orders, and adjustments by federal agencies. Specific legislation returns power by being consistent by abiding by the terms of the "heterosexual ask" and equality governance. Don't ask for too much or stir things up too much. This includes the incremental increase in tax bills, shipping contracts, privatization, gay marriage, and LGB employment rights.

The types of tactics that are most often used within the gay mainstream category include ones that are supported by heteronormative institutions. For instance, there are often fundraisers for certain issues, where politicians appear to help the group raise money. These groups play a large role in picking the leaders on an issue. For instance, I was in a meeting at the Human Rights Campaign building where we were informed that Senators Lieberman and Collins would be the leaders on "don't ask, don't tell" in the Senate. There is also a great deal of staffing staff because the staff trust the heteronormative-aligned group to keep them safe. These lobbyists also provide expertise like issue, legislative, drafting, one-pagers, and talking points (polling). For instance, during much of the marriage equality fight in the states, large LGBTQ groups and funders would hire polling firms to help inform state-wide organizing to defend the issue of marriage.

Lobbyists' gay mainstream tactics also include Dear Colleague letters, and testimony before Congress. Again, their testimony is seen as safe and they are given this opportunity because of the close relationship. This also includes having a chairperson mention your talking points during a hearing; easy, because the point would not be disruptive, and instead would return power to the powerful.

Non-conformist tactics

Low disruption to the return of power to the powerful and high level of political discomfort in achieving the policy. This is perhaps the trickiest category because they are disrupting the system to return power to it. The system may greatly object, but it ultimately accepts the terms of the policy because the policy reinforces the existing power dynamics. Examples include climate change, abortion, immigration, gun control, and health care reform. This category is distinguished from gay mainstream tactics based on the level of the policy threshold. Pepin-Neff (2019: 53) looks at the connection between policy thresholds and emotionality. He states,

> highly emotional issues and events rise on the agenda based on presence of an emotional-political-temporal overlap, where there is an interaction around a problem that matters, to the people that matter, during a time that matters. This compound problem distributes penalties relative to the immediacy or sustainability of the penalty and the strength of the policy domain.

Issues that use non-conformist tactics are controversial issues publicly, but also winners with their personal constituency. Some of these specific tactics include reliance on expert validators with clout, such as scientists to talk about the environmental implications of a policy on wildlife, health care reform on poorer Americans, or gun reform for farmers. Bringing special constituents into the office or agencies are also effective. This may include families of immigrants or refugees who have escaped violence on the left, and adults who regret abortion attempts on the right.

Importantly, for high-discomfort issues like non-conformist tactics and LGBTQ tactics, there is a structural element in Congress and the Executive. Here, the lobbyists use their tactics to try to and survive sub-committee mark up (this is where a bill is discussed and amendments voted on in subcommittee); full-committee markup (this is where a bill is discussed and amendments voted on in before the whole committee); and Rules (if a lobbyist has failed at the sub-committee and full committee, the Rules Committee decides what amendments are allowed for a vote on the Floor of the House of Representatives). Surviving a floor vote puts the amendment in the bill. Finally, the bill is amended in the Senate and a joint committee finalizes the language. The lobbyist tries to influence the members on the Conference Committee so the language "survives conference." Then it just needs to be signed by the President and it becomes law.

Conformist tactics

High disruption to the return of power to the powerful and low level of political discomfort to achieving the policy because these actors are operating within the political system. The shock to power is not a shock to the system. Here we see issues like the War with Iraq, international relations law, NATO, the U.N., and state's rights lobbyists. In this case, conformist tactics may be used by inside players to rearrange power and attempt to seize power.

Conformist tactics present the most favorable situation for the greatest disruption to power. Tactics that are used include political cover:

> Political cover is defined as the tactical protection measures that politicians use or that are afforded to them when they feel their vote or public viewpoint on an issue could result in a political penalty that may reduce their ability to hold onto their office or further their ambitions.
>
> *(Neff, 2016: 191)*

The most famous example of political cover may be the "weapons of mass destruction" (WMD) narrative that was used to mislead the public and led to the war in Iraq.

Conformist tactics rely heavily on select testimony to build their case. An example here is then Secretary of State Colin Powell going to the U.N. to argue the WMD case against Iraq. Importantly, lobbyists who help come up with narratives for war and talking points for the United States demonstrate that the lobbyist is the one inside the system who is lobbying for their bill, that they wrote and introduced, with an issue lead they picked, on after testimony they arranged. These are not outside players.

Data

LGBTQ lobbying and single-issue advocacy pushes back against Diani (1992) and Jenkins (1983) in terms of shared beliefs and solidarity that are part of social movement organizing because the reigning neoliberal movement balances equality for the LGBTQ community with its access to elites. This means resources are directed in ways that are heteronormative and homonormative, and therefore fundamentally racist, sexist, transphobic, and homophobic. I work from the basis that groups are not always optimally rational, and political action is socially constructed in favor of white, gay, cisgender, English-speaking men from the Global North and they receive resources accordingly. Behavior is also error-prone. For instance, a report by BuzzFeed noted a 2014 internal report by the Human Rights Campaign staff that stated "the Human Rights Campaign last fall described the working environment at the nation's largest LGBT rights group as 'judgmental,' 'exclusionary,' 'sexist,' and 'homogenous'" (Geidner, 2015). Geidner adds, "'Leadership culture is experienced as homogenous—gay, white, male,' the report stated." This is consistent with Medina (2015: 53), who writes:

> The LGBT community began to develop its political strategies ... but we Chicanas/os were not part of that leadership. That was the issue for me. We were not part of the inner circle or part of that strategizing. That was all fine and good, because we always found allies, but the larger gay and lesbian movement just did not incorporate us as leaders. And so it was like "Forget them!"

Ferguson (2005: 53) adds to this, stating that "I argue that sociology's understanding of social construction in general and of sexuality in particular arises in the midst of white racial formations."

This analysis of LGBTQ movements relies, in part, on social movements resource mobilization theory (Jenkins, 1983), which Rootes (1990: 7) states

> starts from the very straightforward observation that all political action is socially structured and that the resources available to activists are patterned accordingly. It makes the assumption that movement lobbyists are at least as calculatively rational as are more conventional political actors and that they will, accordingly, devise strategies of action which make best use of the resources they have, and which minimize the requirement for resources they do not have.

In other words, the actions of actors are governed by political gravity.

You can only work with what you have, whether that is money, time, staff, volunteers, or creative ideas. This may also include emotional capacity as a resource.

These are all assets that deplete over time. The resources that emerged in the 1960s and 1970s included locations such as discos, bars, and advertising revenue that allowed print newspapers to advertise LGBTQ events and groups, increasing visibility. Baim (2012: 10) notes, "A good argument can be made that these community-based newspapers played a decisive role in building LGBT organizations and communities and in fostering political mobilization."

Controlling LGBTQ lobbying

Lest these tactics seem one-sided, it is essential to examine the offense, defense, and combination of environments in which political tactics are deployed. For instance, one way to control resources is to limit who is included in the room, or the protest. We see this play out at key moments in LGBTQ history that are noted below. Here we see power in action. The powerful return power to themselves and reproduce heteronormative oppressions of sexism, transphobia, and homophobia.

Throwing out Lee Brewster and Sylvia Rivera from New York pride—1973

Following the Stonewall riots of 1969, a 1973 Pride march in New York City finished with a celebration at Washington Square Park. That year there had been much discussion about prohibiting speeches as a way to celebrate unity. However, once the march arrived at Washington Square Park, activists took to the stage. Among them were hustlers and transgender activist Sylvia Rivera and Lee Brewster, who were protesters at Stonewall. Sylvia Rivera took the microphone and stated:

> I've been trying to get up here all day, for your gay brothers and your gay sisters in jail, that write me every motherfucking week and ask for your help, and you all don't do a goddamn thing for them. Have you ever been beaten up and raped in jail? Now think about it. They have been beaten up and raped after they had to spend much of their money in jail to get their hormones and try to get their sex changes. The women have tried to fight for their sex changes or to become women of the Women's Liberation. And they write Street Transvestite Action Revolutionaries (STAR) because we are trying to do something for them. I have been to jail. I have been raped and beaten by men many times, heterosexual men who do not belong in the homosexual shelter. But do you do anything for them? No. You tell me to put my tail between my legs.

The LGBTQ crowd responded by booing them off the stage. This response is based on stigma against trans, drag queens, the poor, and prisoners. Indeed, these events speak to a number of difficulties in LGBTQ lobbying. The first is that all identities are not valued equally. The hierarchy of identity that put drag queens, femme gay men, and transgender people at the bottom was and is a problem for the LGBTQ community.

Here, the majority at Washington Square Park exercised latent power to reproduce unequal hierarchies of identity that erase the identities of some in the community whilst celebrating others. This is ultimately self-defeating because when we throw someone else off stage, we also throw ourselves off stage. Sycamore (2008: 6) comments that this is systemic, stating "a ravenous gay mainstream seeks control, not only of our bodies and minds, but of the very ways we represent our own identities." In short, there is an LGBTQ normative social coding between the public, groups, political actors, and the media. And when new groups come in, they must abide by these repertoires.

The mainstream movement is more concerned with not losing friends. Wouters (2012: 201) notes that "regimes of emotion" are formed that rely on building trust, which includes

> making friends and acquaintances in the field, those involved customarily invite each other to dinner and to other sociable occasions, such as parties. Thus, by participating in the circles and gatherings of good society, they continue to seek the protection and reinforcement of their occupational and political interests.

Elias (2000: 395) adds that "fear of loss or reduction of social prestige is one of the most powerful motive forces in the transformation of constraints by others into self-restraint." However, to punish is to presume that deviation is doing something wrong, which requires the consent and reinforcement of other groups. "Those who are, thus, excluded have no motivation to cooperate except in order to avoid sanctions" (Ostrom, 1998: 17).

Almost throwing a woman out of the Stonewall, threatening to call the police—2019

In June 2019, at the 50th celebration of Stonewall, literally at the Stonewall Inn, a Black trans woman was heckled by white male patrons for trying to advocate for transgender rights. Reuters reporter Matthew Lavietes (2019) stated, "A Black transgender woman wanted to be heard, but the white men wanted to celebrate." She had interrupted a drag show, which got the patrons riled up. She shouted, wanting a focus at Pride on the deaths of transgender people because they are murders that so often lack attention. Some people were responsive, but others demanded the police be called, seemingly missing the bleak irony of calling the police to the Stonewall to throw out a trans woman of color. The music was turned up to play over her. A group of lesbians got between her and the crowd. She would not be thrown out. Instead she was given a microphone and spoke for 12 minutes. She read the names and gave short obituaries of the trans people killed.

She was a trans activist, seemingly from the radical side of the movement. Power was used by those in power to try and silence someone without power. To erase her and her existence. Her being was in the way of the powerful's pleasure. How fragile that homonormative existence must be. Ultimately, she was protected and *allowed* to speak. This tells us several things:

First, there is a race, gender, cis problem in queer and trans spaces, which speaks to the need for an intersectional approach. Intersectionality (Crenshaw, 1991) holds that people have multiple heterogeneous identities, that oppression is more severe at the intersection of marginalized identities, and that as a result the lived experiences that all men or all women have been different, based on race, sexual orientation, class, and ability. However, rather than simply a list of elements of identity, intersectionality speaks to the way systems and structures in society render some people more vulnerable than others based on a social hierarchy of identities.

Second, power still seeks to reproduce heteronormative oppressions. Here, overt power is used to first silence her and then permit her to speak. In either event, the behavior of the majority at the Stonewall was intended to negatively influence her comments, to shorten her remarks. She was not, in fact, being welcomed by the crowd. She was a guest in the middle of someone else's party. What was really taking place was she, as a member of the radical queer movement, was being placated and pushed aside.

These two examples help illustrate how white, cis, gay activists tried to police the equality of trans people in 1973 and again, how white, cis, gay activists attempted to govern the presence and bodies of trans people in 2019. When people talk about the "gay revolution" and "how far we have come" it is essential to note that many of the same tactics are used to silence the same communities more than 40 years later. The lived experience of trans people and trans people of color, in particular, speaks to how little progress has been made for them, while white, cis, gay, men enjoy the privilege of returning power to power. You must have a modicum of power in order to be able to return it to the powerful.

Discussion

This chapter moves forward by looking at the emotional cost of lobbying tactics on lobbyists who work on LGBTQ issues. This is an under-examined element of lobbying studies and is particularly crucial when considering lobbying by marginalized populations. It then identifies the advocacy tactics that are used in the radical queer and gay mainstream movements. It identifies the type of tactics and their degree of cost to the political system.

Emotional taxation of tactics on lobbyists

Tactics come at a cost or impose a cost. For example, oppressed communities face more *emotional taxation* (Pepin-Neff & Caporale, 2018). In this context, playing defense is more taxing, which may make it more likely for some lobbyists on

LGBTQ issues to have higher rates of burnout. Hegemonic groups manage the nature of the communities, political strategies, and the emotional habitus (Gould, 2009; Pepin-Neff & Caporale, 2018). Emotional habitus may be influenced by straight leaders who ask lobbyists to demonstrate how much an issue means to them and therefore meet an emotional threshold of how much they demonstrably care about an issue before broader attention and consideration is given. For instance, I remember one period of the "don't ask, don't tell" debate where an Obama White House staffer told me that if things did not start moving from the White House's end, then the LGBTQ community should come out in protest to show that we care, in order to convey that they should care, in the White House. However, there are tactics for caring that are seen as respectable and those that are not. When Dan Choi demonstrated in front of the White House, he was federally prosecuted (Marimow, 2013).

In a journal article published in *Politics & Gender*, Thomas Wynter and myself surveyed 1,019 LGBTQ activists and lobbyists from South Africa, the United States, the United Kingdom, and Australia, and asked how "emotionally taxing" it is to work on certain LGBTQ issues (marriage equality, LGBTQ military, senior care, workplace discrimination, youth homelessness, and mental health) and to participate in certain tactics (Tweeting, Facebooking, marches, personal expressions of identity, handing out flyers, attending events, lobbying, and leading a protest). There are three key findings from this study:

First, LGBTQ activists experience a high degree of emotional taxation for their work within the LGBTQ movement. Most interesting was that across all four countries, activist respondents indicated that it was fellow LGBTQ activists who presented the greatest obstacle to achieving equality. This is statistical evidence in favor of the "frenemies" model. In other words, when asked what they thought was the biggest challenge to equality, those answering the survey said the problem was allies. However, this is not entirely surprising. It is consistent with the literature regarding the U.S. civil rights movement, parts of the women's movement, and the peace movement. Indeed, Amin Ghaziani's research into LGBTQ "infighting" is also informative because while infighting can often be generative and help a coalition, it can also stifle progress (Ghaziani, 2008).

Second, young transgender activists of color experienced the worst levels of emotional taxation because these identities are among the most marginalized, and the intersection of age, race, and gender are points of acute oppression, consistent with intersectionality. Even the experiences of white transgender activist respondents were markedly different from those of transgender people of color. This means that the experiences of LGBTQ activists are not evenly shared, with some "groups within groups" paying a higher emotional cost than others.

Third, we found that certain activist issues and tactics distributed emotional taxation unevenly. For intersectionally marginalized groups, particularly transgender activists of color, public-facing activities like Tweeting, posting to Facebook, or leading a protest were more burdensome than marching in a Pride parade or handing out flyers. This may be due to increased trolling and discrimination when they are seen in isolation. In short, we found that costs were greater on the basis of identity, activity, and issue, which means that coalitions of activists and lobbyists face a range of difficult circumstances.

The implications of this research affect the makeup of coalitions, the types of issues that certain populations of activists and lobbyists may select, and the way activists and lobbyists sustain political penalties against opponents on emotionally difficult issues (Pepin-Neff, 2019). To begin, the main goal of social movement lobbyists is to apply political pressure and enforce political penalties. However, this may be more difficult and more harmful to some. Lobbying is a self-selected action with emotional costs and benefits. There may be a filtering effect based on emotional taxation that influences the type of issues that are advocated for on a nonprofit's agenda and the ability of a coalition to maintain advocacy unity and apply political penalties over a longer period of time.

If some tactics and issues impact more marginalized groups more harshly, this may drive them to avoid participation, changing the makeup and agenda of a lobbying coalition, or increase the likelihood of burnout for some more than others. It is valuable to note that those groups that were the most marginalized expressed that they would stay in the LGBTQ advocacy the longest. More research should be done on this subject. It may be that trans women of color feel that they are so at risk that there is no choice but to fight for as long and as hard as possible.

Some issues, like human rights advocacy, are designed by political systems and structures to exhaust most of the lobbyists involved in the policy process, to require sustained emotional opposition in the face of entrenched power. Thus, it is important to know that when lobbyists choose to engage on emotionally difficult issues like responses to school shootings, police violence, and LGBTQ homelessness, and then require tactics like protests, letter writing, or lobbying. These issues and these tactics can deplete the emotional resources of certain populations involved, making change less likely.

Repertoires of contention

This analysis of tactics builds on the concept of "repertoires of contention," which is defined by Tilly (1995: 41) as "the ways that people act together in pursuit of shared interests." Tarrow (1998: 30) notes that "the repertoire is at once a structural and a cultural concept, involving not only what people *do* when they are engaged in conflict with others but what they *know how to do* and what others *expect* them to do." For example, groups that are oppressed are often expected to march in the streets and protest for their rights. Whether it is women's marches or environmental marches, the ritual of walking down the street with signs is seen as a socially understood form of protest.

The way lobbyists choose tactics helps define which social movement an organization belongs to. Armstrong (2002: 9) says that, "by establishing the 'rules of the game,' fields limit the strategies of action that can be pursued. Some forms of action are defined as appropriate and possible, while others are not." Armstrong (2002: 9) adds, "The limiting of appropriate and possible organizational forms tends to produce organizational homogenization." Stepping outside the rules of respectable protest defines a movement as radical. For instance, ACT UP's die-in at St Patrick's Cathedral in 1989 during a mass was seen as rupturing the norms of protest.

Much of this is triggered as a defensive strategy. The adoption of queer non-conforming tools, addressing queer non-conforming targets, and disruption make powerful actors uncomfortable by interrupting the powerful to get an issue addressed. This is radical action because it discomforts heteronormative oppression. In many cases we are talking about lobbying from the outside, activism to maintain queer targets, such as lobbying to keep the bathhouses open in San Francisco or lobbying direct action to gain access to HIV antiretroviral drugs. There may also be lobbying to bring attention to an issue.

The figures shown in Table 3.2 include a number of social movement lobbying tactics. They have been aligned with mainstream activities, radical tools, or shared tactics. They highlight the liberal state model of conformist groups that use different tools to negotiate power. Collecting and collating in this way highlights the functional difference between the two movements while also noting the common spaces where they both work. Most common are the parallel structures that needed to be created to emerge from the closet and build community, as shown in the following section.

Parallel structures

Parallel structures are those tactics which are designed to form an institutional alternative to oppressive elements. For instance, these structures model a celebration of queer life and include: Radical Faeries (Thompson, 2011); agenda-setting photography and zines (Hastings, 2020); books (Ingle, 2020); Queer Shuttle (2009); emotion as an "undetonated device" (Lorde, 1984); comedy (Warner, 2012); teach ins, parties, and affinity groups/Q Street (Palmer, 2009); LGBTQ listservs (Gevisser, 2020); counter symbolism (Chibbaro, 2015); and drag queen story hours (Wronka, 2020).

As a comparison, Table 3.2 looks at tactics from the gay mainstream and radical queer movements. This analysis locates them in a category and then assigns a cost they impose on those with power.

We learn three things by looking at this data. First, LGBTQ tactics put those in power in the toughest positions, with a high cost to the powerful. This is because radical tactics are pushing the most directionally opposite to forces of static power. Second, those tactics come from the LGBTQ lobbying, which is thrust aside. They are pushed aside by hegemons who tap into mainstream efforts because power returns power to the powerful. This exercise reminds us of a few things. Normal lobbying occurs in a manipulative environment, so the point is not always to inflict penalties but often to rub the backs of your friends. This is a low cost to those in power. In short, the direction of costs in Table 3.2 is a reflection of the degree and direction with which institutions and systems redirect from those with more power to those with less power. Lastly, I note the tactics of hegemonic management.

TABLE 3.2 Comparison of tactics across movements

Tactic	Movement	Cost to those in power
Lawsuits	Mainstream	High
Stealth legislation	Mainstream	High
North Carolina	Both	High
Indiana	Both	High
Meals on Wheels	Both	High
Queer shuttle	Both	High
Emotion as an "undetonated device"	Both	High
Comedy	Both	High
ACT UP lobbying the FDA	LGBTQ	High
Glitter bombs	LGBTQ	High
Die-in by ACT UP at church	LGBTQ	High
Occupy	LGBTQ	High
Umbrella revolution	LGBTQ	High
Pie in the face of Anita Bryant	LGBTQ	High
Take my ring—Dan Choi	LGBTQ	High
Commercials	LGBTQ	High
TV interruption	LGBTQ	High
Angels for Matthew	Both	High
Protest songs	Both	Low
Story telling	Both	Low
Bake sale ban	Both	Low
Stopping taking HIV meds as a protest	Both	Low
Faerie communities—Radical Faeries	Both	Low
Zines	Both	Low
Fetish	Both	Low
Kink	Both	Low
Handkerchiefs	Both	Low
Cross-dressing	Both	Low
Teach-ins	Both	Low
Parties	Both	Low
Counter symbolism	Both	Low
Drag queen story hour	LGBTQ	Low
Kiss-in—ACT UP	LGBTQ	Low
Flash mob	LGBTQ	Low
Drag balls	LGBTQ	Low
Having sex as a political statement	LGBTQ	Low
Holding hands	LGBTQ	Low
Kite flying as visibility	Both	Low
Street theatre	Both	Low
Night of noise	Both	Low
Day of Silence	Both	Low
Lobbying	Mainstream	low
Music	Both	Medium
Documentaries	Both	Medium

(continued)

TABLE 3.2 Cont.

Tactic	Movement	Cost to those in power
Chick-fil-A	Both	Medium
Houston	Both	Medium
Agenda-setting photography	Both	Medium
Books	Both	Medium
Messages from Grindr—Australian Marriage Equality	Both	Medium
Form affinity groups/ Q street	Both	Medium
LGBTQ listservs—Insiders Out	Both	Medium
Tweeting	Both	Medium
Micro-funding	LGBTQ	Medium
Counter-protests	LGBTQ	Medium
Ashe action in D.C.	LGBTQ	Medium
Coming out at dinners	Both	Medium
Clicktivism	LGBTQ	Medium
Coming out	LGBTQ	Medium
Folsom Street lobbying the City of San Francisco through street festivals	Both	Medium
Pride parades	Both	Medium
Lobby days	Mainstream	Medium
GAO reports	Mainstream	Medium
Hearings	Mainstream	Medium
Treatment activism—TAG	Mainstream	Medium
Coalition building	Mainstream	Medium
Venue shopping	Mainstream	Medium

Hegemonic tactics

At the movement level, hegemons push one movement to the front over another. Hegemons manage coalition organizations. Hula (1999: 7) notes that "groups join coalitions to pursue strategic goals at reduced costs, to shape public debate, … and to receive symbolic benefits." Within a coalition, there are also norms that govern organizational behavior. Ostrom (1998: 12) says, "they have adopted a norm which serves them well over the long run."

In my experience working on "don't ask, don't tell" there are eight tactics used by hegemons to maintain control of a coalition:

Hegemons seek to control the agenda: gay mainstream tactic

Hegemons announce what the agenda for a community movement should be. For example, on August 7, 2009, Joe Solmonese, then President of the Human Rights Campaign, stated, "I see a road map of six-month windows: the hate crimes bill, then the Employment Non-discrimination Act, then "don't ask, don't tell" (Gilgoff, 2009). In this case, the gay mainstream lobbying led by the Human Rights

Campaign and its President identified the priorities in sequential order for the rest of the advocacy community to align behind.

Hegemons seek control of the emotional habitus: gay mainstream tactic

Hegemons try to control the emotional norms of all groups. This includes when to be outraged and when to be more settled. For example, an interview with Human Rights Campaign President Joe Solmonese entitled "Why Gays Can Trust Obama" set up the emotional norm that the LGBTQ community should have faith and patience with President Obama (Gilgoff, 2009). Emotional norm setting is a key action that was most effective from radical movements like ACT UP, which mobilized around anger; however, mainstream hegemons set the emotional agenda for their movement.

Hegemons control credit on an issue with the media: gay mainstream tactic

For instance, flying people in to take credit for a legislative victory and then using the media connections and more advanced media apparatus to claim credit is one tactic. Hula (1999: 8) argues that "the key enabling strategy revolves around developing a specific reputation through credit claiming, and self-determination." This may also include taking over rallies, displaying an organizational logo out front, putting out a press release that claims credit, showing up on the day of the vote, using media contacts to put pressure on coalition allies, or being able to allocate blame.

Hegemons co-opting issues: gay mainstream tactic

Putting together a project that is essentially what an ally is already doing, so that you can fundraise on it and potentially put them out of business, is one way to co-opt an issue. There may be an ideological alignment if not a previous program alignment that works to their advantage. This is consistent with "venue shopping" (Pralle, 2003) where advocates look for more welcoming political institutions and terrain in which to pitch their issues. Hathaway and Meyer (1993: 161) write, "In order to attract resources, a group must convince potential members and supporters not only of the importance of the issues it addresses, but also of the unique and vital role the individual group plays." This is a fight among a small number of groups, among a small number of potential donors.

Frank (2013) notes that in December 2009, HRC held a meeting with allied groups and donors to organize for the repeal of DADT, an issue that was being led politically by SLDN. He goes on to say, "The [HRC] plan was not to vote in 2010 but in 2011." And he adds, "*Politico* corroborated the charge, reporting in April 2010 that the White House was quietly urging members not to vote on repeal in 2010."

Hegemons direct blockades that keep organizations out of coalition meetings: gay mainstream tactic

In any coalition, there are varying levels of meetings where you invite or avoid allies. The final course of decision-making is not done by the coalition as a whole, but by the hegemon and other elite actors. In the case of "Don't Ask, Don't Tell," the decision-making was run by the hegemon in coordination with the White House. However, coalition allies are expected to keep the hegemon in the loop and not complain when they themselves are cut out of meetings.

Hegemons try to stop alternative coalitions that could challenge the hegemony: gay mainstream tactic

Advocate Dan Choi has also been critical of the Human Rights Campaign, noting that

> The Human Rights Campaign, the biggest, richest gay lobby, kept saying, "There is a plan from the President; the President has a plan." The HRC warning us not to criticize Obama was ridiculous. There was no plan. Left to their own devices, the politicians and lobbyists would never lead on issues like equal rights. Eighty percent of people want to get rid of "Don't Ask, Don't Tell," but HRC didn't even include it at the top of their list of priorities they wanted to accomplish.
>
> *(Streshinsky, 2010)*

Hegemons claim the higher moral ground for their efforts: gay mainstream tactic

Hegemons wish to fight on the high moral ground as a signal of legitimacy and political primacy. Individual activists join this process, for instance, by posting on Facebook to announce which groups are on the right side of an issue or strategy. This is "divine right political activism," where the activists' motives are unquestioned by fellow activists. These divine right activists have three elements: (1) they see themselves as instrumental to policy change. It will not happen without their actions; (2) they often serve as founders of new organizations to acquire personal ownership of the issue; and (3) they stay at an organization long enough to become a member of the executive committee or President. In many cases you see "founders' syndrome" with these actors.

Hegemons protect their own power structures

In the LGBTQ community there are tactics for how they handle those who attempt to speak truth to the power structures, whether about racism, sexual harassment, policy direction, or conflicts of interest. Protecting LGBTQ executive directors, board members, staff, and organizations from criticism is a business tactic that has worked its way into the LGBTQ advocacy community. Defensive tactics include disparaging remarks behind people's backs, non-disclosure agreements, defamation lawsuits, and attempting to get people fired. Again, LGBTQ social justice is a business and a threat to the business will be handled.

Conclusion

This chapter has looked at the different types of political tactics involved in lobbying on LGBTQ issues. Tactics are determined based on the degree of disruption to power they represent and the discomfort or cost that is inflicted on those receiving the tactic. I argue that there are four categories: non-conformist, LGBTQ, Gay Mainstream, and conformist tactics. The most likely to demonstrate "success" are those that return power to the powerful. This indicates that Washington, D.C. politics is often governed by self-interest. LGBTQ lobbying offers an alternative where the system and structure of benefits are not distributed to the powerful. I suggest that considerations of "progress" cannot come at the cost of the marginalized. This means that organizational success cannot profit at the expense of another marginalized group.

To close this chapter, I note that the tactics of hegemons involve the use of gay mainstream tactics. Here, we see hegemons try to protect themselves. A central argument of this book is that gay mainstream lobbying fundamentally helps heterosexual institutions. The same is true for gay mainstream tactics. This chapter has noted that there remain issues of discrimination from within the LGBTQ community that police the lives of trans people. Indeed, LGBTQ lobbying tactics both impose costs on others and receive them as well. The data affirms intersectional frameworks and suggests that those at the margins of LGBTQ face the greatest burdens for participating in lobbying and activism.

In the next chapter, I will look at LGBTQ lobbying and the White House.

References

Aberle, D.F. (1966). *The Peyote Religion among the Navaho*. Wenner-Green Foundation for Anthropological Research.

Armstrong, E.A. (2002). *Forging Gay Identities: Organizing Sexuality in San Francisco, 1950–1994*. University of Chicago Press.

Baim, T. (Ed.) (2012). *Gay Press, Gay Power: The Growth of LGBT Community Newspapers in America*. Prairie Avenue Productions and Windy City Media Group.

Baumgartner, F.R., Berry, J.M., Hojnacki, M., Leech, B.L., & Kimball, D.C. (2009). *Lobbying and Policy Change: Who Wins, Who Loses, and Why*. University of Chicago Press. https://doi.org/10.7208/chicago/9780226039466.001.0001

Carpenter, D. (2012). *Flagrant Conduct: The Story of Lawrence V. Texas: How a Bedroom Arrest Decriminalized Gay Americans*. W.W. Norton.

Chibbaro, L., Jr. (2015, November 11). *Kameny memorial unveiled in LGBT Veterans Day ceremony*. Washington Blade. www.washingtonblade.com/2015/11/11/kameny-memorial-unveiled-in-lgbt-veterans-day-ceremony

Crenshaw, K. (1991). Mapping the margins: Intersectionality, identity politics, and violence against women of color. *Stanford Law Review, 43*(6), 1241–1299. https://doi.org/10.2307/1229039

Diani, M. (1992). The concept of social movement. *The Sociological Review, 40*(1), 1–25. https://doi.org/10.1111/j.1467-954X.1992.tb02943.x

Dye, T.R. (1972). *Understanding Public Policy*. Prentice-Hall.

Elias, N. (2000). *Power & Civility* (The civilizing process, Vol. 2). Pantheon Books.

Ferguson, R.A. (2005). Race-ing homonormativity: Citizenship, sociology and gay identity. In E.P. Johnson & M.G. Henderson (Eds.), *Black Queer Studies: A Critical Anthology* (pp. 52–67). Duke University Press.

Foss, K.A. (1994). The logic of folly in the political campaigns of Harvey Milk. In R.J. Ringer (Ed.), *Queer words, Queer Images: Communication and the Construction of Homosexuality* (pp. 7–29). New York University Press.

Frank, N. (2013, February 19). *Obama's false "Don't Ask, Don't Tell" narrative*. The New Republic. https://newrepublic.com/article/112457/obamas-false-dont-ask-dont-tell-narrative

Geidner, C. (2015, June 3). *Internal report: Major diversity, organizational problems at human rights campaign*. BuzzFeed. www.buzzfeednews.com/article/chrisgeidner/internal-report-major-diversity-organizational-problems-at-h

Gevisser, M. (2020, August 26). *Grindr, PlanetRomeo, Gayglers—Corporate queerness reached India. But many still in closet*. ThePrint. https://theprint.in/pageturner/excerpt/grindr-planetromeo-gayglers-corporate-queerness-reached-india-but-many-still-in-closet/488999

Ghaziani, A. (2008). *The Dividends of Dissent: How Conflict and Culture Work in Lesbian and Gay Marches on Washington*. University of Chicago Press.

Gilgoff, D. (2009, August 7). *Why gays can trust Obama*. U.S. News & World Report. www.usnews.com/news/religion/articles/2009/08/07/why-gays-can-trust-obama

Gould, D.B. (2009). *Moving Politics: Emotion and ACT UP's Fight Against AIDS*. University of Chicago Press.

Hastings, D. (2020, July 7). *In zines, LGBTQ creators find a place to tell their own stories*. PBS News Hour. www.pbs.org/newshour/arts/in-zines-lgbtq-creators-find-a-place-to-tell-their-own-stories

Hathaway, W., & Meyer, D.S. (1993). Competition and cooperation in social movement coalitions: Lobbying for peace in the 1980s. *Berkeley Journal of Sociology, 38*, 157–183. www.jstor.org/stable/41035469

Herrmann, A. (2017). Hegemony. In C. Scott & L. Lewis (Eds.), *The International Encyclopedia of Organizational Communication* (p. 1092). John Wiley. https://doi.org/10.1002/9781118955567.wbieoc094

Hula, K.W. (1999). *Lobbying Together: Interest Group Coalitions in Legislative Politics*. Georgetown University Press.

Ingle, R. (2020, October 10). Roxane Gay: "We need to be more accepting of the choices we make as women." *Irish Times*. www.irishtimes.com/culture/books/roxane-gay-we-need-to-be-more-accepting-of-the-choices-we-make-as-women-1.4374434

Jenkins, J.C. (1983). Resource mobilization theory and the study of social movements. *Annual Review of Sociology, 9*(1), 527–553. https://doi.org/10.1146/annurev.so.09.080183.002523

Lavietes, M. (2019, June 30). Tensions between trans women and gay men boil over at Stonewall anniversary. *Reuters*. https://news.trust.org/item/20190630190335-62bqx

Lorde, A. (1984). *Sister Outsider: Essays and Speeches*. Crossing Press.

Marimow, A.E. (2013, March 28). Daniel Choi, opponent of "don't ask" policy, found guilty in White House protest. *Washington Post*. www.washingtonpost.com/local/daniel-choi-opponent-of-dont-ask-policy-fights-charges-in-white-house-protest/2013/03/28/d6456742-97be-11e2-814b-063623d80a60_story.html

Medina, D. (2015). We are a part of the history of Texas that you must not exclude! In U. Quesada, L. Gomez, & S. Vidal-Ortiz (Eds.), *Queer Brown Voices: Personal Narratives of Latina/o LGBT Activism* (pp. 47–63). University of Texas Press.

Neff, C. (2016). The performance of roll call votes as political cover in the U.S. Senate: Using C-SPAN to analyze the vote to repeal "Don't Ask, Don't Tell." In R.X. Browning (Ed.), *Exploring the C-SPAN Archives: Advancing the Research Agenda* (pp. 191–212). Purdue University Press. https://doi.org/10.2307/j.ctv15wxr41.13

Ostrom, E. (1998). A behavioral approach to the rational choice theory of collective action: Presidential address, American Political Science Association, 1997. *American Political Science Review, 92*(1), 1–22. https://doi.org/10.2307/2585925

Palmer, A. (2009, March 10). Q Street on K Street: New group lobbies for LGBT interests. *Roll Call*. www.rollcall.com/2009/03/10/q-street-on-k-street

Pepin-Neff, C.L. (2019). *Flaws: Shark Bites and Emotional Public Policymaking*. Palgrave Macmillan.

Pepin-Neff, C., & Caporale, K. (2018). Funny evidence: Female comics are the new policy entrepreneurs. *Australian Journal of Public Administration, 77*(4), 554–567. https://doi.org/10.1111/1467-8500.12280

Pepin-Neff, C., & Wynter, T. (2020). The costs of pride: Survey results from LGBTQI activists in the United States, United Kingdom, South Africa, and Australia. *Politics & Gender, 16*(2), 1–27. https://doi.org/10.1017/S1743923X19000205

Pralle, S. (2003). Venue shopping, political strategy, and policy change: The internationalization of Canadian forest advocacy. *Journal of Public Policy, 23*(3), 233–260. https://doi.org/10.1017/S0143814X03003118

Queer Shuttle (2009). *Outright Vermont executive director announces departure, for Australia.* Vermont Business Magazine. https://vermontbiz.com/people/november/outright-vermont-executive-director-announces-departure-australia

Rootes, C.A. (1990). Theory of social movements: Theory *for* social movements? *Philosophy and Social Action, 16*(4), 5–17.

Streshinsky, M. (2010, November). Dan Choi: Fed up with waiting for Congress and the president to repeal Don't Ask, Don't Tell, Lieutenant Dan Choi marched in uniform to the White House and handcuffed himself to the fence. In July, he was discharged from the military for publicly acknowledging that he is gay. *The Atlantic*. www.theatlantic.com/magazine/archive/2010/11/dan-choi/308278/

Stryker, S. (2008). *Transgender History*. Seal Press.

Sycamore, M.B. (2008). There's more to life than platinum: Challenging the tyranny of sweatshop-produced rainbow flags and participatory patriarchy. In M.B. Sycamore (Ed.), *That's Revolting! LGBTQ Strategies for Resisting Assimilation* (pp. 1–10). Soft Skull Press.

Tarrow, S. (1998). *Power in Movement: Social Movements and Contentious Politics*. Cambridge University Press.

Thompson, M. (2011). *The Fire in Moonlight: Stories from the Radical Faeries 1971–2010*. White Crane Books.

Touraine, A. (1981). *The Voice and the Eye: An Analysis of Social Movements*. Cambridge University Press.

Tilly, C. (1995). *Popular Contention in Great Britain: 1758–1834*. Harvard University Press.

Warner, S. (2012). *Acts of Gaiety: LGBT Performance and the Politics of Pleasure*. University of Michigan.

Wouters, C. (2012). The slippery slope and the emancipation of emotions. In S. Thompson & P. Hoggett (Eds.), *Politics and the Emotions: The Affective Turn in Contemporary Political Studies* (pp. 199–216). Continuum.

Wronka, T. (2020, June 9). *Drag queen story hour isn't letting protesters, pandemic stop them from reading to kids*. Spectrum News 9. www.baynews9.com/fl/tampa/news/2020/06/09/drag-queen-story-hour-continues-in-pasco-despite-protesters--pandemic

4

THE WHITE HOUSE AND LGBTQ LOBBYING

Introduction

What does it mean as a lobbyist on LGBTQ issues to disrupt power in one of the three houses of power in the United States?

The Office of the President. LGBTQ lobbying of the White House means you have the opportunity to be the most disruptive to the way power returns to the powerful, to enact the most uncomfortable tactics and the hardest "asks." To center the largest population of the marginalized.

Working at the federal level, lobbyists seek to change the world, from the Presidency of the United States of America. This is an affirmatively U.S.-centric analysis, but it is no small thing to lobby for or against arguably the most powerful political office in the world. Yet, it also underpins the greatest pressures to conform, the enticement to compromise, and the promise of power.

This chapter will note the importance of governance to LGBTQ rights and address the three asks on LGBTQ issues that have been made while I was working as the first lobbyist for the repeal of "don't ask, don't tell" (Neff & Edgell, 2013). I will use as research, those narratives that emerged from my time working with White House staff and use stories as data to highlight the role of LGBTQ lobbying. Through much of this chapter, "don't ask, don't tell" is used to motivate the analysis.

I begin this chapter at the end of the political story: the President of the United States, Barack Obama, was mad.

I could tell. I had seen a lot of speeches from "no drama Obama." But this was drama. It was April 19, 2010. Eight months and one day until President Obama would sign the legislation to repeal "don't ask, don't tell." He was on stage with Senator Barbara Boxer at a re-election rally in California. But a heckler wanted to push Obama on gays in the military (Good, 2010). The President heard the heckler yell, "Repeal Don't Ask, Don't Tell!!" He replied from the podium,

> We are—we are going to do that! Hey! Hold on a second. We are going to do that! So, let's … Alright, guys, guys. Alright. I agree! I agree!! I agree!!! No listen. No, no, no. What the young man was talking about, was, we need to repeal "don't ask, don't tell." Which I agree with. And which we have begun to do.

I had never seen the President so frustrated or mad publicly. Obama had pushed the Chairman of the Joint Chiefs, raised the issue during his State of the Union Address (Goldman, 2010), and moved to stop discharges without the approval of Generals (Emanuel, 2015). He had done more than any President in history to ensure gays, lesbians, and bisexuals could serve in the U.S. military. But here, he was getting yelled at on an issue that was before Congress, not him. So, he was mad. I wrote a piece in April 2010 in response to the Barbara Boxer fundraiser:

> So, I have a suggestion for our next direct-action. Next time we want to inter-rupt the President, I think we make sure to shout this: President Obama— Thank you. We hope you will join us during this Pride season, because we are very proud of you too.

Being a lobbyist means you deliver political packages no matter what. I had spent eight years working professionally on the repeal of "don't ask, don't tell." It was my job to wrap the issue like a Christmas package and deliver it to the President of the United States. To push when they need to be pushed and put on a bow when it's time to put on bows. This included making sure the bill was written and framed in the right way, that it was supported by the White House, that it was a stand-alone bill that could pass Congress, and that the President felt the support of the LGBTQ community. All of these elements were part of getting "don't ask, don't tell" right. It was both legislative and emotional. And so here I was, advocating for a "thank you." To let a pissed-off President know the LGBTQ community appreciated him.

Months went by. But in December 2010, the bill to repeal "don't ask, don't tell" passed the U.S. Congress (Neff, 2016). And a few days later President Obama would sign the legislation. Despite my issues with President Obama on "don't ask, don't tell" (and there are many), it was important for me that the process that followed included healing some of the wounds from the fight over "don't ask, don't tell." I personally had battled with White House staff. The activist community as a whole had really heckled the President hard.

So, when I was invited to the signing ceremony for the repeal of "don't ask, don't tell," I had made a decision that I was going to try and be supportive, to see what I could do to try and frame the signing ceremony as a giant thank you to the President. But there was a lot of history building up to this. I stood in line outside the Department of Interior, where the signing ceremony was held, with LGBTQ White House Liaison Brian Bond and the legendary LGBTQ rights activist, and Air Force veteran Dr. Frank Kameny. We waited for the doors to open on a cold December day.

We were led into a great hall with 700 seats. This historic day would be a celebration. A number of speakers came out and stood at the podium, and then it was time for the President. There were dignitaries on stage, such as Zoe Dunning, who had done so much. Eric Alva, Senator Lieberman, Senator Collins, and the President walked across the stage and greeted each other. The crowd began to chant, "Yes, we did!" "Yes, we did!" Then the President approached the microphone. I was sitting in the second row next to Andy Tobias, the DNC Treasurer:

PRESIDENT OBAMA: "Yes we did. Thank you. I, uhm—"
ME: "Thank you, Mr. President!"
PRESIDENT OBAMA: "You are welcome!"

I had stood up to shout at the President. He had looked at me and replied. I sat back down. We had come full circle. The job of a lobbyist. To make sure the President felt appreciated. In fact, I thought it was important that this be yelled at the President because he'd been yelled at so much about the need for repeal.

The *New York Times* reported it this way:

> He looked relaxed and upbeat as he soaked up the energy from an enthusiastic crowd. For the gay rights movement, which has been frustrated with the pace of progress under Mr. Obama, Wednesday marked a celebratory turning point. "Thank you, Mr. President!" someone shouted, as Mr. Obama took the stage.
>
> *(Stolberg, 2010)*

And my job was done. After eight years, this was the finish line. The package had been delivered. When the White House staff came up to me afterward, I said that I was the one who had said thank you. "Was that ok?" I asked. They said that since the President had responded with, "You're welcome," then yes, it was ok. The White House staff knew that if it was ok with the President, it was ok with them. I breathed a sigh of relief.

History was made. With President Obama's signature, one of the most divisive political issues in a generation had been debated in one of the most divided Congresses in 50 years and became the most pro-LGB congressional vote in American history. With 65 votes from Senators in favor of a stand-alone bill, the "Don't Ask, Don't Tell" Repeal Act received more votes in favor of passage in the Senate than Hate Crimes or ENDA (Hulse, 2010). I conclude that this is in large part due to the way lobbying evolved to focus on "don't ask, don't tell" repeal as a LGBTQ issue needing LGBTQ tactics. The process owned its queerness and challenged the reproduction of heteronormative oppression.

Moving forward, this chapter will review the background on "don't ask, don't tell." It will then look at the specifics on what makes up a White House "ask" including the roles of protocol and location. These are followed by an analysis of the three asks of the White House that were influential on the path toward repeal.

This includes some of the primary documents that led to these events. This analysis relies on my participant-observation lobbying on the issue of "don't ask, don't tell."

The LGBTQ asks of the Obama White House included:

1. An "ask" to sign an executive order to lift the ban on LGB service;
2. An "ask" to include repeal legislation in the Base bill; and
3. An "ask" to lift the ban on transgender service.

There were key factors that made the policymaking process different for "don't ask, don't tell" and separated it from gay mainstream lobbying. This chapter will also look at the tactics that were used specifically with the White House. There are several key points. First, "don't ask, don't tell" was perceived to be a political loser issue, which meant LGBTQ hegemons and other powerful forces initially did not want to touch the issue. As a result, it was left to more radical organizations and LGBTQ lobbying to deal with it. Second, the main issue behind "don't ask, don't tell" was radical queer sexuality, which does not reinforce heterosexuality. Third, the lessons from "don't ask, don't tell" informed many of the same people who worked on the lobbying effort to allow openly transgender military service.

Literature review

The issue of "gays in the military" has involved Presidents for more than 100 years. One of the worst anti-LGBTQ witch hunts in U.S. military history was conducted by a young Assistant Secretary of the Navy, who oversaw personnel issues. His name was Franklin Delano Roosevelt. Roosevelt led the investigation and witch hunts into suspected "queer" sailors in Newport Rhode Island in 1919 (Murphy, 1988).

The modern military personnel policies for LGBTQ military servicemembers came from "the Carter Administration" (Burrelli & Feder, 2009: 1). President George H.W. Bush also had a moment of consideration with LGB service during the Persian Gulf War under a policy referred to as "stop-loss" in 1992, where open service seemed possible for a moment.

In 1993, openly gay, lesbian, and bisexual service rose again on the political agenda. It had a mythical history and was perceived to have damaged the first 100 days of the Clinton Administration.

In an act "verging on insubordination" (Halley, 1999: 20–21), the Joint Chiefs of Staff had "threatened to resign in protest" if President Clinton lifted the ban on gays, lesbians, and bisexuals. A weakened White House then lost healthcare, and the Democratic Congress lost its majority for the first time in 50 years. Democrats blamed the loss on the LGBTQ community, and future LGBTQ issues were seen as "political plutonium" (Neff & Edgell, 2013: 233).

"Don't ask, don't tell" repeal was not an issue whose time had come. This was not inevitable under President Obama. Lobbying played an enormous role in lifting the statutory ban on gay, lesbian, and bisexual service in the U.S. military. To begin, nowhere are frenemies more present than in the White House. In the White House, there are staff working for LGBTQ rights and there are staff afraid of the loser issue status that comes with many LGBTQ issues. Again, the specter of "don't ask, don't tell" as a political catastrophe for Clinton's first 100 days in 1993 looms large.

Since 1994, more than 14,000 lesbian, gay, and bisexual troops in the U.S. military had been mandatorily fired solely on the basis of their real or perceived sexual orientation (Waranius, 2011). This ended in 2010 with the signing of the "Don't Ask, Don't Tell" Repeal Act. A very small list of those grassroots lobbyists who put their careers and their lives literally on the line includes: Allan Schindler, Barry Winchell, Leonard Matlovich, Perry Watkins, Miriam Ben-Shalom, Dusty Pruitt, Joseph Steffan, Margarethe (Greta) Cammermeyer, David Hall, Jack Glover, Alastair Gamble, Shalanda Baker, Dan Choi, Victor Fehrenbach, Stacey Vasquez, Eric Alva, Calpernia Addams, Keith Meinhold, and Jose Zuniga.

It is important to understand what "don't ask, don't tell" was as both a law and a policy. First, "don't ask" was the policy. It was barely enforced. It stated that people should not be asked about their sexual orientation, but, that if an anonymous note was sent to your command stating you were a lesbian you could be investigated. That if someone wrote to your command under an assumed name, or an ex-boyfriend was trying to get even, or if you were beaten by your partner and went to the hospital, those records could be used against you. If you were a female fighter pilot and one of your trainees didn't like the grade they received, they could call you a lesbian and you would be investigated. If you talked to a priest. If you were harassed. If you were asked by your commander and did not believe in lying. All of these mandated under law an investigation. Many times, people looked the other way, but the law stood firm.

"Don't Tell" was the law. That made telling anyone you were LGBTQ, displayed conduct, or tried to get in a same-sex marriage; these were grounds for discrimination and discharge. Under "don't tell" *the law stated* that LGBTQ servicemembers fighting honorably were unfit. Republicans argued that "homosexuality was incompatible with military service." The law was quick and harsh. The "don't tell" policy forced LGBTQ servicemembers to lie as a condition of service.

Data

There are two under-recognized gruesome murders that changed the history of LGBTQ rights in America: Allan Schindler and Barry Winchell.

In 1992, 22-year-old Naval seaman Allan Schindler was beaten to death by his fellow shipmates for being gay (Shilts, 1993). He was murdered in a bathroom in Japan. Schindler's wounds were so severe that the coroner compared the injuries to being hit by a car. The *Los Angeles Times* reported in January 1993:

> Coming as President-elect Bill Clinton is planning to lift the ban on gays in the military, the case is stirring strong feelings. Gay rights advocates are urging Clinton to take swift action to legitimize the presence of homosexuals in the military and have accused the Navy of trying to cover up circumstances of

> the killing. The killing occurred in October, and the Navy waited until gay
> rights groups demonstrated in front of the Pentagon in December before
> announcing a few details of the crime.
>
> *(Reza, 1993)*

Allan Schindler has never received the recognition he deserves for pushing President
Clinton toward acceptance of gays in the military. Nor has his mother Dorothy
Hodges for keeping her son's honorable service and memory alive. However, "don't
ask, don't tell" was not discussed again nationally until 1999.

In 1999, 21-year-old Army soldier Barry Winchell was beaten to death for being
perceived as gay by his fellow soldiers (Pachter, 2001). He was murdered on base at
Fort Campbell, Kentucky. Lying asleep on a bed, he was beaten in the head with
a baseball bat, the first murder under the "don't ask, don't tell" law. One of the
murderers washed the bat.

> *A drawing of the bat used to murder Winchell was scrolled on a wall on base. It had
> the words "fag whacker" written on it.*

The *San Francisco Examiner* (1999) covered the murder, reporting, "The President's
wife, Hillary Clinton, said campaigning last week that the policy wasn't working
and should be replaced. Over the weekend, President Clinton acknowledged that
there were flaws in 'don't ask, don't tell' and vowed to fix them." The law remained
in place.

In 2002, President George W. Bush would nominate the General who
commanded Fort Campbell when Barry Winchell was murdered for a promotion (Neff, 2011). The fight over this nomination and the memory of Barry
Winchell was the single most important factor in the repeal of "don't ask, don't tell."
Neff and Edgell (2013: 236) state that, "This period of congressional dormancy
changed in 2002 with President Bush's nomination for promotion of then Maj.
Gen. Robert Clark, the former Commanding General at Fort Campbell." Indeed,
after 18 months of fighting the nomination, at a pool in Miami on November 9,
2003, Kathi Westcott, Sharra Greer, Karen Armagost, and I decided it was time to
challenge the legislation and repeal "don't ask, don't tell." This motivated the legislative and executive LGBTQ lobbying effort. I started drafting repeal legislation for
Congress the next day.

Leaning into a loser issue

"Don't ask, don't tell" may be perceived as a loser issue, but history shows that it
is not. It was not a mainstream issue that was guided by gay mainstream lobbying.
It was an LGBTQ lobbying issue because it disrupted returning power to the
powerful by making the Pentagon have to support gay sex.

Military readiness was a proxy for the real debate about "gays in the military," which was based on a long-held fear of gay men as predators or willing

participants in affirmative, consensual gay sex with each other. The photo of Republican Senators Sam Nunn and John Warner in a submarine, inspecting the close quarters of the beds, begged the question of how gay men could be trusted to serve without incident. This meant the issue of "don't ask, don't tell" was fundamentally about permitting or banning gay sex. Indeed, in the first hearing about "don't ask, don't tell" repeal the argument was made: that in close quarters where men needed to strip down to save body heat, gay men could not be trusted. Interestingly, congressional members laughed off this specific testimony in the hearing. The public education about gays and gays in the military had moved through radical queer sexuality. "Don't ask, don't tell" was an issue about the acceptability of gay, male, sex in society and the Department of Defense would have to be pro-gay sex in order for it to pass. Repeal won because this issue was about queer sexuality, queer discrimination, and the choice to perpetuate that discrimination or to end it.

Lobbying on "don't ask, don't tell" celebrated queerness and won on those terms. It re-prioritized issues by focusing away from mainstream concerns like ENDA that was part of a large fundraising apparatus (Fox, 2013). And the LGBTQ lobbying around "don't ask, don't tell" made President Obama and the White House uncomfortable for much of the process.

In addition, "don't ask, don't tell" does not meet the criteria for a "loser issue" designation because there are seven attributes needed to qualify. These include: that the issue is "made visible and invisible relative to power." "Don't ask, don't tell" countered this by having attention based around focusing events (Birkland, 1997) which are surprise events that the public and politicians learn about at the same time. An example was the murder of Barry Winchell and the discharge of LGBTQ Arabic linguists. Both disrupted the attentiveness or salience of the issue. The second is that, "there is a political cost for politicians in trying to solve their problem." This has been presumed for decades, but "don't ask, don't tell" polled as high as 79 percent, seven years before the law was repealed.

In addition, perhaps the most important counter-narrative is the argument that loser issues have "a policy monopoly, organizational structure, and resources in favor of the status quo." This is important because it is argued that mainstream loser issues are losers because the system they opt into structurally restricts their political trajectory. "Don't ask, don't tell" policy language was changed shortly before final passage and SLDN shut down soon after repeal took place. On the issue of resources, this is a mixed consideration. While the issue did not present a financially advantageous business model for SLDN and the issue was not controlled by gay mainstream lobbying, there were superstars like Lady Gaga who were prominent in the final years (Bennett, 2014).

Loser issues also promote "a counter-mobilization of discourse, groups, media, and validators against change" or "negative events." This did not happen. Instead, there was a longstanding group of policy entrepreneurs (Neff & Edgell, 2013; Pepin-Neff & Caporale, 2018) at SLDN who worked on the issue for nearly a decade together. They helped build a foundation for the issue that would both limit burnout amongst themselves and create a strong infrastructure for openly LGB service, once enacted.

Instead of being a loser issue, "don't ask, don't tell" successfully navigated the systematic traps that limit gay mainstream lobbying. As a result, LGBTQ lobbying and its fundraising model was not bound to the respectability politics that contain mainstream issues and return power to the powerful.

In its place was a debate about radical queer sexuality beyond the confines of traditional masculine roles, including submissive sexuality, cross-dressers, gender play, feather boas, drag, and a rejection of toxic masculinity and the male gaze. LGBTQ lobbying leaned into gay sex. These are profound disruptions to a military system that is obsessed with heterosexual, male, cisgender, masculinity and the way the military appears.

Methods

The anatomy of a White House "ask"

There is no political "ask" like a White House "ask." The White House staff organizes the operations, systems, and structures around the President to minimize her access, time, and actions in order to maximize the odds of re-election at every level, in every agency, with every hegemon. This is the power of incumbency: to shape the narrative of a Presidency around the alignment and support of an entire government and the limited dissent of most constituencies.

Before the White House

The first "White House ask" happens before she gets there, if the lobbyist is any good. This may be at fundraisers, town hall meetings, campaign debates, or reporter's questions. A good lobbyist will plant a version of the same question to all of these. This may happen when a prominent member of Congress joins a committee, such as Senator Clinton and Harry Truman. When a Cabinet member is appointed like Secretary Julian Castro or a Vice President is nominated like Mike Pence. Another moment is when a member of the Party is seen as a high-profile thinker or fundraiser, like Ronald Reagan, Barack Obama, or Barry Goldwater.

The best time for a "White House ask" is on the campaign trail when candidates are more likely to say "yes." A lot of time is spent trying to lock campaigns into policy positions based on the needs of that constituency. This may be done by using one candidate's statement as a way to get another, or to work within the party to shape the party platform so candidates are forced to adopt it and, if elected, possibly act on it. It creates pressure points for the future. For instance, I met with the Republican National Committee (at RNC headquarters) on March 14, 2003 to address the 2000 language, which stated, "We believe the military must no longer be the object of social experiments. We affirm traditional military culture. We affirm that homosexuality is incompatible with military service" (Peters & Woolley, 2000). This went nowhere.

In 2003, Kathi Westcott and I also went to the Democratic National Committee on April 17, 2003. We had a meeting to discuss putting repeal language in the platform, which was not there in 2000. In addition, we met with the Democratic Leadership Council on April 23, 2003 to discuss framing options for repeal. They suggested creating a narrative around the twenty-first-century advancement plan at the Pentagon so the policy would be seen as an "old backpack on a new soldier." We also discussed access to meetings with Presidential campaigns.

In 2003, Kathi Westcott and I went to Presidential campaign meetings with the staff from Governor Howard Dean and Senator John Kerry's campaign teams. The goal, for example, was a statement in favor or against the repeal of "don't ask, don't tell" in the Democratic Party, which would present a situation where there are two penalties: losing the vote of the LGBTQ community and the nomination of the Party. This is different, however, depending on which political party is being examined. In the case of the Democratic Party in 2003, repeal was not in the 2004 platform.

Protocol

Once in office, the "White House ask" needs to engage skillfully with the White House staff. To begin, you don't meet with the President, the President meets with you. The events that transpire that facilitate a White House "ask" are fluid and change from administration to administration, and over time. My analysis is informed by having been to the White House during the Clinton administration, G.W. Bush administration, and Obama administration.

With a President in office, there are a number of stages to reach before getting to a White House "ask." The first is to reach out to interest group gatekeepers, the large White House surrogates or hegemons. These include the DNC, RNC, CAP, LCCR, NAACP, PFAW, HRC, NCLR, NOW, PPFA, Pew, Brookings, and Heritage, just to name a few. These meetings are meetings for organizations and lobbyists within coalitions.

Once a lobbyist or organization has the goodwill of coalition allies, the next call is to the White House Office of Public Engagement. The Office of Public Engagement is the office that handles special interest constituencies and communities. The Office is very important, but this is an introductory meeting that requires further advancement. From here, the goal is to pull in staff from the White House Counsel's office. This is a serious meeting. The Office of the White House Counsel does not make time for unimportant meetings.

Similar to this, organizations and lobbyists may go from the Office of Public Engagement to an agency meeting. For instance, I have had meetings at the White House on "don't ask, don't tell" and was referred to the Department of Defense— and then went back to the White House as a follow up. As a result, a lobbyist might go from an agency meeting to an agency Counsel meeting.

Meeting with "the White House" in most cases means having the goal of meeting with the Deputy White House Chief of Staff. There are usually several of them with different portfolios. The Deputy Chief of Staff is a stakeholder who can write memos to the President.

Timing

In addition to protocols, time matters. The timeline is often crucial for a White House running for re-election. The re-election campaign starts the moment the election is won. For instance, I was in a meeting at the Obama White House in 2009 and I was giving a staffer a hard time on an issue. They responded that I needed to "get with the program" because "they had a re-election to win." The term had just begun but the pivot to the next campaign was under way. As a result, the lobbying strategy of the White House is to maximize benefits, minimize risks and keep both out of the press (until the campaign). In such circumstances, administrations look to large hegemonic organizations that work within an issue subsystem to dominate the lobbying process, help produce order, protect those in power, facilitate the re-election of the White House, and ensure the cooperation of coalition partners (Pepin-Neff, 2019).

As President, the repeal of "don't ask, don't tell" presents two re-election issues and the same penalty. First, a President may not be in favor. Or second, she may be in favor but not able to accomplish repeal. In reality, "Don't ask, don't tell" ultimately had the pull of White House staff because it was seen as a broken promise and a threat to turn-out by the LGBTQ community for the 2012 election. Here, the penalty is losing the office of the Presidency. Losing the ability to appoint Supreme Court Justices. Being unable to serve as the Commander in Chief. Influencing world events. It is important to keep the stakes in mind for these officials.

Mechanics

Let's say you are going to meet your contact at the White House. The first step is to email the staffer your Social Security number and date of birth so the Secret Service can run a background check on you and make sure you are safe to enter the White House Complex. Importantly, most White House staff do not work in the actual White House. They are on the White House Complex, which includes the Eisenhower Executive Office Building (EEOB).

If the meeting moves forward, your first meeting with staff is most likely at the coffee shop on 17th Street across from the White House. This is not an insult; this is protocol. Very few people make it into the EEOB or the White House in their first or second meeting. I have had many meetings here or down 17th street at the McDonalds.

If your meeting is in EEOB, you need to leave yourself 30 minutes extra to check-in. It is a busy door, of a busy office, in a high-security area. The combination of those elements means that things are slow. You will be emailed by your contact or staffer early that morning with details on the entrance they will meet you at and the time. You will probably enter the EEOB through the Southwest Appointment Gate.

You will show identification as you walk in the gate. I once entered this gate for a ceremony honoring openly LGBTQ Ambassador David Huebner. I was moving slowly at the gate as they checked my ID. I turned to the person standing next to me and asked if they knew Ambassador Huebner. He said: "I am Ambassador Huebner."

In the unlikely event that your meeting is in the White House, you will receive the same email and prepare to be there one hour early. You will likely enter through the Northwest Appointment Gate near the front of the White House (Figure 4.1). There you will be screened by the Park Police and Secret Service. You are now walking toward the West Wing (Figure 4.2). There will be cameras for the television stations on your right. As you approach the White House, you can see the West Wing because there is a United States Marine guarding the door and the crest of the President overhead (Figure 4.3). Yes. It looks just like on television.

The staffer will usually meet you near the door. It would not be unusual for the meeting to take place in the hallway. This is not rude or unusual. In the Congress and the White House this is normal. This is a function of how junior your staffer is more than you. But it is also part of the limits on time and room availability that the White House presents because it is so small.

Lastly, once you are in the hallway or the meeting room, you have seven minutes. The performative nature of the "ask" is seven minutes long. Three minutes for the brief, one minute literally for, "the ask I would like to make of

FIGURE 4.1 White House: Pennsylvania Ave. front entrance

FIGURE 4.2 White House: West Wing entrance

FIGURE 4.3 White House: Entering the White House grounds (Penn. Ave.)

you" and three minutes for their questions and response. You should expect seven minutes of a staffer's time. Anything beyond this is a good sign. If they talk the whole time and there is no time for an ask, then the meeting is over, then you have your answer. This is a bad sign. If they ask you what your ask is, the meeting is over, they know what your ask is and it is too low, or they know what your ask is and it is too high.

The less you speak, the better. I was conference-called into a meeting in the West Wing from the University of Sydney to talk about "don't ask, don't tell." White House Deputy Chief of Staff Jim Messina was running the call. They were discussing legislative reforms to an updated repeal bill, but they kept calling it a "compromise." After the third time this came up, I spoke two sentences. "This is not a compromise. This is the dismantling of "don't ask, don't tell." Jim Messina took over, "That's it. It's the dismantling." The two sentences were the whole point of the call. No more, no less. When newspapers reported on the White House meeting they said:

> By Monday evening, activists were announcing what the Human Rights Campaign's President, Joe Solmonese, said in an official statement was the "brink of historic" action to get rid of "don't ask, don't tell." While legislative language was not available by press time, several prominent activists cheered the White House for clearing the way for what Aubrey Sarvis, an Army veteran and one of the activists who took part in the White House meeting, called "a dramatic breakthrough in dismantling 'Don't Ask, Don't Tell.'"
>
> *(Washington Independent, 2020)*

Location

As a person leaves the White House there are other locations to consider. Now that the formal process has begun and trust established, other venues become possible. There are a number of venues in the White House where lobbying is conducted. The first is the most well-known, the President's office off the Oval. If a lobbyist has access to this location, the deal is probably already done. President Johnson is often photographed in the Oval itself lobbying members of Congress.

There are a number of Presidential venues outside the White House that are also lobbying opportunities. These are much scarcer in the post 9–11, Covid-19 world. One was the President's box seats at the Kennedy Center for the Performing Arts.

I was fortunate to see Yitzhak Pearlman there. Another is the line of donors who go out on the White House lawn to watch the President take off and land in the helicopter Marine One. I did this for President George W. Bush. This also includes golf courses, basketball games, swimming pool, Martha's Vineyard, Mara Lago, and even swimming inside shark net beaches (Pepin-Neff, 2019). These are important locations for lobbying "asks." The location of venues are valuable assets in lobbying, particularly in a profession obsessed with the proximity to power.

But what if you have the opportunity for an "ask" but not for lobbying. Here, we see that individuals without the privileges that are conferred on those who are white, cis, male, not living with a disability. Who are advantaged further with access to organizations, access to coalitions, access to the White House staff, and access to the President. These people understandably jump at opportunities to engage with an elite, restricted system. In fact, for the best lobbyist, an "ask" to the President may only ever happen once. At issue is the governance model that directs a lobbyist's actions—again—if they have access to the lobbying infrastructure.

How hard to push

The phrase "lobbying on LGBTQ issues" is a way of noting once again that there are two lobbying categories and two movements within the LGBTQ advocacy community. LGBTQ lobbying re-centers power on the weak and vulnerable while receiving no benefit. This type of lobbying pursues equality permanence and is part of the radical queer movement. And one profits from the net benefits that come from distributive equality. This is gay mainstream lobbying using equality governance in the gay mainstream movement.

The type of governance that is adopted by a lobbyist within the political system can give them clout over time. Equality governance is designed to manage the proportional redistribution of power as a measure of the discomfort to the powerful. Gay mainstream lobbying is therefore not neutral because groups that engage in equality governance often receive a benefit equal to the net advantage of the compromise that they have arranged. In other words, gay mainstream lobbying gains the benefit of what they hold back when negotiating a situation. For example, if you go to a bar and the drink costs $7 but the bartendress only charges you $5, then you might give both a tip of $2 as well as the $2 that she saved you. The problem with arrangements having to do with the equality from people's lives is that in compromising on the pursuit and delivery of total equality, gay mainstream lobbyists compromise themselves.

The uncomfortable "ask"

As noted, the ask is a calculation, a political equation of what a lobbyist wants, how badly they want it, how soon, and at what cost. Additional factors include the degree of change that the ask requests and how many are being asked to change. And how many people are required to make the change happen (Levine, 2009: 167). As well as the degree of risk the ask imposes. And the degree of difference from a position they hold. She may already hold that position. Below are three notable events in LGBTQ history of activists in the LGBTQ community confronting a President or the White House for HIV/AIDS action, transgender refugee rights, and "don't ask, don't tell" repeal.

Bob Rafsky and Bill Clinton—1992

A contributing factor to coalition management is the way organizations create narratives to care about an issue on which they advocate. In the Advocacy Coalition Framework, the concept of "devil shift" (Sabatier, Hunter, & McLaughlin, 1987) is important because it highlights the way a level of dislike for someone or something serves as an organizing principle to connect members of a coalition. Devil shift also creates a distortion where someone who may be bad is seen as both wildly evil and unbelievably powerful.

This is important to lobbying in the White House because the White House will demand lobbyists demonstrate emotional anguish over their issues before the White House will get involved. For instance, I was in a meeting in the White House where I was told our organization needed to demonstrate how much we cared before the White House demonstrated that they cared. This is emotional agenda-setting.

In 1992, at a Presidential campaign fundraising event, ACT UP activist Bob Rafsky confronted Arkansas Governor and Presidential candidate Bill Clinton on the subject of government inaction on AIDS. The *New York Times* (1992) reported that Clinton stated, "I feel your pain, I feel your pain, but if you want to attack me personally you're no better than Jerry Brown and all the rest of these people who say whatever sounds good at the moment."

This situation saw the exertion of power by then Governor Clinton. There were two messages transmitted to the community. First, activists must demonstrate pain in order to receive reciprocal emotionality from a politician. And second, Bill Clinton is saying that LGBTQ activists need to behave and be respectable. Indeed, to enter politics is to attempt to enter good society on the terms of the hegemonic themes or narrative and to perpetuate self-restraint and manners to the benefit of those in power. Nothing scary or too far out there is welcome or tolerated in this risk-averse, constituent-friendly, and donor-friendly environment. However, this leaves out people who cannot speak up and suffer in silence. This can include people affected by domestic violence who are penalized (i.e. beaten by an abuser) literally for raising their voices. This is consistent with a concept called "security as silence" noted by Lene Hansen (2000). Eggan (2008: 15) addresses gay men in this situation by saying, "We came to understand that our gay rights would be nothing but privileges for the well-to-do unless we acted for the most vulnerable, most easily victimized queers." In short, politicians put the burden on the marginalized LGBTQ community, to emote appropriately. To demonstrate that we cared about an issue sufficiently but not dramatically or suffer the consequences.

Throwing the trans refugee activist out of a Pride reception at the White House

On June 25, 2015, the White House hosted an LGBTQ pride reception for select members of the LGBTQ community (Lee, 2015). As the guests gathered, President Obama came to the podium. However, as he began to speak, Jennicet Gutiérrez, a trans woman of color who was one of the attendees began to shout and raise concerns about trans refugees. President Obama responded, "No, no, no, no. Hey, listen you're in my house. You know what, it's not respectful when you get invited …" (Liptak, 2015). According to media reports, "Attendees drowned out her pleas with chants of 'Obama! Obama! Obama! One attendee shouted at Gutiérrez, 'Enough! Enough. This is not for you. This is for all of us'" (Lee, 2015). Gutiérrez was escorted out of the White House.

Afterwards, Jennicet Gutiérrez made a statement:

> Last night I spoke out to demand respect and acknowledgement of our gender expression and the release of the estimated 75 transgender immigrants in detention right now. There is no pride in how LGBTQ immigrants are treated in this country and there can be no celebration with an administration that has the ability to keep us detained and in danger or release us to freedom.

Here we again see the use of power to return power to the powerful, where the LGBTQ community happily throws out their own for the benefit of the mainstream establishment. Wouters (2012: 202) notes that "helping to identify and exclude undesirables and ensuring that the newly introduced would assimilate to the prevailing regime of manners and self-regulation [is key]. Thus, the codes of good society also function to regulate social mobility and status competition." Indeed, gay mainstream lobbyists often feel like they have a responsibility to manage the social traffic, political manners, respectability, and the behavior of others for those in power. To ensure no disruption for the powerful. In return, gay mainstream lobbyists gain benefits from straight "allies." This compromise of the political market "became a mutually expected self-restraint, which eventually became taken for granted to the extent that it came to function as part of people's conscience" (Wouters, 2012: 203).

Indeed, the punishment of a target population may help a group maintain its reputation as a cooperative partner of the mainstream coalition (Ostrom, 1998: 13). People in attendance may have thought they were doing the right thing for their relationship with the President. To seem respectable. However, it is important to note that rather than LGBTQ lobbying, this is an example of LGBTQ people exiling someone whose expressions did not fit properly into the heteronormative political machine. Sycamore (2008: 2) says that "a gay elite has hijacked the queer struggle and positioned their desires as everyone's needs—the dominant signs of straight conformity have become the ultimate measures of gay success." In the pursuit of an end to alienation and persecution of the members of the community, lobbyists and organizations reproduce it.

The ejection of Jennicet Gutiérrez has profound implications for the negotiation of power among the LGBTQ lobbying community, particularly dominant gay mainstream lobbying. The literature suggests that this behavior falls into a pattern of self-policing, elitism, and respectability politics. They note that there is an alignment between the LGBTQ culture in Washington, D.C., and the political culture in the Capitol that will only accept certain types of identities. Sycamore (2008: 3) notes, "For decades, there has been strife within queer politics and cultures, between assimilationists and liberationists, conservatives and radicals." Normally, being amongst a group of fellow LGBTQ people would be safe and supportive, but here they demonstrated that all queer and trans folk are not created equal and manifested the ejection of one of their own in order to be seen comforting straight people.

Politics in the LGBTQ movement often creates a safe place to talk. Kirsch (2006: 41) adds, "Communities can be sanctuaries for people needing to recover from oppression, and they can provide for collective strategies against those who attempt to destroy and to subjugate their members." However, this was not a safe or supportive place for this trans woman on this day. The communities provide security that affords mutual support and confidence (Kirsch, 2006), which can be lost when a group or member of the group is exiled for "deviant behavior."

Eggan (2008: 17) highlights the biases involved in protective communities, when considering the lived experience for transgender people, stating "the murders of [transgender people] and LGBTQs who can't hide, who can't get into the gated communities, reveal the truth behind the illusion: So-called 'rights' are conveniences granted only to the people who play by the rules."

In response to this terrible behavior, queerness and LGBTQ lobbying speak to an alternative set of options. The LGBTQ lobbyist perspective is the queer perspective. Sycamore (2008: 6) explains the queer path by noting that "the radical potential of queer identity lies in remaining *outside*—in challenging and seeking to dismantle the sickening culture that surrounds us."

Thus, these examples demonstrate that LGBTQ friends, even at the White House, can be more of a problem than our opponents. I argue that seemingly allied coalitions of lobbyists can impose greater penalties on each other in an issue domain or policy subsystem than ideological opponents because they know the weaknesses of their allies, and they have more opportunities to exact a penalty. Frenemies are competitors as groups and lobbyists to establish not simply if an issue is won or lost, but who specifically wins and how it is won or lost. LGBTQ lobbying occurs, but it is often punished from outside and inside.

Dan Choi being arrested after being chained to the White House—2010

On November 15, 2010, Dan Choi suffered for showing he cared "inappropriately." Montopoli (2010) records how gay Army Lt. Daniel Choi handcuffed himself to a White House fence with 13 others and protested the continuing policy of "don't ask, don't tell" by the Obama Administration. Choi was arrested and prosecuted in federal court for "failure to obey a lawful order." This case highlights the use of power, where the White House condemns the actions and the LGBTQ community sweeps it under the carpet. The Obama Administration has never been fully taken to task for the way they singled out Choi for retribution based on his demonstrations and protest of "Don't Ask, Don't Tell."

Choi found little support from the gay mainstream lobbyists. There were also protests in March and April 2010. In March, Choi interrupted a Human Rights Campaign rally to lead a group of protestors to the White House fence. Americablog's Joe Sudbay reported: "Lieut. Dan choi heads to white house to fight for #dadt. Griffin and HRC's Solmonese stay for photo ops. Welcome to gay dc" and "Dan Choi speaking in front of white house. No kathy griffin. She blew him off."

To get a sense of how the Obama White House used power to manage LGBTQ coalitions in this period, a leaked email from Gautam Raghavan, LGBTQ liaison to the President, is illustrative (Geidner, 2014). He addressed recurring leaking of meeting details by allies by cutting them all off from deliberations. He stated, "Apparently one or more of you chose to ignore our request regarding the embargoed nature of this evening's meeting." And he added, "Moving forward, we'll no longer be able to brief any of you in advance of major decisions or developments" (Geidner, 2014). The certain kind of activist was rewarded, and the wrong kind was punished. We used to call this being put in "the deep freeze."

In Washington, D.C., Choi had been seen as a model activist. He had appeared on the Rachel Maddow MSNBC television program and was featured at coalition protests. In being welcomed into the fold as an important LGBTQ activist, this brought with it several assumptions, noted by Wouters (2012: 205):

> [T]o be introduced, accepted and entertained in the drawing rooms and parlours of the respectable or, in other words, to be successful in good society was an important and sometimes necessary condition for success in the business and politics.

Yet, Choi's tactics would violate the membership terms for this bourgeoise collective.

In short, Choi was *unpolitique* to a gay mainstream movement and lobbying community, which is top-down, male, gay, and white. That left him vulnerable inside the community and outside with the Obama Administration. Vaid (1995) notes, "we consciously choose legal reform, political access, visibility, and legitimation over the long-term goals of cultural acceptance, social transformation, understanding and liberation." This access means more than equality or protecting our own. Ward (2008: 4) notes that Vaid added these positions "reflected the movement's largely top-down approach, or the failure of wealthy white gay men and lesbians in national organizations to mobilize a diverse, multi-issue grassroots movement." For Choi, this led to federal prosecution with little support from the LGBTQ community.

Discussion

President Obama believed in the "long game" of politics. He thought that over time and the course of his Presidency, the LGBTQ community would make historic gains on the road to total equality on LGBTQ rights. In his words, the LGBTQ community would be "better off than we were before" (White House, 2012).

Lobbying on "don't ask, don't tell" was frustrating simply because it often involved trying to get politicians and key staff to take a position that they already held. What was missing was political will, not ideological persuasion. The asks below of the Obama White House illustrate the political labyrinth that is often traversed to make even a small step forward.

An "ask" to sign an executive order to lift the ban on GLB service

The first "ask" to the White House was to request that President Obama sign an executive order stopping discharges (i.e. firings) under "don't ask, don't tell" based on the need to keep them, for national security. This ask will not be successful. The White House's position was that a "stop-loss" order was not politically workable and that the issue of "don't ask, don't tell" should be handled by Congress, so it was permanent. The real answer here is that the law allowed it, but it would be difficult for the President with the Pentagon to enact such a policy.

As I entered the White House, I understood that the point person for "don't ask, don't tell" repeal was White House Deputy Chief of Staff David Messina, but Tina Tchen, the Director of the Office of Public Engagement, did the handholding for many of the LGBTQ groups (White House, 2011). Tina was a long-time Obama aide and would go on to be First Lady Michelle Obama's Chief of Staff. She was a key insider who was there to protect the President.

When I think about my nine years working on "don't ask, don't tell," the first thing that comes to mind is my first trip to President Obama's White House. I was going into a meeting arranged by Brian Bond, a smart and trusted LGBTQ liaison who had worked for the Democratic National Committee. I liked Brian and knew he had a tough job. Walking through the West Wing and up the stairs was fascinating. There were frames with blown-up pictures of President Obama on the walls. When we got to the meeting room, MSNBC (specifically Rachel Maddow on mute) played on a big-screen TV in the background. Tina Tchen was in her office. She was mad at us because Rachel Maddow had been raising the issue of gays in the military on her television program for several nights in a row and that was putting pressure on the White House. It had been suggested by the think tank I was working for that with a "stroke of the pen" the ban could be gone, and some of the best legal minds in the LGBTQ community agreed. The law was known as "stop-loss" and resided at 10 U.S.C. § 12305. It stated that

> the President may suspend any provision of law relating to promotion, retirement, or separation applicable to any member of the armed forces who the President determines is essential to the national security of the United States.

This meant that technically if the President declared LGBTQ Arabic linguists as essential to national security, "don't ask, don't tell" would not apply to them and the rationale for the entire policy and law would be called into question.

The White House Counsel's Office had also been invited to this meeting with Tina Tchen and the question was tossed to them. They said there was no "political" way the President could lift the ban through executive action because that would involve invoking national security laws. But, the Counsel's Office added, "legally this is correct." I agreed that this would be difficult politically. However, on a legal basis this was still theoretically possible. I said, "I didn't come here to endorse or blindside the President. We are a think tank and our jobs are to note what options are available, and this is a viable option." We were seen as unhelpful and curtly escorted from the office. Afterwards, I texted with a friend and said, "Brian is a very nice guy. Your advice was helpful. Boy was Tina pissed at us." My friend replied, "oh well—if you are not pissing people off—you are not doing your job."

My friend's advice was valuable. I was going to keep doing my job, and it was clear that there were different types of White House staff to contend with: the staff that were there to protect the President and ensure re-election; the LGBTQ staff who wanted to see this wrong get righted; and those who met in the middle and realized that this was a political headache, but that it could pay off with enthusiasm from the LGBTQ and progressive base.

On January 19, 2010, I put together an analysis regarding the delay in "don't ask, don't tell" action. I noted that the strategy of our right-wing opponents appeared twofold:

> First, rather than arguing directly against the President's position, they [opponents] are attempting to influence the timeline for DADT repeal. Second, opponents are attempting to ensure deference is given to the Pentagon in determining the legislative language and what that language/implementation looks like.
>
> *(personal communication)*

The strategic issue was the timeline, not LGB service. LGBTQ lobbyists were trying to push it up the calendar to counter this. The opponents were trying to push it back. The issue was how many important political pieces would fall in the time that we had. Politics is no chess or checkers. Politics is dominoes. It is about making big things fall. For the President, this includes his key staff, the Secretary of Defense, and Chairman of the Joint Chiefs. These were all big things that we needed to fall and create a cascade of momentum to lift the ban and repeal "don't ask, don't tell."

However, it appeared that LGBTQ lobbyists were seeing a replay in 2010 of efforts to stop openly LGBTQ service, which started in 1993. For instance, there had been historic anti-LGBTQ actions by Colin Powell at the start of this policy and now there was resistance in 2010 from Secretary of Defense Gates.

However, the President made the Joint Chiefs fall. President Obama said, "It's the right thing to do." A sentence that was not in the speech. The speech being the State of the Union, which stated: "This year, I will work with Congress and our military to finally repeal the law that denies gay Americans the right to serve the country they love because of who they are" (Bond, 2010).

This is the most heavily considered speech of a Presidency, and the President was adlibbing. He was talking to the nation about the need to repeal "don't ask, don't tell" but he was looking down at the military chiefs, the Joint Chiefs of Staff. And the President had been having private meetings with the Chiefs, particular Chairman Mike Mullen. History was made between the President's call for action during the State of the Union on January 27, 2010 and February 2, 2010 when Joint Chiefs Chairman Mike Mullen stated:

> Speaking for myself and myself only, it is my personal belief that allowing gays and lesbians to serve openly would be the right thing to do. No matter how I look at the issue, I cannot escape being troubled by the fact that we have in place a policy which forces young men and women to lie about who they are in order to defend their fellow citizens. For me, personally, it comes down to integrity—theirs as individuals and ours as an institution.
>
> *(Terkel, 2010)*

That was just five days. On this ask for the "stop-loss" the President did not budge. But the issue now turned to the Congress and how to make repeal permanent.

Obama: an ask to include repeal legislation in the Base bill

On January 7, 2010 I sent a note to colleagues remarking that "the important 'Ask' here is to Rahm Emanuel to make sure that the MREA language is included in the base bill."

This is the story of a second White House "ask" that was not successful. On February 1, 2010 the White House informed LGBTQ groups that "don't ask, don't tell" language would not be included in the base bill. Following this, on April 26, 2010 the "base bill" was submitted, without the repeal of "don't ask, don't tell" included. There would now only be two ways to pass the legislation through Congress: a stand-alone bill, or an amendment that could be added to the Defense Authorization bill. That would make the larger bill a vehicle for the smaller amendment. And because there is more pressure to pass larger bills with funding in them, this seemed like the best path forward.

But what happened to the "ask"? The story of the base bill has four parts:

1. First, a technical explanation about a "base bill." A base bill is the large memo that the White House outlines and gives to the Pentagon, which they give to Congress as the formal request for military aid for the year. This includes the number of jets the Air Force thinks they will need and the number of tanks the Army will need. This is introduced as the National Defense Authorization Act each year. This is the authorizing legislation which covers policies (like "don't

ask, don't tell") and outlines the needs for the U.S. Armed Forces, which are then fulfilled in the Defense Appropriations bill.

2. Second, is an appreciation of the difficulty and tension between President Obama and the Pentagon. For instance, President Obama struggled to manage Defense Secretary Robert Gates. Gates was supportive of Congress acting on this issue, but not the Pentagon. Gates did not support the repeal of "don't ask, don't tell" included in the Base bill and there was concern among some that Secretary Gates would resign if he was forced to help lift the ban on gays in the military.

This tension was noted in Gates' memoir that included "don't ask, don't tell." Gates wrote about parts of the repeal process, "I was a major obstacle, but he [President Obama] was clearly not prepared to order me to do something I thought was wrong" (2014: 443).

3. Third, the President did not include "don't ask, don't tell" repeal language in the Defense Authorization bill. This meant that repeal language would have to be amended into the bill over a Republican filibuster or that it needed to be part of a stand-alone option or put into something else.

4. Fourth, lobbyists and groups called for a stand-alone bill. On November 15, 2010, LGBTQ lobbyists and organizations proposed a strategy change: to take the "don't ask, don't tell" repeal language out of the Defense Authorization bill (Bolcer, 2010). The analysis (which I led) argued that the repeal of "don't ask, don't tell" would not make it through the Senate in the Defense Authorization "base" bill (O'Keefe, 2010). It was argued that Republicans were holding firm. They had filibustered the bill twice and won. With these groups, I argued that the best chance for passage was to make the repeal of "don't ask, don't tell" an up or down vote in the Senate on supporting or opposing discrimination in the military. This could separate the politics of the Defense Authorization bill from the issue of discrimination.

This was seen as a controversial position. Other organizations had worked hard to put "don't ask, don't tell" repeal language in the Defense Authorization bill as an amendment, and here I was giving opponents the green light to pull it out. In their understandable view, the Defense Authorization bill was the best way forward. Indeed, this was the model that the Human Rights Campaign had used to achieve Hate Crimes success in Congress in 2009. The Hate Crimes legislation was amended into the Defense Authorization bill. The belief was that this could be done again in 2010.

In response to my suggested strategy shift, a number of groups wrote, "Under no conditions should DADT repeal be stripped from the underlying Defense Authorization bill; that is simply a non-starter" (HRC, 2010). However, it is useful to note that "don't ask, don't tell" was *not* repealed as part of the Defense Authorization Act. It was repealed by Congress as a stand-alone bill.

5.   What followed the Defense Authorization discussion was Armed Services Committee Chairman Senator Carl Levin saying that he would in fact remove DADT from the repeal bill. But then something happened. My cell phone rang again. It was a contact at the White House. I was told that President Obama himself had called Senator Levin and asked him to keep the DADT repeal in the bill. The President was engaged in the Senate. But now came a different question. Could the base bill pass the Senate?

I maintained my position on the need for a stand-alone bill. My notes from November 25, 2009 note the plan that I believed the White House and the Human Rights Campaign had put together:

> There seems to be two camps—the one where we all just lie low and then we're able to repeat the Hate Crimes passage in both the House and Senate. And another position (which I support), where stirring the pot to makes (sic) sure we get across the finish line.

Two weeks after this was sent out, the gay mainstream groups noted: "The defense bill failed in a procedural vote on Thursday, which frustrated supporters who said the defeat was the result of bad timing rather than a lack of votes" (O'Keefe & Whitlock, 2010).

6.   The challenges presented with the Defense Authorization bill strategy were twofold: first, Republicans had the votes. Democrats did not have the votes to override a Senate filibuster by Republicans on September 21, 2010. In this vote, there were on 56 of the 60 votes needed. The Republicans filibustered the repeal amendment to the Defense Authorization bill again on December 9, 2010. The second issue was that by having "don't ask, don't tell" repeal included in the broader defense bill there was less pressure to consider the vote a referendum on LGBTQ discrimination.

In response to the two filibusters, Senators Lieberman and Collins introduced a stand-alone bill that solely focused on repeal of "don't ask, don't tell." O'Keefe and Whitlock (2010) note, "Lieberman and Collins hatched their plans during Thursday's defense bill vote, concluding that a standalone measure would succeed if introduced after senators vote on tax cut legislation."

7.   The White House pulled support.

The White House pulled its assistance for the repeal of "don't ask, don't tell."
I was called to the White House for a meeting with Tina Tchen and Aubrey Savis of SLDN. Aubrey and I were told that the White House no longer supported repeal of "don't ask, don't tell" at the moment. They said we had our bites at the apple but had lost two filibusters.

Two factors were key to the White House's argument: first, they were right. There had been two filibusters in the Senate. They believed the prospects were getting weaker not stronger, especially since they wanted to ensure passage of the START treaty with Russia. The legislative calendar was tight. Also, the White House believed that administrative changes to the enforcement of "don't ask, don't tell" that would reduce firings (Bumiller, 2010) would be far enough for the moment.

However, the White House faced opposition to this withdrawal and belief that the Lieberman-Collins stand-alone bill had a chance in the Senate. In short, LGBTQ lobbyists chose tactics that would disrupt power dynamics. Discrimination against LGBTQ servicemembers was put on the ballot. The vote to consider the stand-alone bill would be historic. In fact, it would pass with eight Republican Senators, 65–31.

Obama: an "ask" to lift the ban on transgender service

This "ask" resulted in a yes, that is perhaps more upsetting than any of the nos. This is the consideration of executive power by the Obama White House to lift the regulatory ban on openly transgender military service. This decision was left almost entirely in the hands of the Pentagon. As a result, the military's policy allowed openly transgender service on May 27, 2016. The Presidential election that year was November 8, 2016, a little over five months later.

With no law to be overturned, it was solely up to the President to lift the ban on transgender servicemembers. However, this was done slowly and only after steady lobbying. This slowness set the policy up for failure when newly elected President Trump announced a reversal that would bar transgender people from serving in the military, by tweet.

This "ask" was complicated by a number of factors:

"Don't ask, don't tell"

Sharra Greer and I organized the first meeting on how transgender military service should be addressed in the repeal of "don't ask, don't tell" on September 14, 2004. We invited the leaders of the trans community to SLDN's office and we asked them how they wanted the issue to proceed.

The leaders of the trans community said to leave the "T" conversation out of "don't ask, don't tell" repeal. There was a practical reality that trans service was not included in "don't ask, don't tell" under the law. The law specifically and only banned service by gay, lesbian, and bisexual servicemembers, which meant there was more potential flexibility for dealing with it under regulations. In addition, there was little doubt that Republicans would have passed a new law to statutorily ban transgender service if this issue were public. So, trans in the military was left out of all negotiations, strategies, and lobbying for the next nine years.

The meeting

In 2013, there was the largest meeting of transgender leaders to talk about transgender military service ever assembled. It was in Oakland, California on March 30, 2013. Nearly every transgender rights group in the U.S. was represented. In fact, many of the same people were brought together from the meeting nine years earlier. Attendees included, Kellan Baker, Masen Davis, Jody Herman, Mara Keisling, Dru Levasseur, Sean Lund, Shannon Minter, Paula Neira, Jennifer Pritzker, and Allyson Robinson.

The main item on the agenda was the danger of going forward for lifting the ban on openly transgender service. I raised the issue that Congress could get involved and legislatively ban trans service. I said, "this may be as good as it gets." I added with a question for formal consideration: "would you support a campaign to lift the ban, knowing things could get worse?" Everyone said yes. It was unanimous. It was 2013, and the plan to start advocating and educating the White House on trans in the military set them and us back.

Leap forward

A report and statement by former Surgeon General Jocelyn Elders and Rear Admiral Al Steinman was released on March 13, 2014. The report was a game-changer on public perceptions around trans in the military. It stated, "There is no compelling medical rationale for banning transgender military service, and medical regulations requiring the discharge of all transgender personnel are inconsistent with how the military regulates medical and psychological conditions" (Palm Center, 2014). This study by Dr. Elders and Admiral Steinman was my suggestion, with both of them as co-commissioners. In classic agenda-setting literature, there was a need to change the problem definition. Trans service was not the problem. Transphobia and discrimination were the problems and this report provided the avenue for a framing change about the engagement around this issue.

Everyone was slow

This chapter will close on the "White House ask" by noting that the LGBTQ community was slow to act, and the President was slow to act. Slow is not a word you can use if you are an oppressed and marginalized group and expect to receive benefits. There were three problems.

First, LGBTQ lobbyists failed to keep the trans community in the loop for nearly nine years. After the first meeting, after the trans leaders left the room, there was never any follow up. This meant that congressional offices and the White House were not educated on the issue and lobbyists were not up to speed on the issue. Even if you were not going to include trans issues in the legislation, it would have been prudent to include the trans ban in the conversation.

Second, the failure to incorporate trans in the military in the "don't ask, don't tell" plan was a pattern. A similar set of considerations had been held at the law firm Wilmer Cutler to discuss the sodomy provisions in the Uniform Code of Military Justice, Article 125, that made oral or anal sex between male servicemembers illegal. Other work would be done to challenge the ban in a post-*Lawrence* world. In 2002 and 2003, I testified before the Joint Service Committee on Military Justice, requesting that sodomy be allowed, and SLDN filed a court challenge in the court of appeals. After "don't ask, don't tell" was repealed, Congress acted and today Article 125 is gone. But again, this is an example of not taking an intersectional approach to congressional education and advocacy.

Lastly, the first three years into the effort to lift the ban on trans service looked too much to me like the first three years on "don't ask, don't tell" repeal. It is disturbing to see how hard the LGBTQ community continues to make it on each other. By not including trans groups on "don't ask, don't tell" repeal, we were really helping ourselves, not trans people. Ultimately, it backfired. The first year of education in Congress included staff briefings and meetings in which staff believed that the trans ban had already been lifted when "don't ask, don't tell" was repealed. Diane Mazur and I participated in the first briefing on openly trans service in the House and the attendees were shocked. I began the meeting by welcoming staff whether they were cis or trans and the room fell quiet. This was indicative of a lack of education on these issues. I realized the absence of an inclusive strategy was a mistake that caused lost time, energy, and inevitably opened our community up to our political enemies. President Obama should have acted sooner and the LGB community should have acted sooner. I should have acted sooner.

Conclusion

This chapter examined the "White House ask." It looked at the planning and logistics that go into getting a meeting with White House staff and then executing an "ask." There was then a recap on three LGBTQ stories that illustrate how "asks" are policied by the system in order to return power to the powerful. This chapter then examined the history of "don't ask, don't tell" and the three "asks" that operated in the political constellation.

We have outlined good examples of the need for participant-observation lobbying. The use of stories as data is essential to answering many of these questions. In addition, this chapter uses queer methods to survey difficult questions within a difficult population. It would not have been possible to gain the level of access if the lobbyist was taking notes. In Washington, D.C., when someone starts taking notes, the room gets very quiet. You often have to ask permission to take notes.

LGBTQ lobbying helps us understand the broader literature on lobbying by looking at the LGBTQ cases, the function and added definition of LGBTQ lobbying, and adding the lived experience of a lobbyist to the data on lobbying. Together, this research highlights how the shortcomings of President Obama were not that he said no to "asks." This is an important point. The shortcoming was in the way he said yes. The decision to let the Pentagon run the process provided an opening for opponents to slow down the process, a concern that was raised around "don't ask, don't tell."

The next chapter will address what LGBTQ lobbying in the Congress looks like.

References

Bennett, L. (2014). 'If we stick together we can do anything': Lady Gaga fandom, philanthropy and activism through social media. *Celebrity Studies*, 5(1–2), 138–152. https://doi.org/10.1080/19392397.2013.813778

Birkland, T. A. (1997). *After Disaster: Agenda Setting, Public Policy, and Focusing Events*. Georgetown University Press.

Bolcer, J. (November 15, 2010). *Two groups OK dropping DADT repeal from defense bill*. The Advocate. www.advocate.com/news/daily-news/2010/11/15/two-groups-ok-cutting-dadt-repeal-defense-bill

Bond, B. (2010, December 18). Ending Don't Ask Don't Tell. *The White House*. https://obamawhitehouse.archives.gov/blog/2010/12/18/ending-dont-ask-dont-tell

Bumiller, E. (February 2, 1010). Top defense officials seek to end 'Don't Ask, Don't Tell'. *New York Times*. www.nytimes.com/2010/02/03/us/politics/03military.html

Burrelli, D.F., & Feder, J. (2009). *Homosexuals and the U.S. military: Current Issues* (Report No. RL30113). Congressional Research Service. https://fas.org/sgp/crs/natsec/RL30113.pdf

Department of Defense Authorization Act (1985). Department of Defense Authorization Act of 1985. Pub. L. 98-94, 10 U.S.C. § 12305 (2006). www.govinfo.gov/app/details/USCODE-2011-title10/USCODE-2011-title10-subtitleE-partII-chap1209-sec12305

Eggan, F. (2008). Dykes and fags want everything: Dreaming with the Gay Liberation Front. In M.B. Sycamore (Ed.), *That's Revolting! LGBTQ Strategies for Resisting Assimilation* (pp. 11–18). Soft Skull Press.

Emanuel, M. (2015, December 23). *Gates to make military discharge for being gay more difficult*. Fox News. www.foxnews.com/politics/gates-to-make-military-discharge-for-being-gay-more-difficult

Fox, L. (2013, November 5). LGBT groups outspend opponents on ENDA. *U.S. News & World Report*. www.usnews.com/news/articles/2013/11/05/lgbt-groups-outspend-opponents-on-enda

Gates, R.M. (2014). *Duty: Memoirs of a Secretary at War*. Knopf Doubleday.

Geidner, C. (2014, June 20). *White House threatens to cut out LGBT groups after report*. BuzzFeed. www.buzzfeednews.com/article/chrisgeidner/white-house-threatens-to-cut-out-lgbt-groups-after-report

Goldman, R. (2010, January 28). Gays applaud Obama for pledge to repeal 'Don't Ask, Don't Tell'. *ABC News*. https://abcnews.go.com/Politics/State_of_the_Union/gays-applaud-obama-pledge-repeal-dont-ask-dont-tell-policy-state-of-the-union/story?id=9687078

Good, C. (2010, April 20). Obama heckled over Don't Ask, Don't Tell. *The Atlantic*. www.theatlantic.com/politics/archive/2010/04/obama-heckled-over-dont-ask-dont-tell/39234

Halley, J.E. (1999). *Don't: A Reader's Guide to the Military's Anti-Gay Policy*. Duke University Press.

Hansen, L. (2000). The Little Mermaid's silent security dilemma and the absence of gender in the Copenhagen school. *Millennium: Journal of International Studies, 29*(2), 285–306. https://doi.org/10.1177%2F03058298000290020501

Hulse, C. (2010, December 18). Senate repeals ban on gays serving openly in the military. *New York Times*. www.nytimes.com/2010/12/19/us/politics/19cong.html

Human Rights Campaign (2010, November 15). *Organizations send one message to Capitol Hill&#58 repeal DADT now* [Press release]. www.hrc.org/press/organizations-send-one-message-to-capitol-hill58-repeal-dadt-now

Kirsch, M. (2006). Queer theory, late capitalism, and internalized homophobia. *Journal of Homosexuality, 52*(1–2), 19–45. https://doi.org/10.1300/J082v52n01_02

Lee, E. (2015, June 25). The truth about the heckler at The White House Pride reception last night. Think Progress. https://archive.thinkprogress.org/the-truth-about-the-heckler-at-the-white-house-pride-reception-last-night-1a42f2a6b68d/

Levine, B.J. (2009). *The Art of Lobbying: Building Trust and Selling Policy*. CQ Press.

Liptak, K. (2015, June 25). Obama shuts down White House heckler: 'You're in my house!'. *CNN*. www.cnn.com/2015/06/24/politics/obama-heckler-white-house-lgbt

Montopoli, B. (2010, April 20). Dan Choi, other gay rights protestors arrested after chaining selves to White House fence. *CBS News*. www.cbsnews.com/news/dan-choi-other-gay-rights-protesters-arrested-after-chaining-selves-to-white-house-fence

Murphy, L.R. (1988). *Perverts by Official Order: The Campaign Against Homosexuals by the United States Navy*. Harrington Park Press.

Neff, C.L. (2011, May 25). What does victory on Don't Ask, Don't Tell look like? *Huffington Post*. www.huffpost.com/entry/what-does-victory-on-dont_b_590205

Neff, C.L. (2016). The performance of roll call votes as political cover in the U.S. Senate: Using C-SPAN to analyze the vote to repeal "Don't Ask, Don't Tell." In R.X. Browning (Ed.), *Exploring the C-SPAN archives: Advancing the Research Agenda* (pp. 191–212). Purdue University Press. https://doi.org/10.2307/j.ctv15wxr41.13

Neff, C.L., & Edgell, L.R. (2013). The rise of repeal: Policy entrepreneurship and Don't Ask, Don't Tell. *Journal of Homosexuality, 60*(2–3), 232–249. https://doi.org/10.1080/00918369.2013.744669

The New York Times (1992, March 28). The 1992 Campaign: Verbatim; Heckler stirs Clinton anger: Excerpts from the exchange. www.nytimes.com/1992/03/28/us/1992-campaign-verbatim-heckler-stirs-clinton-anger-excerpts-exchange.html

O'Keefe, E. (2010, November 15). 'Don't ask, don't tell' splitting gay rights groups. *Washington Post*. www.washingtonpost.com/wp-dyn/content/article/2010/11/15/AR2010111506463.html

O'Keefe, E., & Whitlock, C. (2010, December 11). New bill introduced to end 'don't ask, don't tell'. *Washington Post*. www.washingtonpost.com/wp-dyn/content/article/2010/12/10/AR2010121007163.html

Ostrom, E. (1998). A behavioral approach to the rational choice theory of collective action: Presidential address, American Political Science Association, 1997. *American Political Science Review, 92*(1), 1–22. https://doi.org/10.2307/2585925

Pachter, A. (2001). Sexual orientation in the military. *Georgetown Journal of Gender & the Law, 3*(1), 127–134.

Palm Center (2014, March 13). *Former Surgeon General faults military's transgender ban*. www.palmcenter.org/former-surgeon-general-faults-militarys-transgender-ban/

Pepin-Neff, C.L. (2019). *Flaws: Shark Bites and Emotional Public Policymaking*. Palgrave Macmillan.

Pepin-Neff, C.L., & Caporale, K. (2018). Funny evidence: Female comics are the new policy entrepreneurs. *Australian Journal of Public Administration, 77*(4), 554–567. https://doi.org/10.1111/1467-8500.12280

Peters, G., & Woolley, J.T. (2000). *Republican Party Platforms, 2000 Republican Party Platform Online*. The American Presidency Project. www.presidency.ucsb.edu/node/273446

Reza, H.G. (1993, January 9). Homosexual sailor beaten to death, Navy confirms: Crime: Gay-bashing may be motive, activists and family members say. They charge cover-up by military. *Los Angeles Times*. www.latimes.com/archives/la-xpm-1993-01-09-mn-1001-story.html

Sabatier, P., Hunter, S., & McLaughlin, S. (1987). The devil shift: Perceptions and misperceptions of opponents. *Western Political Quarterly*, *40*(3), 449–476. https://doi.org/10.1177%2F106591298704000306

San Francisco Examiner (1999, December 14). Death of a gay in the military. www.sfgate.com/food/article/Death-of-a-gay-in-the-military-3054291.php

Shilts, R. (1993). *Conduct Unbecoming: Gays and Lesbians in the U.S. Military*. St. Martin's Press.

Spade, D. (2015). *Normal Life: Administrative Violence, Critical Trans Politics, and the Limits of Law*. Duke University Press.

Stolberg, S.G. (2010, December 22). Obama signs away 'Don't Ask, Don't Tell'. *The New York Times*. www.nytimes.com/2010/12/23/us/politics/23military.html

Sudbay, J. [@JoeSudbay]. (2010, March 18). *Lieut. Dan choi heads to white house to fight for #dadt. Griffin and HRC's Solmonese stay for photo ops* [Tweet]. Twitter. https://twitter.com/JoeSudbay/status/10679651249

Sycamore, M.B. (2008). There's more to life than platinum: Challenging the tyranny of sweatshop-produced rainbow flags and participatory patriarchy. In M.B. Sycamore (Ed.), *That's Revolting! LGBTQ Strategies for Resisting Assimilation* (pp. 1–10). Soft Skull Press.

Terkel, A. (2010, February 2). *Joint Chiefs of Staff Chairman Mullen: 'It is my personal belief' that repealing DADT is 'the right thing to do.'* Think Progress. https://archive.thinkprogress.org/joint-chiefs-of-staff-chairman-mullen-it-is-my-personal-belief-that-repealing-dadt-is-the-right-2544581edabd

Vaid, U. (1995). *Virtual Equality: The Mainstreaming of Gay and Lesbian Liberation*. Anchor Books.

Waranius, M. (2011). What up with DADT: Addressing confusion from inside the military. *Journal of Law and Social Deviance*, *1*, 56–84.

Ward, J. (2008). *Respectably Queer: Diversity Culture in LGBT Activist Organizations*. Vanderbilt University Press.

The Washington Independent (2020, July 31). Is 'Don't Ask, Don't Tell' on the scrapheap? https://washingtonindependent.com/85605/is-dont-ask-dont-tell-on-the-scrapheap

The White House (2011, January 5). *Tina Tchen to join Office of the First Lady as Chief of Staff*. https://obamawhitehouse.archives.gov/the-press-office/2011/01/05/tina-tchen-join-office-first-lady-chief-staff

The White House (2012, May 7). *Press briefing by press secretary Jay Carney, 5/7/12*. https://obamawhitehouse.archives.gov/the-press-office/2012/05/07/press-briefing-press-secretary-jay-carney-5712

Wouters, C. (2012). The slippery slope and the emancipation of emotions. In S. Thompson & P. Hoggett (Eds.), *Politics and the Emotions: The Affective Turn in Contemporary Political Studies* (pp. 199–216). Continuum.

5

THE CONGRESS AND LGBTQ LOBBYING

Introduction

Lobbyists are legislators. In this chapter, the role of LGBTQ lobbyists as unelected lawmakers who legislate will be examined. Lobbyist-legislators do not function outside the system but on the inside of the political process.

Despite media portrayals and academic literature, lobbying can and does occur as a valuable piece of the lawmaking process. This includes LGBTQ lobbying.

Lobbyist-legislators make up a small proportion of actors in the legislative and executive branches (see Figure 5.1). Indeed, there may only be a brief moment where this designation is accurate. In these episodes, lobbyist-legislators write and pass law. They influence agenda-setting, write speeches, and curate the casting of votes in ways that produce inertia or stasis. In these times, lobbyist-legislators are more important and essential to the making of laws than members of Congress.

As a reminder, I define LGBTQ lobbying as the negotiation of power in the executive and legislative branches, in ways that disrupt the return of power to the powerful, from a position of disadvantage; and the use of the "LGBTQ ask" to re-prioritize issues that center the marginalized and demand total equity, now.

This chapter will note the elements of a lobbyist-legislator and consider this through a LGBTQ lobbying lens. This analysis highlights how these moments come and go, and that lobbyist-legislators act when the opportunities present themselves. Carol Weissert (1991) might call these "policy opportunists."

To analyze the optimal moments and tactics of lobbyist legislating, a framework must be established. I argue that these episodes and actions are fluid and function around the intersections of *capability* (to engage in legislative action), and the degree of *disruption* to power (to stymie the way power is returned to the powerful).

FIGURE 5.1 Policy actions at SLDN

For a lobbyist-legislator, authority comes from expertise, either a knowledge of the process, the institution, or the issue. For elected legislators, authority is derived from legal and institutional rules.

To act, each category of legislators has a repertoire of tactics that are available at the highest levels of Congress. Indeed, rather than focus on the congressional "ask," this chapter is examining the congressional "action." There are four areas (Table 5.1) to consider:

Disruptive and Capable. These are actions by a lobbyist-legislator that have the potential to disrupt the underlying power dynamics and are capable of taking place. This is more than feasibility—this is the capability of execution. Examples include passing legislation through Congress, putting a hold on a nomination in the Senate, swaying the outcome of a vote, bill, nomination, or treaty. In addition, lobbyist-legislators can sway the timing of legislation, write member speeches for the congressional record, or to be delivered publicly. They can also determine which office is the lead on a policy issue. This is the chief category for LGBTQ lobbyists, this is where LGBTQ lobbyists act as lobbyist-legislators.

TABLE 5.1 Categories of legislative LGBTQ lobbying

	Disruptive to power	*Not disruptive to power*

Capable of legislating	*Disruptive and Capable*
	
	Legislation
	Put a hold on something
	Sway votes
	Sway timing of legislation
	Write member speeches
	Determining member leadership/
	    issue lead
		Capable Not Disruptive
		
		List of speakers for hearing
		Get members to not do
		    something—Tom Allen, Ted
		    Kennedy.

Not capable	*Disruptive Not Capable*
	
	Withdraw legislation
	Object on the floor
	Hold a hearing
	Filibuster
	Offer amdt at mark up
	Vote in Committee
	Vote on the Floor
	Political cover to another member
		Not Capable Not Disruptive
		
		Give a speech on the floor or in
		    committee
		Meet with members.
		Member briefings
		Talk to caucus
		Speak at a fundraiser/accept
		    an award
		Talk to someone else

For instance, there was interest in "don't ask, don't tell" over the years from many members of Congress. Some included: Congresswoman Pat Schroeder, Jerry Nadler, Ellen Tauscher, Diane DeGette, Jim Moran, Tom Allen, Alcee Hastings, Patrick Murphy, and Marty Meehan in the House all worked on the issue. In the Senate, Ted Kennedy was the lead until his passing and Senators Lieberman and Collins took over. However, Barbara Boxer, Mark Dayton, Kirsten Gillibrand, Daniel Akaka, and Roland Burris were also active.

Disruptive Not Capable. This is a category where the action being taken must be done by an elected official and that action is disruptive to the way power is returned to the powerful. Included here are actions including withdrawing legislation from consideration, objecting to a motion on the House or Senate floor, holding a hearing (chairing a hearing or asking the chair to hold a hearing), conducting a filibuster in the Senate, offering an amendment during mark up, voting in committee, and voting on the floor. This category is a good example of procedural power.

Capable Not Disruptive. In this category, the actor is capable of action, but that tactic is not disruptive. This would present the highest risk for a lobbyist-legislator. Taking a high-risk move for a low benefit makes little sense. For instance, a lobbyist-legislator may act in these cases to remove items from the agenda. This can include the list of speakers for a hearing or stopping a member from doing something. During "don't ask, don't tell" there was a gay Arabic linguist who was fired in 2002, at a time following 9/11 when Arabic translation was mission-critical. In response, there was national media coverage (Frank, 2013). In response, a number of members of the House and Senate were interested in introducing legislation to lift the ban just for military troops who were Arabic linguists. My colleagues and I talked the offices back from their position. This is an example of Capable Not Disruptive.

Not Capable Not Disruptive. This final area represents ceremonial tactics. Here, only members of Congress can do it, and it yields little benefit. This includes giving a speech on the floor of the House or Senate, or in committee. Meeting with fellow members of Congress, staff or the public. Holding Member-only briefings, talking to their party caucus, and speaking at a fundraiser or accepting an award. This is low-risk, low-reward work that ultimately takes up a lot of time. Lobbying-legislators are not concerned about this last category.

Literature review

There are many different interpretations of what a lobbyist does in Congress. This section focuses on the different ways lobbying in Congress has been constructed. Some of these are based in academia and some are not. The fact that lobbying as a practice is unclear to non-profits, considered swarthy as a profession by the public, and regarded as entirely trustworthy by academia is by design, and affords lobbyists the leverage to normally do as they please.

Public perceptions of lobbyists in Congress have been shaped largely by television and movies. The role of lobbyists has been captured on film, in *Miss Sloane* (2016), *Thank You for Smoking* (2005), *The American President* (1995), and *Born Yesterday* (1993). Lobbyists are pictured in television series such as *K Street*, *West Wing*, *Veep*, *House of Cards*, and *Scandal*. LGBTQ lobbying can also be seen in documentaries, including *United in Anger* (2012), *We Were Here* (2012), *Saving Marriage* (2006), Outrage (2009), Vito (2011), Gay Sex in the 70s (2005), *How to Survive a Plague* (2012), *Pride?* (2017), and *The Strange History of Don't Ask, Don't Tell* (2011). However, there has been little focus on the positive way that LGBTQ lobbyists, and lobbyist-legislators function in Congress.

Moreover, fake movie portrayals of lobbying and highly edited documentary portrayals of lobbyists have been used to inform lobbying and have real-life implications. Neff (2015: 2) notes, "familiar film narratives can serve as the basis for political discourse when they appear to mirror well-known stories, blame marginalized [sic] target populations and provide quick political 'solutions.'"

For instance, the nature of lobbying is seen as illegal and corrupt. In *The American President* Sydney Ellen Wade is a "hired gun"; in *Thank You for Smoking* Nick Naylor is a "Merchant of Death," and in *Miss Sloane*, Elizabeth Sloane is a "cutthroat lobbyist." The response from Government has been to condemn lobbying. President Obama stated, "I intend to tell the corporate lobbyists that their days of setting the agenda in Washington are over." Thurber (2011: 358) notes that "Lobbying is a profession that has been deeply sullied in the last five years by the illegal actions and conviction of Jack Abramoff."

Yet, films and documentaries are not limited to fake historical analogies. They can serve as a meaning-making device. I argue that movies can serve as a political tool to influence the policy process in several ways.

These include Congress as a construct of what rules and procedures they make for themselves. The United States Senate is run by institutional rules among members, or "senetiquette" (Neff, 2016: 192). These rules govern who can stand on the Senate floor, who can be recognized to speak, what type of gavel to use, how high the ceiling is, where people can sit in the gallery and who can ride in an elevator. In short, the House is the House of the People, but the Senate is here for the Senators.

In addition, the location of offices is an example of political construction. One of the more secret venues for lobbying on Capitol Hill are the Senator's "hideaways" located in the Capitol building. The protocol of these offices is based on Senate rules (Neff, 2016: 192). Meetings here are considered rare and special. These hideaways are smaller, more regal offices, in some of the most impressive real estate on the grounds of the Capitol. Lobbyist meetings here are a function of priority and proximity. Important meetings can be held and then members can easily get to votes on the Senate floor. Other prestigious lobbying venues include the Speaker's balcony, the Senate Majority Leader's Office, the Vice President's Office in the House, and the Senate Indoor Tennis Courts in the Hart Senate Office Building.

There is also important political science literature on how lobbyists and interest groups impact agenda-setting in Congress. I have suggested that lobbying-legislators fall into a four-square model where their tactics are determined based on their level of capability to do the task, and the level of disruption to underlying power dynamics. As noted, LGBTQ lobbying would fall under Disruptive and Capable. These actors are able to act as legislators and lawmakers because of their expertise regarding a process or an issue. In this model are factors such as AIDS that devastated much of the LGBTQ community. There is also a high degree of environmental ambiguity about what lobbyists do. Yet, there is an affirmative understanding of the process, structures, and role of loser issues in the policy process. Lastly, this model of lobbying-legislators preferences action that disrupts power dynamics and pick an issue that will inhibit or alter the way power returns to the powerful.

However, comparisons are useful to examine the policy process. To illustrate these ways, I start with a review of agenda-setting theory from the "Multiple Streams Theory" created by John Kingdon in his 1995 book *Agendas, Alternatives, and Public Policies*. In it, Kingdon argues that policy change occurs under conditions of ambiguity and that under these conditions there are opportunities for solutions to problems to take hold. For instance, there is fluid participation (multiple actors at multiple times); problematic preferences (people don't know what they want); and unclear technology.

In Kingdon's view, this is about the power of attention and time rather than rationality. He argues that people have limited processing capacity (Lang, 2010) because of bounded rationality (Jones, 1999) and time constraints. Zahariadis

(1995: 28) states, "Because problems and preferences are not well known, selecting the alternative that yields the most net benefits becomes an impossible task." As a result, the primary goal of actors is to "manage time."

Under this theory, policymakers have not made up their mind so there is little to change. And there are three assumptions: people can only handle one issue at a time as individuals, time pressures drive policymakers, and streams are independent.

The streams can enable policy change and are a combination of three factors: problems (signified by focusing events and negative feedback); politics (the lobbying of groups, national mood, and election results); and policy solutions (that are commensurate with values and technical acceptability). Thomas Birkland has been the main theorist on focusing events, which feature prominently in public policy. For instance, the 9/11 terrorist attacks are the most recognized focusing event. Birkland states that a focusing event is

> an event that is sudden, relatively rare, can be reasonably defined as harmful or revealing the possibility of potentially greater future harms, inflicts harms or suggests potential harms that are … concentrated on a definable geographic area or community of interest, and that is known to policy makers and the public virtually simultaneously.
>
> *(Birkland, 1997: 22)*

When joined, they create a policy stream that can lead to policy change. Bringing them together is a policy entrepreneur. Policy entrepreneurs are the motivating force to the coupling of the streams and the opening of policy windows. Policy entrepreneurship is about giving meaning to events for policymakers who don't have an ability to figure this out for themselves due to time constraints.

A policy stream needs a moment of opportunity to be effective. Kingdon points to these specific times as policy windows. Howlett and Ramesh (2003: 137) as well as Wu, Ramesh, Howlett, & Fritzen (2010:18) identify four different policy windows from Kingdon's (1995) research: routinized windows, discretionary windows, spillover problem windows, and random windows. For our analysis, it is valuable to look at routinized windows, which are governed by procedures and processes such as budget timelines and sunset provisions. Discretionary windows are described as the openings created by decision-makers and may include the introduction of legislation or announcement of a new program (Wu et al., 2010). The latter two windows are created by exogenous factors. During random event windows, unforeseen focusing events prompt the opening in policymaking while spillover windows are noted when a policy window is already open on another issue and the occurrence of another event is brought in for consideration (Wu et al., 2010: 18).

There are a number of useful elements of the Multiple Streams Theory. The first is time being rationed and ambiguity. These are consistent between the two frameworks. In addition, the presence of a crisis or focusing event can lead to the need for lobbyist-legislators because of the need for process and issue experts. However, the Multiple Streams Theory does not consider marginalized groups, or loser issues. In addition, lobbyists are not seen as policy entrepreneurs in this book.

Methods

This book assumes that the behavior of legislative officials is affirmatively self-interested and error prone. I am not diagnosing that which we already know, that politics in the Congress is uncivil. I am stating that, contrary to rational models of elite decision making, what we are more likely dealing with are mass cases of narcissistic personality disorder. This judgment is grounded in the political science and sociology literature. Hatemi and Fazekas (2018: 873) note that "a substantial body of research finds a connection between narcissism and political elites." They highlight Post (1993: 99), who writes,

> It is probably not an exaggeration to state that if individuals with significant narcissistic characteristics were stripped from the ranks of public figures, the ranks would be perilously thinned, for the upper levels of government and industry are filled with 'successful narcissists.'

The literature on narcissistic personality disorder describes it thusly:

> The essential features are a grandiose sense of self-importance or uniqueness and preoccupation with fantasies of unlimited success and power; hypersensitivity to criticism; and a lack of empathy. Self-esteem, while outwardly appearing high, is actually quite fragile, with a need for constant attention.
> *(Post, 1993: 100)*

This presents itself at both the executive and legislative levels.

I remember sitting across from a legislative aide discussing something minor, when suddenly she grabbed my hand from across the table. "You realize my boss is a sociopath, right?" she said. I said, "No, I didn't know." She recalled how he screamed at her and the staff and kept them late into the night to perform minor tasks. I would hear this same story and see narcissism performed hundreds of times, by dozens of elected officials over the next decades.

One way to measure the healthiness of a congressional office is to review their staff turnover. The website LegiStorm ranks office turnover for the top ten offices in the House and Senate (McCaskill, 2018). Congresswoman Sheila Jackson Lee ranks at the top in the House. In the Senate, Amy Klobuchar is the top turnover office. And then there is just the "everyday" behavior, like former Congressman Aaron Schrock designing his office to look similar to the television series *Downton Abbey* or former Vice President Dick Cheney telling Senator Patrick Leahy (on the Senate floor), "Go fuck yourself." The behavior is so aggressive it can be difficult to distinguish between actions that are chronic or just stupid.

To counter this inconsistency, lobbyists step into the gaps. I once formed a shadow organization to use as an umbrella group to lobby on their behalf. I also dressed up to look more Republican and attended a right-wing Republican's congressional meeting on abortion. I pretended to be one of theirs and reported back. Therefore, in the face of an ambiguous environment and errors, lobbyists step in to take control.

Data

LGBTQ lobbying in the Disruptive and Capable category

There is a story that has never been told. There was secret pro-LGBTQ legislation that provided data on "don't ask, don't tell" discharges. It started because the Armed Services used to be in charge of revealing their "don't ask, don't tell" discharge numbers. It was 2003. There was an odious process where we would get piecemeal information that might be improved by requests from a Senate office or by a Freedom of Information request. But every year it was the same stonewalling on the "don't ask, don't tell" discharge data. Even in the best scenario, the data was limited. Servicemembers Legal Defense Network received the number of discharges per Service under "don't ask, don't tell" and nothing else.

So, I had an idea. What if we wrote legislation that was couched as military readiness legislation designed to collect data on "don't ask, don't tell" discharge numbers but under the guise of a broader military readiness narrative during the wars in Afghanistan and Iraq?

The framing went something like this: how can you measure military readiness if you don't know who you lost, and you don't know what they did? This was the pitch that we made for what we called "MOS reporting requirement" legislation. We spoke to Congressman Jim Moran's office who sat on the House Subcommittee on Defense Appropriations and a friendly congressional office on the House Armed Services Committee. It was a better fit for House Armed Services.

Servicemembers Legal Defense Network attorney Sharon Alexander and I worked with the House Legislative Counsel's Office to write up the legislation that would give us all the data that we needed. For instance, how many discharges were there for "don't ask, don't tell," what was the person's job specialty, how many years had they been in the military, what units were they in, where were they deployed? This was a lot more data than we ever had before, and we would get it from 2004 to 2011. This changed our approach to repeal by giving us a broader picture and narrative for those being fired under "don't ask, don't tell". For instance, the bill provided us with the jobs that LGBTQ servicemembers held, where they were deployed, and how long they had been serving. This added to the impact of the stories we could tell, and the DOD was now forced by law to give us this information.

We wrote the bill, selected the office, selected the committee, pitched it to the ranking member, wrote the talking points and followed up with staff to make sure the bill was packaged to pass. We worked with committee staff in both the Senate and the House. As a result, the Chairman of the personnel subcommittee liked the idea (it was good for military readiness) and it passed during mark up. Then it went to the full committee and passed there, with the support of the Republican Chairman. Once in the National Defense Authorization Act, it passed the full House and Senate. President George W. Bush signed it into law. Now we had all of the data on LGBTQ service we would need to fuel the repeal of "don't ask, don't tell" from the secret bill that was written, managed and passed by LGBTQ lobbying-legislators in 2004.

Disruptive and Capable

In the long history of "don't ask, don't tell," there is one mistake that produced the most positive benefit for servicemembers that should be noted. In 2002, during Major General Clark's nomination fight, there was an intense push inside the Senate for a hold (a Senate procedure that puts a stop to the consideration of a nomination) to be placed on the General's nomination. But it was unclear what Senate office would step forward to implement the hold. Senator Susan Collins's office had been helpful on LGBTQ issues in the past but was not willing to do it. Senator Gordon Smith's office was also helpful on this issue but was unwilling to do it. And Senator Kennedy's office had been a lead office in dealing with the nomination, but he was also reluctant because as a leading liberal he wanted to make sure the issue had bipartisan support.

However, there was an error that was more important than a member of the Senate. A Senate office had phoned the Senate Cloakroom (which often manages Senate business) to see if a hold had been placed. There was a miscommunication between the clerk and the office and the Cloakroom thought a hold was being placed on the Major General's nomination. It was not. However, as a result, a hold was put on General Clark's nomination. This is the only documented Senate hold in history that was not done not by a Senator. What we saw was a strategy to place a hold that created enough pressure to produce an error. The production of the error was just as good as writing legislation and it demonstrated the ability to hold a nomination without a Senator being directly involved. In short, the LGBTQ lobbying-legislator did not need a Senator to produce the kind of error that would deliver the desired result. The actions were Disruptive and Capable.

Disruptive and Capable

The hold on Major General Clark caused a stir among Republicans and resulted in Senator Jim Bunning of Kentucky placing a counter-hold on all Department of Defense nominations until the nomination was resolved. This meant that the entire Department of Defense was aware of Major General Clark's nomination now, and it posed a historic precedent for the treatment of LGBTQ troops. A general's job had been put on the line as had every nomination, promotion, and bill in all of the

Department of Defense because a *gay* soldier was murdered. This set a new standard for the entire military. If LGBTQ troops faced harassment or died under someone's command, it could cost a General or Admiral their job. Now any General's nomination could now be placed on hold if they didn't look after their LGBTQ troops. This was an issue that was not lost on the senior leadership in the Pentagon and meant a little more protection for LGBTQ troops.

The hold was lifted when the Senate Cloakroom realized there had been a mistake. Here, Senator Bunning had acted on something that was capable for him and lobbyist-legislators. However, this case is a good example of the fluidity involved. The nature of the hold (all Department of Defense nominations) may have raised a clarifying question and removing the hold may have required some political gymnastics. In other words, it is possible that these actions also fall into the Disruptive Not Capable category. These actions may have been linked in time.

Indeed, a debate was then held, and that debate reopened the conversation about the repeal of "don't ask, don't tell." While the law was not repealed until December 2010, this eight-year period changed the climate for LGBTQ troops. We will never know how important the hold was, but it happened, and it happened because a clerk misheard what a Senate office said in the Cloakroom.

It was resolved when the same Senate office called to find out who had placed the hold on the General's nomination and was told that it was them. They clarified that it was not them, that they were not placing a hold and hadn't intended to do so in the first place. The hold was lifted. By this time Democratic Senator Tom Daschle had stepped in to negotiate a final lifting of the Bunning hold to give the General a vote. The condition of lifting the hold would require two hours of Senate debate on the treatment of LGBTQ troops in the military. This would be the first debate on LGBTQ troops since "don't ask, don't tell" was debated in 1993. This was a historic moment for the Senate. Seven years later, this issue would come up again and the Senate would pass the most pro-LGBTQ bill in American history when they passed the "Don't Ask, Don't Tell" Repeal Act in December of 2010.

Bunning lifted his hold, the two hours of debate happened, the General was confirmed, but history was changed on the issue of gays in the military. A resistance had been formed based on this success. There were positive meetings across congressional offices, which had built a lobbying effort that was ready to repeal "don't ask, don't tell." From this moment, SLDN would shift organizationally from the Clark nomination to the legislative repeal of "don't ask, don't tell" in Congress.

Disruptive Not Capable

It was 2010, and late in the lobbying process to repeal "don't ask, don't tell." We felt like we had the votes, but we were asking everyone and especially the more conservative Democrats where they stood. Once we had the votes to win, we wanted to pile on and try to make it hard for the moderate Republicans to sit this one out. These moments reveal the most about the policy process. Three examples come to mind. Two of them highlight the role of the West Virginia delegation, which has not been widely addressed.

First is senior Democratic Senator Robert Byrd from West Virginia. Senator Byrd was the 15th vote on the Senate Armed Services Committee to add repeal legislation as an amendment to the Defense Authorization Bill. This vote was conditional on an important addition that became law. He asked for a 60-day delay and review period (Memmott, 2010). His support was seen as an indicator that gay rights had evolved. This change was complicated, however. I was told by one of his staff that this change of heart came on a "lucid day" when he was feeling all right and was asked if he wanted to support the amendment and he said yes, but only if there was a greater level of oversight. After his death, Senator Chris Dodd stated, "Here was a man unafraid of progress, a man who, in one of his final acts in the Senate, voted to overturn the 'don't ask, don't tell rule' in our military." This is an example of Senator Byrd being disruptive on something a lobbyist-legislator would not have been capable of doing.

Second is junior Democratic Senator Joe Manchin, also from West Virginia. He played a role in the final floor vote. He had a Christmas party and missed the most historic LGBTQ rights vote in U.S. history. His vote was a no. Senator Manchin had publicly opposed repeal, but apparently didn't want to be seen voting no by his colleagues or cajoled into yes by his colleagues. Manchin's spokesperson stated the Senator had "planned a holiday gathering over a year ago with all their children and grandchildren" (Bolton, 2010). Senator Manchin is an example of doing something a lobbyist-legislator is not able to do, with no disruption to the process.

Lastly, there is North Carolina Republican Richard Burr. A few details stand out for this vote. He is the only Republican Senator from a Republican state to vote for repeal of "don't ask, don't tell." While North Carolina voted for President Obama in 2008, it has voted Republican nine out of ten Presidential elections. I have previously argued (Neff, 2016) that Burr was given political cover when he voted "yea" by voting alongside Senators Collins and Snowe. This is an example of being disruptive by voting on an issue that only he could, and that issue and vote disrupt the underlying power dynamics.

Following this vote, Senator Burr supported same-sex marriage benefits. This shows the importance of unconventional political science mixed-method approaches. Here we see in-depth participant-observer data, unique empirical data, and queer methods. This book models the importance of applying queer mixed-methods to answer research questions about LGBTQ lobbying in the United States.

Capable Not Disruptive

The classic action by a lobbyist is the delivery of talking points, in a one-pager. These talking points are the basis for congressional speeches and building a legislative history. This act of deciding what talking points a member of Congress will use makes the lobbyist capable and their effort not disruptive. This is a cultivation exercise that is not intended to upend power dynamics.

TABLE 5.2 Comparison of "don't ask, don't tell" talking points

2002	2010
Keeping good troops is good policy	Don't Ask, Don't Tell is a failure
No national security interest is served by spending millions of taxpayer dollars to fire gay linguists and doctors who can do the job	We can stop losing good troops today
U.S. forces are already serving alongside openly gay International troops	Kick out bad troops for poor conduct
We thank our veterans; we don't discriminate against them:	Nat. Security is hurt by keeping DADT

Table 5.2 identifies the first set of talking points I developed in 2002 and the last set of talking points in 2010. Here we see that the 2002 narrative is more conservative. It talks about veterans, international troops, and taxpayers. In the 2010 talking points, there is a more aggressive stance. The narrative is centered around "don't ask, don't tell" hurting the military. It notes how "don't ask, don't tell" is a failure, how we lose good troops, how it hurts national security, and how most troops don't care. The first set of talking points are designed to solicit asks to gain information (to fill a need that in organizations). The second set is telling someone that continuing with "don't ask, don't tell" makes you a failure. You are complicit in losing good troops you are hurting national security all the while troops don't care. Again, these 2010 talking points are statements of action.

Not Capable Not Disruptive

Sometimes Senators ask each other for help. In many cases, help includes political cover to mitigate any political damage from a vote on a controversial topic. I argue that political cover can be seen in the vote to repeal "don't ask, don't tell" in the Senate. In December 2010, the vote took place in the Senate. A number of vulnerable Senators voted to repeal "don't ask, don't tell." However, the way in which they voted was unique. I argue that there was a degree of political cover that was afforded to vulnerable Senators during this vote. This cover presents a situation where a lobbyist is not capable of taking action, but the result is not disruptive. We see a space only for members of Congress. In fact, the reason the political cover is not disruptive is that it cannot be in order to work. Political cover is something that is afforded quietly.

In Table 5.3 there is a series of highlighted boxes which note the timescale for the vote to repeal "don't ask, don't tell" which was 30 minutes.

An interesting variable for looking at the votes to repeal "don't ask, don't tell" can be seen in Table 5.3. There was a meeting with Senator Dick Lugar of Indiana before the vote. Senator Lugar had a 60 percent rating from the Human Rights Campaign; however, he faced a primary challenge. As a result, he is among the very first to vote

TABLE 5.3 Senate analysis of "don't ask, don't tell" repeal vote

Time	Senators Voting Yea					
03:00	Bayh (D)					
03:01	Kerry (D)	Webb (D)				
03:02	Franken (D)					
03:03	Inouye (D)					
03:04	Lieberman (I-D)	Casey (D)				
03:05						
03:06	Schumer (D)	Reed (D)	Gillibrand (D)	Shaheen (D)		
Nays	McCain (R)	Lugar (R)	Cornyn (R)	Sessions (R)	Kyle (R)	
03:07						
03:08						
03:09						
Nays	Cochran (R)	Roberts (R)				
03:10	Scott Brown (R)					
	26 = Yeas	14 = Nays				
03:11	Klobochar (D)	Durbin (D)				
Nays	Lugar (R)	Bond (R)				
03:12	Snowe	Collins (R)	Burr (R)			
Nays	Lemieux (R)					
03:13	Sanders (I)	Harkin (D)	Rockefeller (D)	Cardin (D)	Conrad (D)	
03:14	Sherrod Brown (R)	Wyden (D)	Merkley (D)	Begich (D)	Feingold (D)	Dorgan (D)
Nays	Brownback (R)	Graham (R)	Wicker (R)			
03:15	Ensign (R)	Voinovich (R)				
Nays	Rich (R)	Bennett (R)	Grassley (R)	Crapo (R)		
03:16	Ben Nelson (D)	Johnson (R)				
Nays	Chambliss (R)					
03:17	Kirk (R)					
Nays	Alexander (R)	McConnell (R)				

TABLE 5.3 Cont.

Time	Senators Voting Yea				
03:18	Aaka (D)	Bill Nelson (D)	Feinstein (D)	Whitehouse (D)	Lincoln (D)
03:19	Murkowski (R)	Menendez (D)	Dodd (D)	McCaskill (D)	
Nays					
03:20	Coons (D)	Specter (D)	Kohl (D)		
Nays	Inhofe (R)				
03:21	Bachus (D)			Thune (R)	
03:22	Udall (D)	Stabenow (D)			
03:23	Pryor (D)	Lautenberg (D)			
Nays	Hutchison (R)				
03:24					
03:25					
03:26					
03:27					
03:28					
03:29	Carper (D)				

to oppose the repeal of "don't ask, don't tell." Other Senators who voted in favor of repeal of "don't ask, don't tell" from Republican seats included Scott Brown, Olympia Snowe, Susan Collins, and Senator Burr. I have noted that Senator Burr voted with Senators Snowe and Collins as an example of this political cover. There were also pairs that voted together, such as Senator Ensign and Senator Voinovich.

However, the most dramatic cover appears to be Democrats giving other Democrats cover. The last Democratic vulnerable seat to vote for repeal of "don't ask, don't tell" was Senator Mark Pryor of Arkansas. The vote appears to have been both Not Disruptive, Not Capable for a number of Senators, while it was also a Disruptive Not Capable vote for a number of other Senators. Some Senators were seeking political cover, while others were giving cover. These Senators were Not Disruptive, Not Capable. However, there were also those who were making a statement. Whether it was Senator Lugar voting no, or Senator Brown voting yes. In short, two things were going on at the same time among members that become visible when you look at the process and consider the roles of inside actors and outside actors.

Discussion

The repeal of "don't ask, don't tell" was House Majority Leader Steny Hoyer's legislative victory, and Senator John McCain's defeat.

Congressman Hoyer, a Democrat from Maryland, is one of the longest-serving members of the House of Representatives. In 2010, Hoyer introduced the last version of the "Don't Ask, Don' Tell" Repeal Act as a stand-alone bill in the House. He introduced the bill at a time when it was unclear if it could get through the Senate. As a result, he worked with Democratic Senate Majority Harry Reid of Nevada (disclosure: I used to work for Senator Reid) who was worried about making sure there was enough time on the legislative calendar for consideration and passage of the START treaty with Russia. Hoyer worked with Senate Republicans to get the numbers and led the passage of the bill in the House. This was a mammoth last-second approach, which worked. This occurred despite efforts of Senate Republicans John McCain and Lindsey Graham, who were hinting at a horse-trade. They offered support for START in exchange for dropping "don't ask, don't tell" in the Senate. This was an enticing option for skittish Democrats.

In the Senate, there was a fight between Independent-Democratic Senator Joe Lieberman and Majority Leader Reid. Senator Lieberman thought the final stages of repeal on the Senate floor were a set up by Reid so he would fail. In turn, Senator Reid's office was openly saying that Lieberman's efforts could cause major problems for the end of the legislative session.

Three asks will be reviewed:

1. "Ask" to vote against the Major General Clark nomination;
2. "Ask" to meet with Senator Warner's office; and
3. "Ask" to cosponsor bill to repeal "don't ask, don't tell.

"Ask" to vote against the Major General Clark nomination

The first "ask" in Congress that I worked on was the request to vote against the nomination of then Major General Clark. Here, we see asks given to Senators and their action is disruptive and not capable. This is a situation where a lobbyist-legislator is not capable of acting but the action that is taken is disruptive to the way power is returned to the powerful.

To begin, one of the first meetings on this nomination was with Senator Daniel Akaka of Hawaii on January 8, 2003. Senator Akaka will be the lead Senator behind the scenes to oppose the Major General Clark nomination. At the end of the process when committee members sit in Executive Session to consider the nomination in private there is a motion for a confidential vote, Senator Akaka objects. When there is a public vote, Senator Akaka votes no. His is one of the most pro-LGBTQ records that is underrepresented in politics.

"Ask" to meet with Senator Warner's office

There also was a scene with Senate staffer Dick Walsh, who appeared to be aggravated by the opposition to the Major General Clark nomination. Dick Walsh worked for the Senate Armed Services Committee. I called Dick Walsh to set up a staff meeting with him, just between the two of us, and he told me "you will never meet with me."

It is the height of a lobbyist's career, not to pass legislation, but to get around a staffer that has decided you will never meet with the office. In this situation, I reached out to Pat and Wally Kutteles, Barry Winchell's parents. I decided that if Dick Walsh was going to block me from having a meeting with him, then I would go above his head and arrange a meeting between Pat and Wally and the Senator. In this case that was Senator Warner of Virginia. Pat and Wally met with Senator Warner and Senator Levin on May 14, 2003.

On the day of the Executive Session in the Senate Armed Services Committee and Senate floor vote, I was in the Russell Senate Office Building. I was standing in the hallway outside the hearing room. In my overly large suit, I stood alone in the marble hallway. A group of Generals, including Major General Robert Clark, emerged from a side door. They stood across from me on the other side of the hallway. As a group of seven they looked at me derisively. Just then, Republican Senator John Warner of Virginia came out of his office. He walked toward both of us, and then he turned. He came up to me. He put his hand on my shoulder, just as if I was still working for him, and said, "Hey Chris, I need to go down to the floor for a vote, so it'll probably be 15–20 minutes before things start." And then he was off. The Generals all stared at me, presumably wondering what the hell was going on. As Chairman of the Senate Armed Services Committee he was the only one who could reach out to me. He didn't rock the boat, but the gesture was appreciated. He voted in favor of the Major General Clark promotion.

Senator Levin is one of the more unfortunate stories around the repeal of "don't ask, don't tell." He publicly supported the Major General Clark nomination, he was reluctant to include "don't ask, don't tell" in the base bill, and he was generally mediocre in advocating for repeal. In addition, his committee staff were there to keep the LGBTQ in line, for nearly a decade. Of the Clark nomination, Levin stated, "I think it is appropriate we now confirm this nomination."

"Ask" to co-sponsor legislation to repeal "don't ask, don't tell"

One of the key elements of lobbying is getting co-sponsors for a bill. This happens in a number of ways. First, you build confidence with an office. At SLDN, we referred to these as basic introductory meetings. In our introductory meetings we would introduce ourselves and create a space for congressional work on repeal of "don't ask, don't tell." This included raising questions about the Arabic linguists who had been fired, the Major General Clark nomination, complaints about anti-gay harassment, and any personal stories about gay servicemembers from that state. The first question that every congressional office asked, was where is the Human Rights Campaign on this?

In response, we told them that we were engaged with them, but were not occupied on this issue. In addition, we also had meetings on anti-gay harassment and

AHAP implementation. These meetings were designed to also build confidence, to give offices something to do, educate their staff, and demonstrate that we could follow through. Lastly, we were building relationships with individual congressional offices. This involved very specific targets. Committee members, military bases, large veteran populations, and high rates of "don't ask, don't tell" discharges. For example, we reached out to Marty Meehan, Susan Davis, Ellen Tauscher, all members of the House Armed Services Committee. We also reached out to Mary Bono in Palm Springs given her relationship with Chaz Bono Anne Ileana Ros-Lehtinen in southern Florida and openly gay members such as Barney Frank and Jim Kolbe.

We also used a target list, a scorecard put together by our intern Sarah Einowski, who put together a series of votes (Table 5.4), which provided us the most likely targets for co-sponsoring a bill to repeal "don't ask don't tell." This included previous support for the Boxer amendment in 1993, whether or not they sponsored ENDA in 2003, opposition to the Major General Clark nomination, if it was the Senate, and support for Hate Crimes legislation.

Together, these provided a snapshot that allowed us to move forward with our outreach and education efforts on the Hill. We also had meetings to stop offices from taking seemingly helpful steps. There were a number of offices that were interested in what they called a "carve-out" that would have allowed different service members (doing different jobs) to remain in the military.

We had to stop all of these efforts to ensure that the timing, the messaging, and the stakeholders, were all ready for a full-frontal attack on "don't ask, don't tell." Our concern was that there would be a backlash against us. And we were concerned that the backlash would be worse than the existing policy. As a result, Servicemembers Legal Defense Network had more than 200 meetings in Congress between November 2002 and March 2005. These meetings included basic introductory meetings, meetings about anti-LGBTQ harassment, meetings to stop offices from introducing legislation, opposition to Major General Clark and lastly explanations about article 125. This last point was important, because of the *Lawrence* decision in 2003 that argued that sodomy was legal. However, according to the military's Uniform Code of Military Justice, sodomy was illegal. As a result, this was being reviewed by the Department of Defense.

We also developed a core group of 13 offices that did the heavy lifting for most of the different issues we worked on, particularly in the House. We met with these offices, we shared our introduction strategy, draft legislation, and our plans to secure leadership within caucuses and delegations and the support of the House and Senate leadership. When the bill to repeal "don't ask, don't tell" was introduced, in March 2005, the bill had 48 co-sponsors and was bipartisan with the support of Congressman Chris Shays of Connecticut and later Congressman Jim Kolbe of Arizona.

TABLE 5.4 2005 SLDN Senate "don't ask, don't tell" vote count

U.S. Senate Vote Count 109th Congress on "don't ask, don't tell"

1 = Support Boxer Amendment? Pro Open Service. 1993
2 = Did they sponsor ENDA? 5/1/03
3 = Opposed General Clark Nomination? 11/03
4 = Support DOD Hate Crimes and Authorization Act? 6/15/04

	Yes **1**	**1**	**2**	**3**	**4**	**5**		**SLDN Met w/?** (how many)/(most recent)
1	Akaka(HI)	Y	Y	Y	Y	Y	1	1 – 1/8/2003
2	Biden (DE)	Y	Y	NV	Y	Y	2	2 – 5/24/2004
3	Bingaman(NM)	Y	Y	NV	Y	Y	3	1 – 5/24/2004
4	Boxer(CA)	Y	Y	Y	Y	Y	4	3 – 5/24/2004
5	Cantwell(WA)	NIS	Y	NV	Y	Y	5	3 – 5/24/2004
6	Clinton(NY)	NIS	NIS	Y	Y	Y	6	5 – 5/24/2004
7	Corzine(NJ)	NIS	Y	Y	Y	Y	7	1 – 10/29/2003
8	Dayton(MN)	NIS	Y	Y	Y	Y	8	6 – 9/13/2004
9	Dodd(CT)	Y	Y	NV	Y	Y	9	No
10	Durbin(IL)	NIS	Y	Y	Y	Y	10	2 – 5/24/2004
11	Feingold(WI)	Y	N	Y	Y	Y	11	4 – 10/31/2004
12	Feinstein(CA)	Y	Y	Y	Y	Y	12	3 – 5/24/2004
13	Harkin(IA)	Y	Y	NV	Y	Y	13	No
14	Inouye(HI)	Y	Y	NV	Y	Y	14	No
15	Jeffords(I-VT)	Y	Y	NV	NV	Y	15	No
16	Kennedy(MA)	Y	N	Y	Y	Y	16	9 – 9/10/2004
17	Kerry(MA)	Y	Y	Y	NV	NV	17	5 – 9/27/2004
18	Lautenberg (NJ)	Y	Y	Y	Y	Y	18	1 – 10/31/2003
19	Leahy(VT)	Y	Y	NV	Y	Y	19	No
20	Levin(MI)	Y	Y	N	Y	Y	20	3 – 5/24/2004
21	Lieberman(CT)	Y	Y	NV	Y	Y	21	2 – 7/4/2003
22	Mikulski(MD)	Y	Y	NV	Y	Y	22	2 – 5/24/2004
23	Murray(WA)	Y	Y	NV	Y	Y	23	3 – 5/24/2004
24	Obama (IL)	NIS	NIS	NIS	NIS	NIS	24	No
25	Reed(RI)	NIS	Y	N	Y	Y	25	1 – 1/8/2003
26	Sarbanes(MD)	Y	Y	NV	Y	Y	26	2 – 5/24/2004
27	Schumer(NY)	NIS	Y	NV	Y	Y	27	3 – 5/24/2004
28	Stabenow(MI)	NIS	Y	Y	Y	Y	28	2 – 5/24/2004
29	Wyden(OR)	NIS	Y	NV	Y	Y	29	No

Conclusion

Members of Congress are not the only lawmakers in Congress. Lobbyist-legislators provide an essential function adding technical expertise of the processes and issues that rise on the agenda. Sometimes these are complex incremental changes and sometimes they are dramatic focusing events. LGBTQ lobbying plays a key role in defense and offense when these moments arise. Indeed, they also include nominations, which are an understudied area of lobbying research. Moving forward, this book will look at the "White House ask" rather than the congressional action. Both involve lobbying and both provide windows into LGBTQ lobbying.

To close this chapter, it is important to note that the motivating story of this book, the repeal of "don't ask, don't tell," is a story about people. It is the story of servicemembers who lived in the closet while fighting abroad, at the direction of those in power. The politics of repeal will always matter less than the reality of their service. It is important, however, to honor their service and use these examples as a way to prepare for the LGBTQ battles that are yet to come.

References

Birkland, T.A. (1997). *After Disaster: Agenda Setting, Public Policy, and Focusing Events.* Georgetown University Press.

Bolton, A. (2010, December 18). GOP slams new Dem senator who skipped votes to attend Christmas party. *The Hill.* https://thehill.com/blogs/blog-briefing-room/news/134379-gop-slams-new-dem-senator-who-skipped-votes-to-attend-christmas-party

Frank, N. (2013, February 19). *Obama's false 'Don't Ask, Don't Tell' narrative.* The New Republic. https://newrepublic.com/article/112457/obamas-false-dont-ask-dont-tell-narrative

Hatemi, P.K., & Fazekas, Z. (2018). Narcissism and political orientations. *American Journal of Political Science, 62*(4), 873–888. https://doi.org/10.1111/ajps.12380

Howlett, M., & Ramesh, M. (2003). *Studying Public Policy: Policy Cycles and Policy Subsystems* (2nd ed.). Oxford University Press.

Jones, B.D. (1999). Bounded rationality. *Annual Review of Political Science, 2,* 297–321. https://doi.org/10.1146/annurev.polisci.2.1.297

Kingdon, J.W. (1995). *Agendas, Alternatives, and Public Policies* (2nd ed.). Harper Collins.

Lang, P.J. (2010). Emotion and motivation: Toward consensus definitions and a common research purpose. *Emotion Review, 2*(3), 229–233. https://doi.org/10.1177/1754073910361984

McCaskill, N.D. (2018, March 21). *The "worst bosses" in Congress?* Politico. www.politico.com/story/2018/03/21/worst-bosses-congress-476729

Memmott, M. (2010, May 27). *"Don't ask, don't tell" repeal gets critical 15th vote.* NPR. www.npr.org/sections/thetwo-way/2010/05/dont_ask_dont_tell_repeal_byrd.html

Neff, C. (2015). The *Jaws* effect: How movie narratives are used to influence policy responses to shark bites in Western Australia. *Australian Journal of Political Science, 50*(1), 114–127. https://doi.org/10.1080/10361146.2014.989385

Neff, C. (2016). The performance of roll call votes as political cover in the U.S. Senate: Using C-SPAN to analyze the vote to repeal "Don't Ask, Don't Tell." In R.X. Browning (Ed.), *Exploring the C-SPAN archives: Advancing the Research Agenda* (pp. 191–212). Purdue University Press. https://doi.org/10.2307/j.ctv15wxr41.13

Pepin-Neff, C. (2019). *Flaws: Shark Bites and Emotional Public Policymaking*. Palgrave Macmillan.

Post, J.M. (1993). Current concepts of the narcissistic personality: Implications for political psychology. *Political Psychology*, *14*(1), 99–121. https://doi.org/10.2307/3791395

Smith, S.L., Choueiti, M., Pieper, K., Case, A., & Choi, A. (2018). *Inequality in 1,100 Popular Films: Examining Portrayals of Gender, Race/Ethnicity, LGBT & Disability from 2007 to 2017*. USC Annenberg. http://assets.uscannenberg.org/docs/inequality-in-1100-popular-films.pdf

Thurber, J.A. (2011). The contemporary presidency: Changing the way Washington Works? Assessing President Obama's battle with lobbyists. *Presidential Studies Quarterly*, *41*(2), 358–374. https://cces.gov.harvard.edu/publications/contemporary-presidency-changing-way-washington-works-assessing-president-obama%E2%80%99s-

Weissert, C.S. (1991). Policy entrepreneurs, policy opportunists, and legislative effectiveness. *American Politics Research*, *19*(2), 262–274. https://doi.org/10.1177%2F1532673X9101900207

Wu, X., Ramesh, M., Howlett, M., & Fritzen, S.A. (2010). *The Public Policy Primer: Managing the Policy Process*. Routledge.

6

SEX AND LGBTQ LOBBYING

Introduction

People are viewed as sex objects within the political system in the United States. This chapter reviews the way hierarchies of identity about perceived attractiveness, sex (as an act), and gender identity all reduce people down to a one-dimensional version of who they are. These essentialized constructions are used to rank identities in ways that return power to the powerful.

The implication of sexual hierarchies includes the way organizations are staffed and developed, as well as activist burnout. I argue that the way norms are placed upon LGBTQ identities are designed to benefit institutional heterosexuality. This includes the structure of lobbying, agenda-setting, and policy areas, which prioritize mainstream heteronormative issues. Put another way, preferencing certain identities leads to preferencing the political issues connected with those identities. To analyze this, the lens from the "social construction of target populations" developed by Anne Schneider and Helen Ingram (1993) helps look at the way identities impact lobbying and distribute political power.

For this discussion, the chapter is divided into six sections, outlined below:

1. Sexual hierarchy: This element helps make certain identities political priorities and others invisible. We see a reliance on a sexual hierarchy that reproduces oppression in the LGBTQ community by preferencing gay, white, young, cisgender, able-bodied, English-speaking males, from the Global North based on socially constructed perceptions of sexual attraction. Here, we also see fatphobia, which has been addressed by Roxanne Gay;
2. Impossible people: Where the system is functioning when it refuses to accommodate, and intentionally obstructs, the lives of trans and non-binary people. Whether this is licenses, bathrooms, passports, health care, employment, or

prison accommodation, these systems render trans and non-binary people vulnerable as citizens. The literature on "impossible people" advanced by trans law scholar Dean Spade (2010) helps articulate the way structures are designed to deny access, particularly to transgender and non-binary people;

3. Sexual harassment: Where the business model privileges white, cis, young, able-bodied, English-speaking, males from the Global North; and there are high rates of sexual harassment on the basis of these identities in LGBTQ organizations. It is also important to note that sexual harassment targets vulnerability so this may include volunteers and staff who are poor, do not speak English, and are from the Global South;

4. LGBTQ philanthropy: Low levels of funding for the LGBTQ non-profit community can exacerbate high instances of burnout. For instance, according to data from the Equality Federation, Executive Directors in LGBTQ state-wide organizations turn over every two or three years (Snyder, 2015), which makes planning and strategy more short-term in focus, in the face of long-term systemic oppression;

5. Respectability: This is the dominance of heteronormative behavior as a means of accessing social acceptance. This may include clothes, manners, speech, and the types of political issues and tactics employed; and

6. Burnout: Lastly, burnout looks at the factors that contribute to staff, volunteers, and board members leaving an organization and a movement. The most common cause in the LGBTQ advocacy community is infighting within the movement. The lowering of morale is more influential than opposition from anti-LGBTQ groups.

Literature review

Sexual hierarchy

Perceptions of beauty are statements of political power

Sexual hierarchies deliver power to the one making the judgement about beauty, not simply to the one about whom beauty is being attributed. The flow of power begins with the one establishing the dominant perceptions about identity in society. As a result, we can see how perceptions of beauty return power to the powerful. Hierarchies that establish who is attractive, whose sexual activity is celebrated, and whose identity is validated by the State can all be seen in racism, sexism, classism, fatphobia, serophobia, homophobia, transphobia, and ableism.

Sexual hierarchies are based on three factors: the organization of physical features in a way that orders their perceived attractiveness (i.e. male gaze); the hierarchy of hegemonic masculinity (Connell, 2002); and the hierarchy of sexual activities (Rubin, 2007).

The "male gaze" is a concept developed in feminist literature and refers to the idealized version of women for the purpose of satisfying men's sexual desires. In this model, the representation of women is heterosexual, and the hierarchy of sexual attractiveness is based on what will please the heterosexual male.

First, hierarchies of lesbian beauty are often dominated by the male gaze. Zipkin (1999) wrote an article entitled, "The Myth of the Short-Haired Lesbian" for the *Journal of Lesbian Studies.* In it, she notes,

> A number of myths and misperceptions related to images of lesbian beauty surround hair length. Short hair has become a symbol of being a lesbian, and many lesbians with long hair have felt pressured to cut theirs when they come out.
>
> *(Zipkin, 1999: 91)*

She adds that the heterosexual male gaze is still a factor in lesbian perceptions of beauty. By adopting short hair as a "masculine" signal of lesbian beauty, "lesbians are still reacting to male-defined images and standards and may be internalizing and perpetuating sexism" (Zipkin, 1999: 91). Here, we see how the male gaze is driven by masculinity for both men and women.

Yet, it is important to note that lesbians diverge from both the male gaze and heterosexuality at key points. Taub (1999: 28) notes that "lesbians have their own beauty standards within their communities, standards that differ from heterosexual ones." Importantly, Mitchell Wood adds in his article "The Gay Male Gaze: Body Image Disturbance and Gender Oppression Among Gay Men" that, "whereas feminists have fought passionately against the male gaze, many gay men are still fighting passionately for it, striving to extend its reach, wishing to partake of its power" (Wood, 2004: 45).

There is a privilege toward young, white, gay, English-speaking, cisgender, males from the Global North. Central to this are perceptions of a highly masculine appearance, voice, and behavior. Ziv (2011: 125) notes that there is a "gay social hierarchy" with stigma inside and outside the LGBTQ community toward effeminate men. Appearing to be effeminate is the stigma. Ziv (2011: 125) states:

> As such, he occupies the bottom of the gay social hierarchy, since many gay men (and lesbians too) wish to distance themselves from this stigma-bearing figure. One of the things that make gay men uncomfortable about drag queens is their visibility. While most lesbians and gay men can pass as heterosexual, most drag queens cannot, thus they in effect wear their stigma for all to see. This visibility has made them symbolize the potential vulnerability of all gays, but on the other hand it also made them adopt and represent a stance of proud defiance: it is no coincidence that drag queens played a major role in the Stonewall riots.

An additional physical feature is someone's face. Ralph Geiselman, Nancy Haight, and Lori Kimata wrote in 1984 about the "Context Effects on the Perceived Physical Attractiveness of Faces" in the *Journal of Experimental Social Psychology*, noting, "it is inevitable that physical appearance will have an important social impact on people's lives. Past research illustrates that physically attractive people are assumed to possess more socially desirable personality traits (Dion, Berscheid, & Walster, 1972)." This maladaptive set of preferences within the sexual hierarchy is ultimately harmful and can lead to the perpetuation of heteronormative structural stigmas as well as anti-LGBTQ violence against others or ourselves.

In January 2020, the BBC reported (Hunte, 2020), "Manchester-based charity the LGBT Foundation has warned that body image issues are becoming more widespread in gay communities. It says gay and bisexual men are 'much more likely' than heterosexual men to struggle with them." It added, "A number of gay men have told the BBC they are going to extreme lengths to change their bodies—including using steroids and having plastic surgery—just to become 'accepted' by others in the LGBT community."

Second, there is a hierarchy of hegemonic masculinity. Raewyn Connell came up with the term and notes that "it embodied the currently most honored way of being a man, it required all other men to position themselves in relation to it, and it ideologically legitimated the global subordination of women to men" (Connell & Messerschmidt, 2005: 832). The idea that to be masculine and male is the normal way to express gender and that men are superior to women is central to this form of masculinity.

Attractiveness is designed by hegemonic masculinity and the heterosexual male gaze. This can be seen in the halo effect and attractiveness effect. The halo effect is a cognitive bias, a misjudgment, that is made about someone as a whole person or someone's personality based on one leading characteristic. This may be height, weight, sex, race, gender, gender identity, expression, or ability. We see this in taller people who are often judged to be more trustworthy based on their height.

The focus on race as a signifier of masculinity or attractiveness is particularly corrosive. Here, we see the prominence of sexual racism. Sexual racism is racism in a romantic or sexual context. It is more common among gay and bisexual men than straight men, it frequently happens online, and it reinforces hierarchies of identity. To begin, Callander, Newman, and Holt (2015: 1991) state that "sexual racism" is the "discrimination between potential sexual or romantic partners on the basis of perceived racial identity." Stember (1978: xi) first defined sexual racism as "the sexual rejection of the racial minority, the conscious attempt on the part of the majority to prevent interracial cohabitation."

Thai (2019: 347) notes that sexual racism is common in the gay and bisexual male community, "This type of discrimination is prevalent, especially within the community of men who have sex with men." Callander, Newman, and Holt (2016) build on all of this to note the implications of sexual racism. That sexual racism is a type of harm that subjugates most populations. They note, "the fetishization of racial identities is another potent expression of sexual racism, which reproduces hierarchies of race often under the guise of personal preferences towards particular racial 'types'" (Callander et al., 2016: 4–5).

Racial or sexist interpretations of sexual desire (the male gaze) are often found in movies. In the LGBTQ community, a prominent symbol of gay, male, able-bodied life are Tom of Finland pictures. In these illustrations, many men have bulging muscles, mustaches, and leather outfits. Yet, there are problems with this Tom of Finland look. Mann (1998: 352) states, "The inherent racism in the prevailing ideal of gay male beauty is obvious." Mercer and Julien (1994: 132) add that "the racist and fascist connotations of these new 'macho' styles escaped gay consciousness, as those who embrace the 'threatening' symbolism of the tough-guy look were really only interested in the eroticization of masculinity." Lahti (1998: 197) adds that "these images are embedded in a cultural tradition that has sexualized the oppression of women." In addition, Lahti (1998: 197) notes that

> while the drawings by Tom of Finland attempt to empower the gay male body, they are also in complicity in the binary opposition instituted by the dominant culture according to which the core of (heterosexual) masculinity consists of muscles and a hard body.

Third, we see sexual hierarchies played out through sexual activity that are seen as more or less acceptable, as outlined by scholar Gayle Rubin (2007). However, what people and sex acts are allowed to be perceived as attractive are defined by the straight world. Attractiveness in the LGBTQ world is most often seen through the male gaze of what straight white men find attractive.

Dr. Joseph Osmundson (2019) has written about the role of circuit parties in the LGBTQ (but mostly gay and mostly male) community. He highlights the rules of perceived attractiveness as well as the politicization of beauty.

> Circuit parties are damn near body-fascist. They worship—because the people within them worship—tall, angular, muscled men. Men who have this look wander a circuit party in a special way. There seems, to me, to be a small wake around them; no one dares get too close. At the same time, men follow them around, from point A to B to C on the dancefloor, waiting for the perfect moment to try to talk, or, more likely, to dance. And this beauty—who owns it, and why—is of course political, and is also the nucleation point of the pleasure we go to the circuit party seeking.
>
> (Osmundson, 2019)

The continued objectification of Black women and men, invisibility of the disabled and indigenous is not evidence of the LGBTQ revolution. Sexual racism against Asian women and men, transphobia, hetero-sexism and misogyny, and the reproduction of male, cis, whiteness as the apex of sexual desirability is a step backwards in LGBTQ rights.

Methods

Certain people, and the sex they have, are celebrated while others are punished as deviants. And this perception influences their relationship with the State. The social construction of target populations (Schneider & Ingram, 1993) helps provide a framework to understand this.

The most important point to remember about the social construction of target populations is that each social construction allocates benefits or burdens.

Under this model, the social construction of groups happens across an axis of power (high or low) and perception of the group (positive or negative). This is a distributive framework, which means that we are looking at what comes out of the policies that affect them. What does it mean to fine the homeless for sleeping on the sidewalk or to give a tax break to the wealthy? This policy activity produces rules of participation that rewards and encourages some to participate while punishing others, discouraging their engagement in the policy process. This creates a pattern of participation that privileges or dishonors citizenship based on your group. In short, policies are designed to send a message and produce an experience that influences the target group's behavior.

People are classified into four categories: advantaged, contender, dependent, and deviant. Again, people and issues are placed in each category based on two factors: the level of power afforded to the group and the way they are positively or negatively perceived. The first two categories are for the powerful. For instance, a group that was positively perceived and given a high degree of power by society would be in the advantaged category. In short, these are people that we like and that we give power. This might include people like celebrities, certain politicians, military veterans, people perceived as patriots, married people, the nuclear family, certain sports figures, doctors, and firemen and firewomen.

The contender category includes people who we don't like but who are afforded a lot of power by society. This may be lawyers, oil barons, big corporations, unions, Congress as a whole, and lobbyists. In LGBTQ politics, this may include rich major donors and granting agencies like the government or private foundations. As a lobbyist, I frequently had to note that I was "using my powers for good and not for evil." While an organization may be perceived as positive, their fundraising or lobbying staff are a different story. To compensate for these negative connotations many organizations work in coalitions with more positively perceived groups such as the NAACP, AARP, or the ACLU. This is a form of non-profit statecraft and socially conscious marketing. A key element to remember here is that this is done in most cases to obscure the fact that contenders are still intent on returning power to the powerful, they just need a disguise to do it.

The dependent classification involved people and groups who everyone likes, but who are not allowed a lot of power. This includes people like nurses, teachers, scientists, and stay-at-home mothers. This is a particularly sexist category. Adopted children, and victims of domestic violence are other groups that are supported by the public but given little power. Issues like gun control, climate change, and support for the homeless reside here. The public broadly supports these issues, but political structures give them no real chance to achieve change. In the LGBTQ community, this is where intersectional causes go to die. Generally speaking, the public likes feminism but not feminists and marches but not protesters. Issues that look at violence against transgender people of color are a prime example of a dependent target population that engender support but not change. Because these alternative structures and issues are not designed to return power to the powerful, they are pushed aside.

When a group is more positively or negatively perceived and is seen to have moved from one category to another, but it does not receive corresponding power, this is referred to as degenerative politics under the social construction of target populations. People living with HIV/AIDS are a good example here. They are viewed more as dependent victims, not deviants, but there are still structures and systems that criminalize HIV in many states. There is a pharmaceutical structure that allows for a lack of access to PrEP and other preventative drugs, and there is ongoing stigma and serophobia against people living with HIV/AIDS.

In the LGBTQ community, another example of degenerative politics is the little political power that is afforded to transgender people. Transgender Americans have moved in large part from the deviant category to the dependent category. They are more well-liked than 20 years ago, but they still lack power. As a result, this is degenerative to the issues they work on like homelessness, sex work, employment, adoption, housing, and eldercare. In all these areas trans people are rendered mostly powerless and are defined by the State as lesser citizens.

Lastly is the deviant category, which is the target population that is the least well-liked and who receive the least power. This is a particularly racist category, that includes immigrants, drug users, prison convicts, atheists, environmental protestors, sex workers, and LGBTQ lobbyists. This is the central category of the "other" because it challenges the hetero-state. Violations of social and political norms are to be punished including being flagrantly transgender (i.e. impossible people), attempting change (i.e. loser issues) and being at the bottom of the sexual hierarchy, where—for instance—BDSM, nudity, bathhouses, promiscuity, and polyamory reside. These are not in line with the male gaze. They do not produce male, cis, hetero, desire in the prescribed manner and therefore are punished. To come to the aid of an undesirable issue or an undesirable population is to incur penalties.

In LGBTQ politics, we see here how deviant issues are perceived to come at a political cost. There is a high level of emotional taxation for working on queer and trans issues. Or put another way, the emotionality of the issues distributes political penalties toward those perceived as vulnerable, deviant, and subversive political actors. When you organize and you are harassed or arrested, the costs are greater. Costs may also be greater based on how you identify.

The regulation of norms is very present here. For instance, radical queerness, gender expression, and sexuality are often celebrated by society during a Pride march, but these features of humanity are otherwise seen as a problem to be corrected, with order restored by a gay mainstream hegemon. The way social construction happens also allocates membership or resources proportionally along each category. Social constructions also inform future policies. This is called a "feed forward" effect because by entrenching the importance given to one group over another and the value of the problems they face over others there are preferred kinds of solutions. This creates path dependency and degenerative politics.

The political patterns that preside over the social construction of target population is best understood in LGBTQ public policy as equality governance, which was noted previously. Here we see non-profits (particularly hegemons) create a distributive formula for the delivery of equal rights that is consistent with which category a group or issue falls in. Social constructions matter because politicians and organizations rely on them to determine their level of risk within a political environment. They gain rewards or funding by continuing the patterns of benefits and burdens. In fact, changing how they respond to a group may result in a politician incurring a cost when they deviate from the pattern. The pattern provides predictability. And social constructions of target populations provide political equilibrium.

Everyone is set in their own category. This political dynamic makes changing things hard. Consistent with the discussion of loser issues, attacking certain advantaged groups is harder and attacking certain deviant groups is easier. Powerful hegemons determine what issues are on the agenda, in what order, and at what cost.

Finally, in LGBTQ lobbying, I would modify the social construction of target populations' framework based on several points. To begin, this book argues that the heteronormative mainstream gay movement is more advantaged because it adopts an assimilationist model that is most similar to the most advantaged—the white, male, cisgender, heterosexual community. This is why the gay mainstream lobbying as an advantaged group abides by respectability politics and reproduces power dynamics for the powerful. Galas that attract celebrities connect the gay mainstream lobbying with the most advantaged group in society. This is a white, male, cisgender moneyed interest within the political system that only allows certain types of neoliberal mainstream solutions or issues to reach the political agenda. Those solutions don't challenge the status quo and therefore don't really change the underlying issue.

Viewing the gay mainstream lobbying as an advantaged category under the social construction of target populations is consistent with hegemonic heterosexuality. The groups that are most positively perceived and garner the most societal power are embedded within heterosexual norms. I argue that hegemonic heterosexuality relies on institutions and structures to enforce the ideals of heterosexuality on individuals in society. This includes LGBTQ organizations within the gay mainstream lobbying. Assimilation means affirming that heterosexuality is morally superior to any other sexuality. And lastly, this advantaged status renders all alternative sexualities as "the other."

Data

Heteronormative examples of racist, sexist, ableist advertising

An example of gay nightclub racism, sexism, transphobia, and ageism was on display in 2019 with "Poof Doof," a gay club based in South Yarra near Melbourne, Australia. Promoters have admitted the document (see Box 6.1), which says men with "bad skin" should also be avoided, as well as "skinny boys in burgundy T-shirts and chinos," is genuine.

Australia writer Dejan Jotanovic (2019) addressed this, noting:

> "Poof Doof is a gay club for homos. No-one is here to see girls. Ever." The implications of this briefing was fascinating. Are people with vaginas not welcome? Or just those overtly feminine, or coded as women? In a more visible queer society where people are increasingly free to present their most authentic gender expression, an "anti-women" stance seems curious. But what's also curious is that entertainment at our clubs is almost entirely predicated on women's involvement and representation. It's in the way we continue clinging onto straight cis women as our "gay icons", spinning Kylie on the decks, and accepting hyper-femininity and feminine parody through our drag. But women in the club? Unacceptable.

He added, "I fear that we're becoming siloed in our desire. What's the cost? Aside from inflated gym memberships it means that our barriers to entry for desirability are higher, access is more difficult, and the pressure to conform is steep" (Jotanovic, 2019). The bar scene is consistent with the market it serves. Sexual racism can also be seen on Grindr and digital ghettoization of social networking apps. The comments "not into Asians" or "rice queen" are common. Each racialized identity is done so relative to white supremacy. Raj (2011: 1) notes, "Whiteness, in particular, becomes a privileged form desiring capital, enabling bodies that 'pass' as 'White', while marking out bodies which do not. Racial 'others' become produced in this economy of desire as fetishes or repugnant objects." Lahti (1998: 198) adds to this specifically with Asian identities: "At the level of representation this means assigning the Asian a role which connotes to-be-fucked-ness. He often comes to represent a figure of fantasized passivity betraying that these movies are often primarily about white power over Asians."

It is also important to note how often ableism is overlooked in conversations about sexuality. Wood (2005: 52) provides an entry point into disability theory:

> Disability theory is grounded in the social model of disability, which above all maintains that society disables individuals, not bodily impairments. The social model is based on a fundamental distinction between impairment and disability, in which impairment denotes physiological disorder in mind or body, while disability refers to restrictions placed on persons with impairments due to social, economic, and political barriers.

BOX 6.1 POOF DOOF ADVERTISEMENT, SYDNEY AUSTRALIA

POOF DOOF: A GAY CLUB FOR HOMOS

BRIEF FOR PHOTOGRAPHER

Photos are only to be taken of:

- Boys. Poof Doof is a gay club for homos. No one is here to see girls. Ever. Boys with Muscles. Big ones. The kind of muscles that come about from spending at least 5 sessions a week at the gym.
- Hot Boys. If you want to lick their faces because they look so delicious, take a photo.
- Drag Queens. But ONLY the BEST. And never more than 3. And once they've had their photo taken once, that's it. Forever. (Exception: Fag Drag and Poof Doof Family Members.)

Photos are NOT to be taken of:

- Skinny boys in burgundy t shirts and chinos. They are a dime a dozen. There is nothing interesting nor cool about them.
- Boys with Bad Skin.
- Messy Boys. Anyone who looks like they've poked down a 10-pack is OUT.
- Indi boys. They are not Power Poof worthy unless they are BREATHTAKINGLY good looking or epically stylish.
- Any boys that have previously had Power Poof photos. Repetition is unimaginative and boring.
- Number of photos to be submitted: 50.
  Submit to: Hockers. Levi. Dynon and Susie.
  Deadline 6pm on Mondays.

Please note:

- You must be at the club from 12am to 3am every week without fail.
  It is your responsibility to ensure you have the correct equipment and backups in case of equipment failure.
- Your primary focus is Power Poof focus. Your secondary focus is venue shots.
- All photos taken at Poof Doof are the property of Poof Doof. Absolutely no photos are to be distributed to any other individual or business without written consent from Poof Doof Management.
  The decision regarding which photos get turned into Power Poof photos is made by Poof Doof Management only.

The restrictive perception of attractiveness was also on display at D.C.'s gay bar JR's. Rodriguez (2017) noted, "The manager of Washington, D.C., gay bar JR's is defending himself against charges of racism after a leaked email from 2012 showed him requesting a 'hot white guy' instead of a black man on an advertisement." The manager stated: "'I don't know how to be [politically correct] about it but do you have a hot white guy?' reads the email from David Perruzza. 'That's more our clientelle [sic].'"

This type of restrictive perception of conventional attractiveness gives rise to unhealthy and destructive groups like the "gaycels" on Reddit. This extreme point of view is fanatical, but it is not asymptomatic. In 2019, Buzzfeed conducted a survey of 801 LGBTQ respondents. They asked how social media affected mental health. Interestingly, 38% of trans respondents reported a positive experience while only 17% of gay, cis respondents reported positive feedback. However, negative sentiments were more evenly shared, with 41% of transgender respondents indicating a negative impact and 38% of gay, cis respondents indicating negative effects.

This plays into "respectability politics," where perception is the most important issue. It is more important that you are perceived as "normal"—but more than this, that you are not perceived as the "other." Under this analysis the problem is with personal behavior, not anti-gay discrimination, transphobia, or homophobia. So, there is a latent and insidious problem that homophobia is the fault of the homosexuals.

Discussion

Implications on LGBTQ lobbying

Some in the LGBTQ community face the stress of "compulsory heterosexuality." Adrienne Rich coined the term as "the cluster of forces within which women have been convinced that marriage, and sexual orientation toward men, are inevitable, even if unsatisfying or oppressive components of their lives" (Rich, 1980: 640). While some have to deal with the aforementioned sexual racism.

All members of the LGBTQ community navigate sexual rules that can often be seen in "*hierarchies* of beauty" (Mann, 1998: 347) that exist within all facets of the LGBTQ community and that come together in national LGBTQ organizations. There is also ageism in the selection of staff. Age is one of the strongest sexual characteristics in the LGBTQ community. Specifically, I should say the issue of "youth" and the gay community in particular. For instance, there is a common saying in the gay, male, cis, white community that "30 is gay death." However, there is something else at work with older, more masculine men. Lahti (1998: 187) notes that "the gay male leather subculture is an important example of an attempt to capitalize on the body's potential for simultaneous pleasure and resistance."

Hierarchies of beauty in the organization of movements

I argue that the heteronormative mainstream gay movement is organized around hegemonic masculinity and the male gaze: the desire for young, white, English-speaking cis, able-bodied, masculine men from the Global North. This is the heteronormative mainstream preference, which influences the staffing of LGBTQ non-profit organizations.

Here, the staffing for an organization is based on perceptions of conventional heterosexual masculine attractiveness, or what is often referred to as "straight-acting." It means that pockets of the LGBTQ community privilege "beauty" as established through the heteronormative "male gaze," and this makes it that much easier to base an agenda on heteronormative factors. Indeed, if an organization is willing to objectify women and men, to take some people and dismiss others, then it becomes easy to see how an entire movement agenda can be compromised. For instance, Vaid (1995: 276) recounts that, as the incoming executive director of NGLTF, it was recommended that she hire a "nice white man with a cute ass as your development director."

In addition, coalitions are selling an issue to Capitol Hill and they want it to be the best-looking issue possible. It is nothing new to use good-looking people to try and sell things. We "package" pop stars, sodas, political issues, and organizations all the time. Nor is it a crime to try and create an atmosphere of attractiveness around your brand so that it is perceived as attractive. Indeed, we see this with integration theory: "One implication of integration theory is that the perceived attractiveness of any one member of a group will shift toward the value of the other members" (Geiselman, Haight, & Kimata, 1984: 410). The complication is when this is a well-curated front that is designed to manipulate and exclude others.

Here we see the re-emergence of the attractiveness effect: for people who are enticed by aesthetics and beauty, physical attractiveness holds numerous advantages, rewards, and value (Etcoff, 1999). Psychological research has labelled this phenomenon "the attractiveness effect." Chaiken (1979) and Horai, Naccari, and Fatoullah (1974) note that attractive people are judged as more trustworthy and are more persuasive. Probably as a result of these advantages (Mobius & Rosenblat, 2006), attractive people receive many rewards: they get better grades in school, have more friends, receive lighter sentences from the courts, and are treated better by the job market (Hamermesh & Biddle, 1994; Hosoda, Stone-Romero, & Coats, 2003; Judge, Hurst, & Simon, 2009).

Consistent with these findings, political scientists have found that good-looking politicians enjoy more electoral success (Surawski & Ossoff, 2006). This is consistent with the "halo effect." Thorndike (1920: 27) was the first to articulate the halo effect, where they note that "a halo of general merit is extended" toward those seen as deserving. Skin color, height, weight, hair color, or eye color may be biased characteristics that are used to assume that someone is "good" or smart.

So, the halo effect and attractiveness effect contribute to who becomes a high-profile activist. Urvashi Vaid (2012: 15) adds, "The default of the definition of community from which the mainstream LGBT movement speaks is white and most often male." Therefore, patterns of conventional attractiveness, namely white men, often receive the support of the organization and activist community, lessening the burden on them and reducing the chances of burnout.

Sexual harassment and abuse in the LGBTQ advocacy community

Charity First stated in 2019 that,

> According to the *Journal of Philanthropy*, one in three instances of nonprofit sexual harassment involved a donor. And this type of harassment is disproportionately experienced by women—only 7% of male fundraisers reported it, while 25% of female fundraisers did.

Donors are the key constituency of nearly all non-profits. The data on LGBTQ groups is consistent with this. According to the Movement Advancement Project's (MAP) 2014 report, individual giving is the largest source of funding (37%) for LGBTQ advocacy organizations. In 2020, MAP's report on the impact of COVID-19 found that individual giving to community centers was the most resilient, with only a 22.8% drop in revenue. In other words, individual giving by donors is the highest amount of giving and the most sustainable, making it the most valuable for a nonprofit organization. As a result, it is important to note the impact this can have on individuals and organizations.

To begin, the EEOC (n.d.) defines sexual harassment, stating:

> It is unlawful to harass a person (an applicant or employee) because of that person's sex. Harassment can include "sexual harassment" or unwelcome sexual advances, requests for sexual favors, and other verbal or physical harassment of a sexual nature.

The National Council of Nonprofits (2020) add to this by noting, "Nonprofit leaders have an obligation to prevent, investigate, and address sexual harassment. Harassment can take place in nonprofit workplaces, and board rooms." Sexual harassment can occur from senior staff, board members, and donors toward junior staff that are male, female, or nonbinary. Given the way organizations hire, package, and promote attractive staff, volunteers, and interns, LGBTQ organizations could put their people at risk of sexual harassment or sexual abuse. There are several considerations in looking at sexual harassment in the LGBTQ advocacy community:

1. Reliance on major donors
2. Harassment and abuse by major donors
3. Retaliation to protect major donors
4. Burnout where staff leave the movement

Reliance on major donors

There are some of these donors who think it is their right to sexually harass and abuse young female, male, and non-binary staff, interns, and volunteers, that they perceive as attractive, because they write big checks to that organization.

A 2020 article in the *Harvard Business Review* noted that "They [nonprofits] need to go where the money is." The piece by Alan Cantor notes that reaching out to major donors is the way forward during the current downturn (Cantor, 2020). This reliance on major donors is not neutral to an organization.

Nonprofit Quarterly notes, "Ethical choices regarding gifts have always been hard, but in the current dynamic of declining numbers of smaller donors, consciousness about the costs of overdependence on large grants has been brought into greater focus" (Levine, 2019). This is true for the LGBTQ advocacy community. Major donors are increasingly important but the reliance on them and their money puts them in a position of power that makes incidents of sexual harassment a complicated endeavor even for those organizations with a zero-tolerance policy.

Harassment and abuse by major donors

In 2018, Anne Wallestad wrote for the *Nonprofit Quarterly* and noted, "The American Red Cross has come under fire for providing a glowing reference to a senior leader who resigned after allegations of sexual harassment from a subordinate." Wallestad adds that *Inside Philanthropy* has noted, "when it comes to sexual misconduct— board members themselves are sometimes the problem, propositioning or other- wise harassing nonprofit employees." So here we see examples of senior staff and board members engaging in sexual harassment.

Ian Kullgren wrote a piece in 2018 for *Politico Magazine* on sexual harassment at the Humane Society. He notes the pressures that male major donors can put on younger women and how the organization may be complicit. Kullgren notes that the female staffer being harassed was told she "should 'take one for the team' by having sex with a donor …. His alleged behavior, staffers say, led to the resignations of no fewer than five employees from 2015 to late 2017."

In LGBTQ organizations, the same incidents are taking place. Some of these young people are coerced into sex out of perceptions of power, concern for their jobs, or the impact of alcohol or drugs (which may be provided by the major donor). In these situations, the staffer, volunteer or intern cannot provide consent. The disproportionate power dynamics do not allow consent to be given.

Retaliation to protect major donors

The National Council of Nonprofits (2020) addresses the issue of retaliation to sexual harassment, noting, "State and federal laws also prohibit retaliation against someone for complaining about sexual harassment, or other types of illegal discrimination."

Young people are often packaged as organizational commodities that are directed at attracting major donors. This may also be seen in the discourse about hierarchies of identity. LGBTQ non-profit lobbying and media relations are sanitized for political consumption. Nardi (2000: 5) says that "the rhetoric about gender in many gay organizations and communities has often been oppositional in its tone and it questions the role of effeminate men, drag queens, and 'fairies' in the political strategies and media images." It is a worthy question to trouble the assumption that hegemonic groups discipline other individuals and organizations in ways that normalize them, commoditize identities, and "reproduce a liberal model of tolerance that stresses patriarchal forms" (Bennett, 2006: 116).

However, if the staff are harassed and complain, they can be moved from one position to another or when they leave asked to sign a non-disclosure agreement (NDA) because the funding from the donor is more important than the impact of harassment or abuse.

It is imperative that LGBTQ organizations protect all of their staff and act transparently about the way they address abuse and harassment. One request from this book is to the LGBTQ community. I am asking all of us to make sure that our representative organizations in the MeToo era of Harvey Weinstein are not using NDAs to silence staff.

Indeed, LGBTQ organizations, in this scenario, can be essentially trapping staff into inappropriate situations, leaving them to be preyed upon, and punishing them when they report it.

Burnout where staff leave the movement

The Nonprofit Law Blog notes, "For nonprofits, a harassment scandal will not only erode public trust, a vital aspect of an organization's support and success, it will also demoralize employees in a way that contravenes our shared values of equal opportunity" (Berger, 2018).

The combination of LGBTQ organizations using staff, volunteers, and interns who convey heteronormative standards of beauty to gain the financial support of donors, who then harass and abuse them, and if staff, volunteers or interns report it are punished by the same organization does not look like the picture of the LGBTQ revolution. In this scenario, heterosexuality benefits. This has implications for the structuring of LGBTQ organizations around elements.

LGBTQ lobbying loses people in this scenario. The work environment for staff at LGBTQ organizations may be toxic or hostile and this creates low morale for all staff, while forcing some staff to leave. This has implications because sexual harassment imposes emotional taxation and emotional labor on staff and drives burnout. Therefore, sexual harassment may reshape the nature of staffing at LGBTQ advocacy organizations and their reputation on Capitol Hill.

Unlivable people and impossible people

There are many elements of literature on the transgender and non-binary experience that are important to understanding the additional costs placed on the trans community. Here, I focus on two. The first is the concept of "unlivable" people (Butler, 2004). Here Judith Butler (2004: 2) states:

> Certain humans are recognized as less than human, and that form of qualified recognition does not lead to a viable life. Certain humans are not recognized as human at all, and that leads to yet another order of unlivable life. If part of what desire wants is to gain recognition, then gender, insofar as it is animated by desire, will want recognition as well. But if the schemes of recognition that are available to us are those that "undo" the person by conferring recognition, or "undo" the person by withholding recognition, then recognition becomes a site of power by which the human is differentially produced. This means that to the extent that desire is implicated in social norms, it is bound up with the question of power and with the problem of who qualifies as the recognizably human and who does not.

The second concept is specific to the bodies of transgender and non-binary activists. DeFilippis and Anderson-Nathe (2017: 113) note that "the queer liberation organizations draw on this notion of impossible personhood to illustrate [bell] hook's call for movement from the margin to the center, naming the majority of their constituencies as impossible people." Dean Spade (2015: 120) discusses "impossible people," stating:

> Contemporary political conditions terrorize and shorten the lives of trans people and threaten to subsume trans resistance. Trans people are told by legal systems, state agencies, employers, schools, and our families that we are impossible people who are not who we say we are, cannot exist, cannot be classified, and cannot fit anywhere. We have been told by lesbian and gay rights organizations, as they continually choose to leave us aside, that we are not politically viable and that our lives are not a political possibility that can be conceived. At the same time, we are told that we have to run our resistance organizations like businesses, that participatory or collective models of governance are inefficient and idealistic, that we must tailor our messages to what the corporate media can understand, and that our demands need to fit within the existing goals of the institutions that are killing us. The demands that are emerging from the most vulnerable trans communities for the abolition of prisons, police, and borders, and for full trans-inclusive health-care and food, housing, and education for everyone are the kinds of demands that are incomprehensible to heteronormative mainstream movements focused on rights claims. These broader, transformative demands cannot be won in courts, and they emerge from those for whom narrow legal reform demands have little to offer. White-led, lawyer-dominated lesbian and gay rights organizations—even those that have added a "T" to their mission statements—cannot comprehend these demands and cannot win them using narrow elite media and law reform strategies focused on inclusion. To the extent that they try to incorporate trans people into their work, they will do so narrowly, focusing on

those deemed "deserving" and/or "innocent," ignoring the actual conditions facing the most vulnerable trans people. The inconceivability of the very lives of trans people, especially trans immigrants, trans people of color, indigenous trans people, and trans people with disabilities, and the perceived impossibility of the demands and methods of resistance emerging from the most targeted and impacted populations, are symptomatic of the inherent conflicts and divides produced (and often hidden) by the philanthropically controlled models of advocacy that dominate today's social movements.

What Dean Spade is describing is a series of structural traps that transgender and gender non-conforming people face every day by a heteronormative-cisgender system that intentionally harms them. This additionally neoliberal system is designed to oppress the "other." The traps are in the attempts to enter the bureaucracy, ask to be an equal citizen, petition for human rights.

LGBTQ lobbying, therefore, should be addressing the letter of the law, but also the power dynamics imposed on the implementation of the law. Changing birth certificate laws may not be enough if the administrative process renders trans and non-binary people ineligible to access the policy, even when it is directed at them.

Respectability politics in sexual hierarchies

If "respectability politics" in the LGBTQ advocacy community were on Grindr, its profile would be "heteronormative for heteronormative." It is essentially a white, gay, male, cis, English-speaking, Global North, able-bodied, social, and professional network. Hire the right people, sleep with the right people, drink with the right people, and you are seen as respectable in a dominantly acceptable frame. However, here we see the performance of sexual activity also being connected to community approval.

At the peak of the "erotic pyramid" (Rubin, 2007: 151) are those who are married heterosexuals whose purpose is reproduction. Below are those who are unmarried but monogamous, and monogamous homosexuals, a category which includes transsexuals, transvestites, prostitutes, and porn models. Adding to this is Koopman (2017), who notes, "Bio-power does not forbid sexuality, but rather regulates it in the maximal interests of very particular conceptions of reproduction, family and health."

Respectability changes over time. Gay, HIV-positive author Andrew Sullivan was criticized for interest in gay HIV-positive bareback sex, which caused a scandal in 2001. Indeed, sometimes using a condom is considered respectable, and sometimes not using one is considered respectable. A 2014 study of 18–24 year-old young men who have sex with men found that 20 percent of those who use Grindr had unprotected sex with people they met through the app, and that this was true the longer they had the app and the more they used shirtless pics (Winetrobe, Rice, Bauermeister, Petering, & Holloway, 2014).

This respectability politics extends to other considerations of dating and sex. For instance, there is a type of relationship where larger people date smaller people, which is referred to as "big spoon, little spoon." The data collected by Valentova and his co-authors in a 2014 study is compelling:

> However, these preferences were dependent on the participant's own height, such that taller men preferred shorter partners, whereas shorter men preferred taller partners. We also examined whether height preferences predicted the preference for dominance and the adoption of particular sexual roles within a couple.

Conceptions of self also implicate sexual liberation. The data from Anthony Bogaert in 2007 shows that gay men overestimate the size of their penises (France, 2007):

> Anthony Bogaert re-sorted Kinsey Institute data—in which 5,000 men answered detailed questions about their sex lives, practices, fantasies, and, it turns out, measurements of their erect organs—along sexual-orientation lines. Gay men's penises were thicker (4.95 inches versus 4.80) and longer (6.32 inches versus 5.99).

Again, we also see the data supporting considerations of sexual hierarchy based on who people date relative to body type. Considerations of someone as "gay thin" means that they are skinnier than an average person. In turn, "gay fat" is not fat but rather normal size. Here the data reads, "Men in particular were found to prefer attractive partners, regardless of sexual orientation" (Legenbauer et al., 2009: 228).

Legenbauer et al. (2009: 228) add, "weight/shape dissatisfaction was found to be a negative predictor for heterosexual men and women. For gay men, preferences were better explained by internalization and weight/shape dissatisfaction. No such associations were found in the lesbian group." This disqualifies trans people because they are the wrong shape. Indeed, Roxane Gay notes the opposite can be true. Being fat is beautiful. She stated, "When you're talking about fat positivity, it's a radical thing: the idea that fat is neither negative nor neutral, but a positive thing, and [something that] you don't need to explain or justify" (Okwodu, 2017).

The data is also consistent in "masc for masc" considerations. A study of Chinese men by Zhang, Zheng, and Zheng (2019: 1) found that men who considered themselves more attractive

> showed stronger preference for lower pitched voices compared with self-perceived less attractive individuals. In addition, we found that gay men's sociosexuality score was positively correlated with their preference for masculine cues in male voices, indicating that gay men who were less sociosexually restricted preferred lower pitched voices over higher pitched versions compared with men who were more restricted.

So, Chinese gay men who thought they were attractive preferred deep-voiced partners, which is a socially constructed element of conventional masculinity.

Finally, overall sexual activity may look different than expectations of respectability. Rosenberger et al. (2011: 3040) found that of nearly 25,000 men who have sex with men, about 37% report engaging in anal sex with their last partner. Sewell, McGarrity, and Strassberg (2017: 825) also found that

> The behaviors in which participants were most likely to have engaged were manual-genital (82%) and oral-genital stimulation (79%). Regarding definitions of sex, a clear 'gold standard' emerged for men, with 90% endorsing penile-anal intercourse as sex. No equally clear standard existed for women.

Respectability politics puts pressure on LGBTQ people to conform to heteronormative standards and this can lead to burnout. There are connections between the distributive benefits of sexual hierarchies and political burnout from those who receive burdens because they are considered lower on the sexual hierarchy. Gorski (2019: 669–670) looks at race and states that activists of color "carry the burden of structural understanding on top of the challenge of coping with the grind of racism in their own lives, often referred to as racial battle fatigue." He goes on to say,

> Specifically for activists of colour … their engagement in racial justice activism often is directly associated with the accumulative trauma of the racial battle fatigue they experience; those who perceive the most traumatic accumulative experiences with racism are most likely to become activists.
>
> *(Gorski, 2019: 670)*

This link between race (sexual racism), burnout, and sexual hierarchies can also be seen in Srivastava's (2006) analysis of how feminist activists of color have to expend their emotional and activist energies attending to the emotional needs of white feminist activists. Gorski (2019: 671) notes, "These threats are not equally distributed. Marginalized-identity activists are targeted at higher rates than privileged-identity activists."

In all, the respectability of sexual hierarchies is about making a good impression on your oppressor (Strange, 2018), even when they are not in the room. This is a problem with white, cis, gay, male, English-speaking, Global North, hegemony. The adoption of heteronormative norms like the male gaze, hegemonic masculinity, respectability politics, and the halo effect play to the power of institutions of heterosexuality and corrupt real LGBTQ liberation. Indeed, the gay mainstream movement's willingness to reproduce oppressions in social life translates into political life. This is a fundraising method, lobbying method, and organizing principle. Attractiveness is seen as a coalition-building strategy.

LGBTQ philanthropy

There are fundamental issues regarding LGBTQ philanthropy that cause problems for LGBTQ organizations. To begin, there isn't enough charitable giving relative to consumer spending. Also, grant requirements often force organizations to alter or change their mission because the terms of the grant are different from the goal of the organization. Scholar Myrl Beam addresses this in his book *Gay, Inc* by analyzing the non-profit industrial complex. Here they identify a model where non-profits make little money and have a tendency to spend most of their time chasing grants (Beam, 2018). This is a position they are forced into because the neoliberal model favors corporations over non-profits and has created a tax system that does not fund social safety net projects. The result is that non-profits are in perpetual financial crisis.

A study in the United States by the LGBT Chamber of Commerce found that LGBTQ Americans contribute $917 billion in "buying power" to the economy (Witeck Communications, 2016). This is larger than the GDP of Ohio, New Jersey, Georgia, or Washington state. This buying power of the "pink dollar" should mean that there is ample funding for LGBTQ non-profit organizations from individual donors in the community.

However, a report by the Movement Advancement Project found that in 2015, "The total number of people who gave $35 or more to a participating organization represents approximately 3.1% of the total number of LGBT adults in the U.S." (MAP, 2016: 1). This is about 274,180 individual donors out of more than 9 million total LGBTQ adults, which means 97% of the LGBTQ community are non-donors (MAP, 2016: 9). However, a report by Pew found that 31% of LGBTQ respondents have donated in their lives to organizations or politicians who support LGBTQ rights (Pew Research Center, 2013). This stands in contrast to the overall amount of annual philanthropy by all taxpayers. A study by the *Chronicle of Philanthropy* found that "24 percent of taxpayers reported on their tax returns that they made a charitable gift in 2015" (Lindsay, 2017).

According to Nielsen research, LGBTQ households are 55% more likely to shop at a liquor store than the average U.S. household (Campbell, 2015). More specifically, LGBTQ households spend 48% more on wine than non-LGBTQ households. In addition, BuzzFeed's survey of the LGBTQ community also showed that overall, 58% drink alcohol (Holden, 2019). This is consistent with data from the 2015 National Survey on Drug Use and Health (NSDUH), which showed that 56.2 percent of all respondents reported that they drank in the past month (Medley et al., 2016). In short, if the LGBTQ community invested what it spends on alcohol in one month on its own equality, political candidates, and LGBTQ organizations we would see a radically different level of LGBTQ political power.

Mainstream versus LGBTQ burnout

LGBTQ burnout is unique to an individual. For some, activism is endlessly liberating, for some it is an act of survival, while for still others it is exhausting. I look at LGBTQ burnout relative to its causes and buffers. One thing is clear from the literature: most often burnout is caused by the conflict between coalition actors. This is true across movements outside of the LGBTQ community. Infighting in the "Peace Movement," "Environment Movement," and "Civil Rights Movement" points to conflicts from within as major sources of burnout. In the LGBTQ community, this means that both movements lose.

To begin, "burnout is defined as long term involvement in situations that are emotionally demanding and is caused by 'a combination of very high expectations and chronic situational stresses'" (Slackers, 2007: 13). Burnout is an equation between mental and physical renewal and exhaustion. However, burnout is not always negative. "Burnout often affects people who are very skillful, trustworthy, and hardworking … we [should] consider burnout not as a sign of weakness but rather as being out of balance" (Koster, 2007: 168). The connection to heteronormativity is that issues which impose greater burdens on activists and are more likely to produce burnout are radical issues, and the ones that receive the most public support and financial reward are neoliberal heteronormative issues.

There are three elements to consider regarding lobbying tactics. The first is the cost or discomfort that is imposed on the lobbyist relative to other penalties they are experiencing at that period of time. These costs come in many forms. This is consistent with the literature on intersectionality, which argues that people experience more acute oppression at the intersection of multiple marginalized identities (Crenshaw, 1991; Pepin-Neff & Caporale, 2018). A lobbyist who is fighting racism or sexism may find this harder if they are a Black female. In addition, activists experience "emotional taxation" for their choice of LGBTQ issues and tactics (Pepin-Neff & Wynter, 2020).

Again, emotional taxation is the emotional cost, intentional or not, that a policy, program, or scheme places on an individual or group for entering into the political process or addressing a political issue. The cost is relative to an individual or group's political power, capacity to pay the cost, and collective support (Neff, 2016).

Some LGBTQ lobbyists will face a greater or lesser cost for undertaking their tactic. The issue is whether a lobbyist has the capacity to absorb the cost. This includes time, resources, and political capital. Two important points to note are that lobbyists for hegemonic organizations have more capacity and the ability to deal with more relative costs; therefore, hegemons experience fewer costs and greater capacity. In addition, gay mainstream lobbyists choose heteronormative issues, tactics, and norms because it affords more power and imposes fewer costs. The result is more capacity to deal with other issues and have a wider portfolio. In addition, lobbyists work on multiple issues with multiple offices, and multiple branches of government. Having the capacity to endure the cost of a tactic is only as good as the frequency with which a lobbyist needs to execute it. Frequency is a key measurement in its own right as well as a measure of capacity.

Causes of burnout

Infighting may be one key factor in burnout. As Maslach and Gomes (2006) note, in one study of 1990s peace activists "relationships with other activists" emerged as both the most common reward and the most common stressor in their activist work. Gorski (2019: 672) adds to this by pointing to similar conditions in the Black Lives Matter movement, saying "research suggests in-movement causes may be more responsible for burnout than internal or external causes." This is consistent with Pepin-Neff and Wynter (2020: 22) who report,

> We asked respondents to indicate the most significant obstacles to LGBTQ progress: "What would you say are the biggest obstacles to winning LGBTQ equality?" Respondents from every country nominated allies (i.e., equality groups and non-LGBTQ progressive groups) over enemies (i.e., anti-LGBTQ religious groups and opponents) at a rate of 62% versus 38%, respectively.

In addition, Hargons et al. (2017) pointed to conditions in the Black Lives Matter movement. They add a point about the nature of inter-group agitation and dissent which is shared by Gorski (2019: 681), who reports, "the most impactful burnout causes revolve around how activists treat one another." He also says,

> participants attributed their burnout to how activists treat one another. Many became worn down attempting to navigate activist communities in which in-fighting and ego clashes were commonplace. They entered racial justice movements to work with like-minded people, but found movements full of competition, not cooperation.
>
> *(Gorski, 2019: 679)*

There are also situations where stress and burnout can be heightened: Fillieule and Broqua (2005) note the complexities of burnout using the example of AIDS activism due to the scope of the epidemic. They add that longer-standing and older activists are among those affected most by burnout and fatigue. Similar to this, Maslach and Gomes (2006: 43) note that

> activists also have other unique characteristics that can make them vulnerable to burnout. The very nature of activist work involves cultivating and maintaining awareness of large and overwhelming social problems, often carrying a burden of knowledge that society as a whole is unable or unwilling to face. This can lead to feelings of pressure and isolation that easily feed into burnout.

However, the data from Pepin-Neff and Wynter (2020) showed something else. Transgender respondents who felt the most under threat indicated they would stay in LGBTQ advocacy the longest. This suggests that when in danger trans activists may feel they have nothing to lose.

In addition, burnout can come from internal stress. Gorski (2019: 672) states that "another in-movement burnout-exacerbating condition is a culture that quiets concerns about the toll activism can take on activists." Rodgers (2010: 279) calls this "the ubiquitous discourse of selflessness" wherein "displays of personal strain, sadness, or depression, while perhaps understandable, are viewed … as unnecessary and self-indulgent." Burnout is carried like a "badge of honor" (Pigni, 2016) as a symbol of commitment (Rodgers, 2010).

There is also a category of activist who may be "high-risk" because of the frontline nature of their activism. Jones (2007: 43–44) defines high-risk activists as those "whose work for peace and freedom for people, animals, or ecosystems jeopardizes their physical, emotional, or spiritual balance. At particularly high risk are those who encounter injurious violence as well as those whose work involves repetitive or ongoing upsetting experiences."

Similarly, Plyler (2009: 125–126) notes that "radical activism inherently carries with it a certain level of risk of confrontation and repression, because it directly threatens the functioning of systems and groups who profit from exploitation and injustice." This was apparent in 2020 as activists and protestors stood against police during the Black Lives Matter protests, following the murder of George Floyd.

Buffers to burnout

Buffers to burnout vary from case to case. Regarding persistent activists, Rettig (2006: 20) notes that "their activist work doesn't drain them, it sustains them." This can also be seen in what I call divine right activism: the belief that you know things that others don't know, that you are best suited (above others) to do the work, and that you have been selected to complete this mission, to work on this issue. Gorski (2019: 677) says, "Many described similar examples of self-imposed martyrdom syndromes tied to their passion and emotional investment." This connects with liberation activism in that the heightened struggle renews these activists rather than burning them out.

The high adrenaline life of activists may be self-renewing and allow them to continue working at a high rate. High-profile activists often gain emotional rewards from their activism (such as praise and support, as well as engagements with the world outside their organizations) that are not available to others, enabling them to continue in ways that would otherwise be unsustainable, and are in fact unsustainable for other activists who do not receive these rewards.

The type of activity one does may also lessen burnout. Cox (2011: 16) notes that there can be an "'activist majority,' where certain *kinds* of activism (e.g. demonstrations) are normal, non-stressful, and broadly acceptable, activities that most people might consider doing themselves." This is consistent with emotional taxation; however, it is important to note that each activity registers a different cost based on intersectional identities. For instance, going on Twitter was seen as a more difficult front-facing activity for trans activists because of trolling.

There is also the role of support structures. Lester, Lamson, and Wollman (1997) note that "some psychologists identify social support and sense of accomplishment as the two most important buffers against stress." In this case, the lack of support from family may increase burnout, but support from a group may support anti-burnout efforts.

Another buffer may be time. Cox (2011: 30) states, "A temporary break from movement work occasionally appears as a valued strategy for combating burnout." Fillieule and Broqua (2005: 192) refer to green card measures of an AIDS activism organization, where volunteers were given the opportunity to negotiate a 3–6 month duration free of activity; then, they could either resume activism or leave the organization.

In short, elements that create hierarchies of identity such as sexual racism, administrative barricades creating "impossible people," sexual harassment of staff, volunteers, and interns, and respectability politics all contribute to burnout. Each chips away at who can participate in the LGBTQ advocacy community. In other words, the politics of sex and gender identity influence the lobbying on sex and gender identity.

Conclusion

In this chapter, I highlight the way heteronormativity advantages the gay mainstream lobbying through heterosexual institutions. In addition, I illustrate how heteronormative oppressions such as racism, sexism, and ableism are reproduced by gay mainstream lobbying. Examples include sexual hierarchies that both privilege white, male, cis, English-speaking, Global North, able-bodied people and set them up for harassment, abuse and burnout. The structures preference these identities (in many cases young and poor people) and then create power dynamics so they can be taken advantage of by individuals within the system. This harassment and abuse is propped up by norms of respectability that place wealthy individuals at the top of social settings and the poor and the young at the bottom.

The consequence of heteronormative dominance is that it damages LGBTQ lobbying and marginalized groups. For instance, transgender communities (particularly communities of color) face disproportionate oppressions from social, political, and bureaucratic systems that are intentionally designed to leave them out of the political process, including day-to-day life. As non-profits work to address these issues, they confront a safety-net model that provides little funding and high degrees of burnout. The result is a non-profit industrial complex unable to fix problems, underfunded and often understaffed.

References

Beam, M. (2018). *Gay, Inc.: The Non-Profitization of Queer Politics*. University of Minnesota Press.

Bennett, J. (2006). A Queer anxiety: Assimilation politics and cinematic hedonics in *Relax… It's Just Sex*. *Journal of Homosexuality, 52*(1–2), 101–123. https://doi.org/10.1300/J082v52n01_05

Berger, M. (2018, May 17). Protecting your nonprofit from sexual harassment. *The Nonprofit Law Blog*. https://nonprofitlawblog.com/protecting-nonprofit-sexual-harassment/

Butler, J. (2004). *Undoing Gender*. Routledge.

BuzzFeed (2019). *LGBTQ in America survey*. https://assets.documentcloud.org/documents/6175837/Withman-Insight-Strategies-LGBTQ-in-America.pdf

Callander, D., Newman, C.E., & Holt, M. (2015). Is sexual racism *really* racism? Distinguishing attitudes toward sexual racism and generic racism among gay and bisexual men. *Archives of Sexual Behavior, 44*, 1991–2000. https://doi.org/10.1007/s10508-015-0487-3

Callander, D., Newman, C.E., & Holt, M. (2016). 'Not everyone's gonna like me': Accounting for race and racism in sex and dating web services for gay and bisexual men. *Ethnicities, 16*(1), 3–21. https://doi.org/10.1177%2F1468796815581428

Campbell, A. F. (2015, November 27). LGBT families shop more, spend more. *The Atlantic*. www.theatlantic.com/politics/archive/2015/11/lgbt-families-shop-more-spend-more/433485

Cantor, A. (2020, September 17). In a k-shaped recovery, nonprofits should lean on major donors. *Harvard Business Review*. https://hbr.org/2020/09/in-a-k-shaped-recovery-nonprofits-should-lean-on-major-donors

Chaiken, S. (1979). Communicator physical attractiveness and persuasion. *Journal of Personality and Social Psychology, 37*(8), 1387–1397. https://doi.org/10.1037/0022-3514.37.8.1387

Charity First (2019, January 1). The dynamics of sexual harassment in nonprofit environments. charityfirst.com/blog-posts/the-dynamics-of-sexual-harassment-in-nonprofit-environments/

Connell, R.W. (2002). On hegemonic masculinity and violence: Response to Jefferson and Hall. *Theoretical Criminology, 6*(1), 89–99. https://doi.org/10.1177%2F136248060200600104

Connell, R.W., & Messerschmidt, J.W. (2005). Hegemonic masculinity: Rethinking the concept. *Gender and Society, 19*(6), 829–859. https://doi.org/10.1177/0891243205278639

Cox, L. (2011). *How Do We Keep Going? Activist Burnout and Personal Sustainability in Social Movements*. Into-ebooks.

Crenshaw, K. (1991). Mapping the margins: Intersectionality, identity politics, and violence against women of color. *Stanford Law Review, 43*(6), 1241–1299. https://doi.org/10.2307/1229039

DeFilippis, J.N., & Anderson-Nathe, B. (2017). Embodying margin to center: Intersectional activism among queer liberation organizations. In M. Brettschneider, S. Burgess, & C. Keating (Eds.), *LGBTQ Politics: A Critical Reader* (pp. 110–133). New York University Press.

Dion, K., Berscheid, E., & Walster, E. (1972). What is beautiful is good. *Journal of Personality and Social Psychology, 24*(3), 285–290. https://doi.org/10.1037/h0033731

Etcoff, N. (1999). *Survival of the Prettiest: The Science of Beauty*. Doubleday.

Fillieule, O., & Broqua, C. (2005). La défection dans deux organisations de lutte contre le sida. In O. Fillieule (Ed.), *Le désengagement militant* (pp. 189–228). Belin.

France, D. (2007, June 21). The science of gaydar. *New York Magazine*. https://nymag.com/nymag/features/33520/index1.html

Geiselman, R.E., Haight, N.A., & Kimata, L.G. (1984). Context effects on the perceived physical attractiveness of faces. *Journal of Experimental Social Psychology, 20*(5), 409–424. https://doi.org/10.1016/0022-1031(84)90035-0

Gorski, P.C. (2019). Fighting racism, battling burnout: Causes of activist burnout in US racial justice activists. *Ethnic and Racial Studies, 42*(5), 667–687. https://doi.org/10.1080/01419870.2018.1439981

Hamermesh, D., & Biddle, J. (1994). Beauty and the labor market. *American Economic Review, 84*(5), 1174–1194. www.jstor.org/stable/2117767

Hargons, C., Mosley, D., Falconer, J., Faloughi, R., Singh, A., Stevens-Watkins, D., & Cokley, K. (2017). Black Lives Matter: A call to action for counseling psychology leaders. *Counseling Psychologist, 45*(6), 873–901. https://doi.org/10.1177/0011000017733048

Holden, D. (2019, June 24). *Most LGBTQ Americans actually love having cops and corporations in Pride parades.* BuzzFeed News. www.buzzfeednews.com/article/dominicholden/lgbtq-poll-pride-month-cops-coprorations

Horai, J., Naccari, N., & Fatoullah, E. (1974). The effects of expertise and physical attractiveness upon opinion agreement and liking. *Sociometry, 37*(4), 601–606. https://doi.org/10.2307/2786431

Hosoda, M., Stone-Romero, E.F., & Coats, G. (2003). The effects of physical attractiveness on job-related outcomes: A meta-analysis of experimental studies. *Personnel Psychology, 56*(2), 431–462. https://doi.org/10.1111/j.1744-6570.2003.tb00157.x

Hunte, B. (2020, January 29). The gay men risking their health for the perfect body. BBC News. www.bbc.com/news/uk-51270317

Jones, P. (2007). *Aftershock: Confronting Trauma in a Violent World: A Guide for Activists and their Allies.* Lantern Books.

Jotanovic, D. (2019, February 1). The problem when gay culture fetishises masculinity above all else. *The Guardian.* www.theguardian.com/commentisfree/2019/feb/01/the-problem-when-gay-culture-fetishises-masculinity-above-all-else

Judge, T.A., Hurst, C., & Simon, L.S. (2009). Does it pay to be smart, attractive, or confident (or all three)? Relationships among general mental ability, physical attractiveness, core-self-evaluations, and income. *Journal of Applied Psychology, 94*(3), 742–755. https://doi.org/10.1037/a0015497

Koopman, C. (2017, March 15). Why Foucault's work on power is more important than ever. Aeon. https://aeon.co/essays/why-foucaults-work-on-power-is-more-important-than-ever

Koster, F. (2007). Insight meditation as a remedy for burnout symptoms. In. F. Koster (Ed.), *Buddhist Meditation in Stress Management* (pp. 190–210). Silkworm.

Kullgren, I. (2018, January 30). Female employees allege culture of sexual harassment at Humane Society. *Politico.* www.politico.com/magazine/story/2018/01/30/humane-society-sexual-harassment-allegations-investigation-216553

Lahti, M. (1998). Dressing up in power: Tom of Finland and gay male body politics. In J. Löfström (Ed.), *Scandinavian Homosexualities: Essays on Gay and Lesbian Studies* (pp. 185–206). Routledge.

Legenbauer, T., Vocks, S., Schäfer, C., Schütt-Strömel, S., Hiller, W., Wagner, C., & Vögele, C. (2009). Preference for attractiveness and thinness in a partner: Influence of internalization of the thin ideal and shape/weight dissatisfaction in heterosexual women, heterosexual men, lesbians, and gay men. *Body Image, 6*(3), 228–234. https://doi.org/10.1016/j.bodyim.2009.04.002

Lester, N., Lamson, M., & Wollman, N. (1997). How staff get burned (out) by social change work. *Journal of Community Advocacy and Activism, 2*(1), 83–93.

Levine, M. (2019, March 26). Concerns about large donor dependence heat up as small donorship wanes. *Nonprofit Quarterly.* https://noanprofitquarterly.org/concerns-about-large-donor-dependence-heat-up-as-small-donorship-wanes/

Lindsay, D. (2017, October 3). Fewer Americans find room in their budgets for charity, Chronicle data shows. *Chronicle of Philanthropy.* www.philanthropy.com/article/Share-of-Americans-Who-Give-to/241345

Mann, W.J. (1998). Laws of desire: Has our imagery become overidealized? In D. Atkins (Ed.), *Looking Queer: Body Image and Identity in Lesbian, Bisexual, Gay, and Transgendered Communities* (pp. 345–354). Haworth Press.

Maslach, C., & Gomes, M. (2006). Overcoming burnout. In R. McNair & Psychologists for Social Responsibility (Eds.), *Working for Peace: A Handbook of Practical Psychology and Other Tools* (pp. 43–59). Impact.

Medley, G., Lipari, R.N., Bose, J., Cribb, D.S., Kroutil, L.A., & McHenry, G. (2016). Sexual orientation and estimates of adult substance use and mental health: Results from the 2015 National Survey on Drug Use and Health. www.samhsa.gov/data/sites/default/files/NSDUH-SexualOrientation-2015/NSDUH-SexualOrientation-2015/NSDUH-SexualOrientation-2015.htm

Mercer, K., & Julien, I. (1994). Black masculinity and the sexual politics of race. In K. Mercer (Ed.), *Welcome to the Jungle: New Positions in Black Cultural Studies* (pp. 131–170). Routledge.

Mobius, M.M., & Rosenblat, T.S. (2006). Why beauty matters. *American Economic Review*, *96*(1), 222–235. https://doi.org/10.1257/000282806776157515

Movement Advancement Project (2014). 2014 National LGBT movement report: A financial overview of leading advocacy organizations in the LGBT movement. www.lgbtmap.org/file/2014-national-lgbt-movement-report.pdf

Movement Advancement Project (2016). 2016 National LGBT movement report: A financial overview of leading advocacy organizations in the LGBT movement. www.lgbtmap.org/file/2016-national-lgbt-movement-report.pdf

Movement Advancement Project (2020). Understanding the impact of COVID-19 on the LGBTQI movement. www.lgbtmap.org/file/2020-report-covid-impact.pdf

Nardi, P.M. (2000). "Anything for a sis, Mary": An introduction to gay masculinities. In P.M. Nardi (Ed.), *Gay Masculinities* (pp. 1–11). Sage.

National Council of Nonprofits (2020). Sexual harassment in the nonprofit workplace. www.councilofnonprofits.org/tools-resources/sexual-harassment-the-nonprofit-workplace

Neff, C. (2016). Emotional taxation lecture [Blackboard slides]. University of Sydney GOVT 6159 Emotions, Agendas and Public Policy. www.blackboardconnect.com

Okwodu, J. (2017, June 18). In *Hunger*, Roxane Gay says what no one else will about being fat in America. *Vogue*. www.vogue.com/article/roxane-gay-interview-hunger-memoir

Osmundson, J. (2019, October 22). Circuit: Queer pleasure as queer memory. *Los Angeles Review of Books*. https://lareviewofbooks.org/article/circuit-queer-pleasure-as-queer-memory

Pepin-Neff, C., & Caporale, K. (2018). Funny evidence: Female comics are the new policy entrepreneurs. *Australian Journal of Public Administration*, *77*(4), 554–567. https://doi.org/10.1111/1467-8500.12280

Pepin-Neff, C., & Wynter, T. (2020). The costs of pride: Survey results from LGBTQI activists in the United States, United Kingdom, South Africa, and Australia. *Politics & Gender*, *16*(2), 1–27. https://doi.org/10.1017/S1743923X19000205

Pew Research Center (2013, June 13). A survey of LGBT Americans. www.pewsocialtrends.org/2013/06/13/a-survey-of-lgbt-americans

Pigni, A. (2016). *The Idealist's Survival Kit: 75 Simple Ways to Avoid Burnout*. Parralax Press.

Plyler, J. (2009, October 26). How to keep on keeping on: Sustaining ourselves in community organizing and social justice struggles. *Upping the Anti: A Journal of Theory and Action*, (3). https://uppingtheanti.org/journal/article/03-how-to-keep-on-keeping-on/

Raj, S. (2011). Grindring bodies: Racial and affective economies of online queer desire. *Critical Race and Whiteness Studies*, *7*(2), 1–12. www.academia.edu/941246/Grindring_Bodies_Racial_and_Affective_Economies_of_Online_Queer_Desire

Rettig, H. (2006). *The Lifelong Activist: How to Change the World Without Losing Your Way*. Rudolf Steiner Press.

Rich, A. (1980). Compulsory heterosexuality and lesbian existence. *Signs*, *5*(4), 631–660. www.jstor.org/stable/3173834

Rodgers, K. (2010). "Anger is why we're all here": Mobilizing and managing emotions in a professional activist organization. *Social Movement Studies, 9*(3), 273–291. https://doi.org/10.1080/14742837.2010.493660

Rodriguez, M. (2017, January 29). D.C. gay bar JR's under fire after manager requests "hot white guy" instead of black model on ad. Mic. www.mic.com/articles/166954/dc-gay-bar-jrs-under-fire-after-manager-requests-hot-white-guy-instead-of-black-model-on-ad

Rosenberger, J.G., Reece, M., Schick, V., Herbenick, D., Novak, D.S., Van Der Pol, B., & Fortenberry, J.D. (2011). Sexual behaviors and situational characteristics of most recent male-partnered sexual event among gay and bisexually identified men in the United States. *Journal of Sexual Medicine, 8*(11), 3040–3050. https://doi.org/10.1111/j.1743-6109.2011.02438.x

Rubin, G. (2007). Thinking sex: Notes for a radical theory of the politics of sexuality. In R. Parker & P. Aggleton (Eds.), *Culture, Society and Sexuality: A Reader* (2nd ed., pp. 143–178). Routledge.

Schneider, A., & Ingram, H. (1993). Social construction of target populations: Implications for politics and policy. *American Political Science Review, 87*(2), 334–347. https://doi.org/10.2307/2939044

Sewell, K.K., McGarrity, L.A., & Strassberg, D.S. (2017). Sexual behavior, definitions of sex, and the role of self-partner context among lesbian, gay, and bisexual adults. *Journal of Sex Research, 54*(7), 825–831. https://doi.org/10.1080/00224499.2016.1249331

Slackers (2007, October 25). One Slacker's account of singing, pedagogy and sustainable activism. https://lambethbandofsolidarity.wordpress.com/2007/10/25/slackers-singing-pedagogy-and-sustainable-activism/

Snyder, M. (2015, September 24). *Board of directors.* Equality Federation Blog. www.equalityfederation.org/?s=executive+director+tenure

Spade, D. (2010). Keynote address [Symposium]. *Columbia Journal of Gender and Law, 19*(4), 1086–1110.

Spade, D. (2015). *Normal Life: Administrative Violence, Critical Trans Politics, and the Limits of the Law.* Duke University Press.

Srivastava, S. (2006). Tears, fears and careers: Anti-racism and emotion in social movement organizations. *Canadian Journal of Sociology, 31*(1), 55–90. https://doi.org/10.2307/20058680

Stember, C.H. (1978). *Sexual Racism: The Emotional Barrier to an Integrated Society.* Elsevier.

Strange, S.E. (2018). "It's your family that kills you": Responsibility, evidence, and misfortune in the making of Ndyuka History. *Comparative Studies in Society and History, 60*(3), 629–658. https://doi.org/10.1017/S001041751800021X

Surawski, M.K., & Ossoff, E.P. (2006). The effects of physical and vocal attractiveness on impression formation of politicians. *Current Psychology, 25*(1), 15–27. https://doi.org/10.1007/s12144-006-1013-5

Taub, J. (1999). Bisexual women and beauty norms: A qualitative examination. In J.C. Cogan & J.M. Erickson (Eds.), *Lesbians, Levis and Lipstick: The Meaning of Beauty in Our Lives* (pp. 27–36). Routledge.

Thai, M. (2019). Sexual racism is associated with lower self-esteem and life satisfaction in men who have sex with men. *Archives of Sexual Behavior, 49*, 347–353. https://doi.org/10.1007/s10508-019-1456-z

Thorndike, E. (1920). A constant error in psychological ratings. *Journal of Applied Psychology, 4*(1), 25–29. https://doi.org/10.1037/h0071663

U.S. Equal Employment Opportunity Commission (n.d.). *Sexual harassment.* www.eeoc.gov/sexual-harassment

Vaid, U. (1995). *Virtual Equality: The Mainstreaming of Gay and Lesbian Liberation*. Anchor Books.

Vaid, U. (2012). *Irresistible Revolution: Confronting Race, Class and the Assumptions of Lesbian, Gay, Bisexual, and Transgender Politics*. Magnus Books.

Valentova, J.V., Stulp, G., Třebický, V., & Havlíček, J. (2014). Preferred and actual relative height among homosexual male partners vary with preferred dominance and sex role. *PLoS One, 9*(1), 1–9. https://doi.org/10.1371/journal.pone.0086534

Wallestad, A. (2018, February 22). It's time for nonprofit boards to have a conversation about sexual misconduct. *Nonprofit Quarterly*. https://nonprofitquarterly.org/time-nonprofit-boards-conversation-sexual-misconduct/

Winetrobe, H., Rice, E., Bauermeister, J., Petering, R., & Holloway, I.W. (2014). Associations of unprotected anal intercourse with Grindr-met partners among Grindr-using young men who have sex with men in Los Angeles. *AIDS Care, 26*(10), 1303–1308. https://doi.org/10.1080/09540121.2014.911811

Witeck Communications (2016, July 20). America's LGBT 2015 buying power estimated at $917 billion [Press release]. www.witeck.com/pressreleases/2015-buying-power

Wood, M.J. (2004). The gay male gaze: Body image disturbance and gender oppression among gay men. *Journal of Gay & Lesbian Social Services, 17*(2), 43–63. https://doi.org/10.1300/J041v17n02_03

Wood, M.J. (2005). The gay male gaze: Body image disturbance and gender oppression among gay men. In B. Lipton (Ed.), *Gay Men Living with Chronic Illnesses and Disabilities* (pp. 43–62). Routledge.

Zhang, J., Zheng, L., & Zheng, Y. (2019). Self-rated attractiveness and sociosexual behavior predict gay men's preferences for masculine cues in male voices in China. *Evolutionary Psychology, 17*(2). https://doi.org/10.1177%2F1474704919847430

Zipkin, D. (1999). The myth of the short-haired lesbian. *Journal of Lesbian Studies, 3*(4), 91–101. https://doi.org/10.1300/J155v03n04_12

Ziv, A. (2011). Diva interventions: Dana International and Israeli gender culture. In T. Peele (Ed.), *Queer Popular Culture: Literature, Media, Film, and Television* (pp. 119–136). Palgrave Macmillan.

7

THE HUMAN RIGHTS CAMPAIGN AND LGBTQ LOBBYING

Introduction

I argue that the Human Rights Campaign (HRC) engages in gay mainstream lobbying, which is designed to reward heterosexual institutions over LGBTQ interests. The Human Rights Campaign's lobbying is considered gay mainstream lobbying in three ways:

1. The Human Rights Campaign is not intersectional because its lobbying priorities place one set of issues over another, highlighting some and diminishing others;
2. The Human Rights Campaign's political "ask" can demand less than full equality immediately, because asking for equality would upset the powerful; and
3. In both the issues selected (or not selected) and the "ask," power is returned to the powerful—heterosexual institutions.

The systems and structures of the Human Rights Campaign consist of an approach to policy change motivated by "equality governance," a term for the way political "asks" are made by lobbyists to the legislative and executive branches on LGBTQ issues. Importantly, as a result, the "ask" in gay mainstream lobbying is designed to be relative to the degree of discomfort it imposes on those in authority.

These structures at the Human Rights Campaign include the class-based business model that funds lobbying efforts; a pattern of norm-setting in its lobbying, events, and outputs that is at odds with an intersectional approach; and educational programs like the Corporate Equality Index whose 100 score recipients engage in unacceptable behavior.

These issues are important because which issues are highlighted, how norms are set, who receives power, how hard the LGBTQ community pushes are all influenced by the leadership of the Human Rights Campaign. As a hegemon, state-wide and federal groups look to the Human Rights Campaign to set the strategic path toward LGBTQ rights.

However, the Human Rights Campaign's political management confronts and opposes the more intersectional visions, initiatives, and discourses of LGBTQ lobbying. In this analysis, LGBTQ lobbying is a category of lobbying that centers the marginalized and imposes penalties that disrupt power dynamics in the name of full equality. However, this is not the case with the Human Rights Campaign's practice of gay mainstream lobbying. For instance, Lilian Faderman notes in her 2015 book *The Gay Revolution: The Story of the Struggle*, that the Human Rights Campaign is among "mainstream gay and lesbian groups" (Faderman, 2015: 514). Senator Bernie Sanders stated in 2015, "Human Rights Campaign and Planned Parenthood are 'part of the establishment'" (Flores, 2016). Urvashi Vaid, in her 1995 book *Virtual Equality: The Mainstreaming of Gay and Lesbian Liberation* states, "The organizational history of the Human Rights Campaign Fund illustrates the conservative worldview of this gay upper middle class" (Vaid, 1995: 91). Vaid adds that "throughout the eighties, at a time of enormous challenge for gay and lesbian people, the fund consistently took a safe, middle-of-the-road approach" (1995: 92).

Table 7.1 locates the Human Rights Campaign's lobbying on LGBTQ issues in the typology established in Chapter 2. Here I argue that the Human Rights Campaign issues (1) "heterosexual asks" and (2) prioritizes issues that return power to the powerful. That places the Human Rights Campaign in the category of gay mainstream lobbying. These elements are examined in this chapter.

Importantly, it appears that the Human Rights Campaign is also a political branding enterprise, based on its structural design. For instance, in 2019 the Human Rights Campaign generated about $2.2 million of income from HRC-branded merchandise (InfluenceWatch, 2020). This is approximately the same amount that the Human Rights Campaign spent on in-house lobbying:

1. HRC-branded Merchandise Sales in 2019: $2.2 million;
2. HRC Lobbying Expense: (2019—Open Secrets) $1,390,000—$1,880,704;
3. HRC: Budget: (2019 990) $48,000,000.

TABLE 7.1 The Human Rights Campaign in the categories of lobbying

Issue:	*Tactic: Heterosexual Ask*	*LGBTQ Ask*
Prioritize issues that return power	*Gay Mainstream Lobbying* **The Human Rights Campaign**	*[Where the public thinks gay groups are]* X
Prioritize issues that center marginalized	*Non- Conformist Lobbying*	*LGBTQ Lobbying*

Therefore, approximately 6% of the Human Rights Campaign's income is HRC-branded merchandise sales and approximately 4.6% of their expenses make up their federal lobbying efforts. Put another way, the Human Rights Campaign could fund much of its federal lobbying for 2019 on t-shirts and other merchandise sales.

Another comparison might note that state activism expenses should be counted, and that the total for federal and state advocacy should be considered relative to the smaller "program" expenses budget. In this case, federal lobbying by the Human Rights Campaign is around 16% of program spending in 2019. However, total budgets direct the priorities of every organization, as do program budgets.

The Human Rights Campaign's consumer business model has also been noted by others. Business interests incentivize political backing and support corporate models. In Amin Ghaziani's 2008 book *The Dividends of Dissent: How Conflict and Culture Work in Lesbian and Gay Marches on Washington*, he notes,

> The organization symbolically marked the expansion of its mission statement on August 7, 1995, by dropping the word *Fund* from its name, making them the Human Rights Campaign (HRC). HRC launched a new website, a flashy magazine, and engineered a slick logo.
>
> *(Ghaziani, 2008: 229)*

This was also noted at the 2000 Millennium March, where this came up again. Ghaziani (2008: 238) refers to a letter to the Human Rights Campaign that states, "'Participation in this march uncritically replicates and propagates the racism, elitism, and consumerism that need to be confronted'" (Ghaziani, 2008: 238). Ghaziani notes that Gamson's (2000) position on the march was that it should be opposed because it represented "a movement dominated by arrogant, corporate style, money-driven organizations geared toward assimilation through the marketing of acceptable gayness."

The implications of the Human Rights Campaign's use of equality governance in lobbying and corporate education is that it provides political cover for politicians and companies to be both pro-gay and anti-intersectional. The Human Rights Campaign is a large, dominant hegemonic organization in the LGBTQ community. Its systems and structures are designed to inhibit or encourage widespread intersectional thinking. Picking one identity over another (i.e. white and cis over Black and trans) or any number of lived experiences (monogamy vs polyamory) is the opposite of intersectional sensibility. This system provides cover when the Human Rights Campaign supports political candidates who vote for LGBTQ legislation but also right-wing Supreme Court Justices, like Senator Susan Collin's vote for Justice Alito.

The Human Rights Campaign structurally reproduces oppression for several reasons. First, it perpetuates the sexual hierarchy that reproduces oppression. Robinson (2012: 333) adds that "this feat of regulating gender nonconformers is accomplished through marginalizing and silencing them within the community." Second, issue selection within the non-profit structure reproduces oppression.

Beam (2018: 7) notes that "the non-profit structure actually entrenches the very inequalities that it purports to ameliorate." Third, the essentializing of issues and people allows for the reproduction of oppression. In short, the corporate model of many organizations privileges white, gay, cis, men. This reproduces inequality and racism in LGBTQ institutions.

The result, in part, is an approach to lobbying on LGBTQ issues that uses heteronormative tactics. The Human Rights Campaign's prioritization of issues deploys resources back to the State, like Hate Crimes. Murib (2017: 21) notes that "these negotiations over priorities often result in the reproduction of marginalization *within* these coalitions, as leaders elevate the concerns of more advantaged subgroups over those members with less power and influence." In addition, the Human Rights Campaign's "asks" reinforce heterosexual institutions, like marriage. Spade and Willse (2013) likewise argue that marriage advocacy has created "a world of representations of gay and lesbian couples who are monogamous, upper class, tax-paying, obedient consumers." And most importantly, these efforts come at the expense (i.e. opportunity cost) of other issues, which are more dire, more deadly, and less heteronormative.

Consumerism is an economic philosophy that was designed to protect the straight world and encourage participation in the straight economy. It returns power to the structures of capital that keep it in power. Put another way, the historical tradition of consumerism is not designed to look out for the needs of queer or trans consumers or to return power specifically to queer and trans people. Consumerism operates in response to heterosexual markets and institutions. This can be seen in many of the actions that organizations take. Human Rights Campaign Fund Co-founder Steve Endean notes in his edited memoir, *Bringing Lesbian and Gay Rights into the Mainstream: Twenty Years of Progress* that he helped name the organization the Human Rights Campaign Fund in part because, "I did feel the name would make it a little easier to make the initial breakthrough and get candidates to take our money" (Endean, 2006: 89). Here we see the need to enable actors to accept queer and trans money by making it sound less queer or trans.

The fundamental question for the Human Rights Campaign today is whether gay mainstream lobbying can disrupt the benefits, rewards, and privileges that racism, sexism, classism, homophobia, transphobia, and ableism confer on identities of whiteness, straightness, cisness, maleness, and of ability that exist as a product of their organization. This would include dismantling a business model that can advantage white people. LGBTQ lobbying offers first steps. DeFilippis and Anderson-Nathe (2017: 114) note that "these organizations are committed to the belief that the interests of people who experience the greatest oppressions must be prioritized over those of the most privileged."

Importantly, this analysis argues that the systems and structures of the Human Rights Campaign reproduce oppression and are inconsistent with intersectionality. The argument is not that current or former staff do this specifically. It would be unfair to the hard-working staff at any LGBTQ organization. The structures at the Human Rights Campaign can be seen in a number of empirical data points:

(1) historic narratives from the 1980s and 1990s with comments from early leaders such as Steve Endean and Vic Basil; (2) newer data, including comments from recent Presidents Joe Solmonese and Chad Griffin; and (3) patterns across the 40-year history of the organization.

To look at these elements, two points from Chapter 2 are important to revisit:

1. There are two types of "asks:" the "heterosexual ask" and the "LGBTQ ask." The "ask" as a concept of agenda setting is an understudied area. The "heterosexual ask" is designed to prioritize or avoid certain issues, set limits on the degree of change, and contain the discomfort of the powerful. The "LGBTQ ask" chooses issues that center the marginalized and is motivated to ensure discomfort and disruption with intersectional asks for permanent, unreserved, and immediate equality.
2. Equality governance is a lobbyist's negotiation of power in ways that request limited equality, relative to the discomfort of the powerful. It has roots in the literature on incremental policy change, and Charles Lindblom's 1959 research on "The Science of 'Muddling Through.'" In Duberman's 2018 book, *Has the Gay Movement Failed*, they look at the Human Rights Campaign's strategy. They note that it "is what Signorile has aptly characterized as 'incrementalist' ('winning a little bit at a time') a political philosophy that accurately reflects the limitations of the 'official' gay movement" (Duberman, 2018: 105).

Literature review

The Human Rights Campaign is the largest LGBTQ organization in Washington, D.C. with more than 3 million reported members (Ring, 2020). According to HRC's annual tax documents, it had a budget of more than $48 million in 2019 (HRC, 2020b). The Human Rights Campaign stands out as one of the dominant organizations in the LGBTQ community. It was the lead LGBTQ organization working for the successful passage of Hate Crimes legislation (CNN, 2009). It has also been a chief advocate of the Equality Act (Riley, 2019), which would "prohibit discrimination on the basis of the sex, sexual orientation, gender identity, or pregnancy, childbirth, or a related medical condition of an individual, as well as because of sex-based stereotypes." The Human Rights Campaign has worked on marriage equality, pushed back on efforts to establish a Federal Marriage Amendment, and opposed anti-LGBTQ Trump nominees. In addition, part of HRC's strategy was the development of a political action committee (PAC) that would provide money to certain political candidates. It was about fundraising and the distribution of money by "contributing to the candidacies of our friends and trying to defeat our enemies" (Endean, 2006: 107).

In August 2019, Human Rights Campaign's new President Alphonso David took over the organization. He has addressed a number of issues regarding race in America. In June 2020, he stated, "This moment requires that we make explicit commitments and take action to embrace anti-racism and end white supremacy, not as necessary corollaries to our mission, but as integral to the objective of full equality for LGBTQ people" (Bibi, 2020). This is important commentary from the largest LGBTQ advocacy organization in the United States. This section looks at the structural patterns of behavior that constitute an equality governance model at the Human Rights Campaign.

The structure of the Human Rights Campaign

Staffing

Internal data from the Human Rights Campaign points to a preference for conventionally attractive staff. In June 2015, Buzzfeed reporter Chris Geidner reported on an internal workplace culture analysis of the Human Rights Campaign: "'Leadership culture is experienced as homogenous—gay, white, male,' the report stated. 'Exclusion was broad-based and hit all identity groups within HRC. A judgmental working environment, particularly concerning women and feminine-identified individuals, was highlighted in survey responses'" (Geidner, 2015). The report added, "'There is a general perception that current diversity efforts are not working and that there's a lack of diversity understanding broadly.' A participant in a focus group noted, 'A lot of folks are personally invested in diversity inclusion but their voices have been smothered or pushed away'" (Geidner, 2015).

Geidner writes, "Among those issues highlighted repeatedly in the more than 30 pages of Pipeline Project report documents obtained by BuzzFeed News was what one subsection of the reported called a 'White Men's Club' environment at HRC" (Geidner, 2015).

The report states, "'One of the most frequent concerns that rose was the sense of an organizational culture rooted in a white, masculine orientation which is judgmental of all those who don't fit that mold.'" Finally, the report notes, "'Seven out of 31 men who have been promoted have been on staff less than two years (some promoted two times). No women under two years have been promoted'" (Geidner, 2015).

Galas

The structure of the Human Rights Campaign's lobbying efforts rely on a fundraising model with a major focus on major donors. Early on, the Human Rights Campaign Fund (HRCF) based its fundraising on gala events. "The Campaign Fund's anticipated fund-raising strategy—modeled after the large banquets of the local gay PAC in Los Angeles, the Municipal Elections Committee of Los Angeles—would rely on black-tie dinners and/or concerts" (Endean, 2006: 93). Endean (2006: 95) adds, "we had to hope our idea for major 'big ticket' banquets would catch on in cities with no track record of raising funds from the sort of affluent donors on which we'd have to depend."

In Myrl Beam's 2018 book *Gay, Inc.: The Nonprofitization of Queer Politics*, he identifies the non-profit model, stating that it was "adopted by most organizations in the 1980s and 1990s" to include "gala fundraisers, mass mailings, corporate sponsorships, foundation funding, donor tracking databases, and logic models" (Beam, 2018: 49). There are also characteristics like professionalization, performance management, and rating systems that are consistent with neoliberal business models.

Having events, like galas, that feature the whiteness of others celebrates whiteness for the sake and comfort of other white people. This complements the celebration of wealth or greater perceived status with the rich, not the poor. You would not highlight and celebrate richness with those living in poverty. These are structures that reinforce and reproduce oppression. This can be seen in the black-tie dinners that the Human Rights Campaign is a part of today, in places like Dallas, where the DFWFC puts together the "Luxury Live Auction Package" and other locations like Cleveland and Atlanta.

Ramirez in their 2015 book chapter, "The Queer Roots of the Esperanza Peace and Justice Center in San Antonio, Texas" states,

> In 2001 the Human Rights Campaign Fund (HRCF) of San Antonio honored Graciela Sánchez at their annual Black Tie Dinner in November, but did not acknowledge that some of the very same white men of their organization were the ones who ultimately caused the defunding of Esperanza. HRCF, which had allowed grapes at its functions, denying the validity of the United Farm Workers movement as a human rights issue, never got the significance of multi-issue organizing and the need for diversity in organizations.
>
> *(Ramirez, 2015: 169)*

This fundraising model complaint does not solely rest with the Human Rights Campaign, but is emblematic of many organizations. Evans, Richmond, and Shields (2005: 73) argue that "the neoliberal model of market-based regulation has moved many nonprofit service organisations away from their community oriented focus and towards a 'business model.'"

Intersectionality

The Human Rights Campaign's gay mainstream lobbying efforts have not demonstrated a prioritization of intersectionality. "Intersectionality is not additive. It's fundamentally reconstitutive," according to race and law scholar Kimberlé Crenshaw, who coined the term in her 1989 academic article, "Demarginalizing the Intersection of Race and Sex: A Black Feminist Critique of Antidiscrimination Doctrine, Feminist Theory and Antiracist Politics." Intersectionality speaks to the way systems and structures are designed to render certain people vulnerable on the basis of their identities. An LGBTQ organization, therefore, should recognize the patterns of power that render some people exposed and act to celebrate the reconstituted identity.

Intersectionality is a lens through which people can examine the idea that we cannot be reduced to one facet of our identity. We may be white, male with a mental health disability, or black, female, and straight, or Asian, transgender and straight—for instance. We exist as all of these things at the same time. By abandoning the essentialist hierarchy of identities that are designed through structures to contain our humanity, we reconstitute both ourselves and our society. We contest power and see where "power collides" (Crenshaw, 1989). We see a different picture of ourselves and without the systems of oppression, our trajectory is unlimited.

The gay mainstream model is not intersectional. Vaid (1995: 92) quotes former Human Rights Campaign Fund executive director Vic Basile,

> I recognize my limitations. I mean, you have the power to change certain things, and I think we develop power by learning how the system works and being able to manipulate it. And not to think about changing the system. It's too big a task. I don't think we can make any difference in that equation.

In December 2009, Chicago Congressman Gutierrez introduced immigration legislation in Congress, but this legislation did not address LGBTQ issues. Representative Gutierrez had received approximately $15,000 from the Human Rights Campaign. However, when asked about the intersections of sexual orientation and immigration, he told Roll Call,

> There has never been a serious, in-depth discussion between the gay and lesbian community and the immigrant community. It's never existed .... It's a new conversation, but not one that I'm fearful of. I welcome it. But you can't expect after nearly two decades of struggle for a new component—to be quickly embraced.
>
> *(Bendery, 2009)*

The gay mainstream lobbying model is a trickle-up model identified by DeFilippis and Anderson-Nathe (2017: 116): "A trickle-up social justice framework informs not merely *who* these groups mobilize but also *what* they mobilize around." Here, we see how groups reproduce inequalities. The staff they hire, the issues for which they fight, and the careerist pursuits they explore.

This is about more than dismantling the structures and systems of oppression that are created by those in power. The task is greater than this. Intersectionality teaches us that the systems and structures of oppression reduce people down to a consumable portion by those in power. We are essentialized and compartmentalized. Therefore, to be intersectional means to take down both the systems of oppression *and* the structural hierarchy on which it is built. The Black community, the Women's Movements, and HIV/AIDS activists have been doing this for decades.

Therefore, an intersectional approach to lobbying disrupts the paths of power that structurally reproduces oppression by making requests on political issues that return power to the powerful and provide partial equality relative to the discomfort of those in authority. Put another way, lobbying is the choice about what issues to prioritize and which to diminish and this action either disrupts power or returns power to the powerful.

The next task of this chapter is to look at the implications of the Human Rights Campaign on the success and failures of the LGBTQ advocacy community. This is especially important because the Human Rights Campaign is a hegemon. Which issues are highlighted, how norms are set, who receives power, how hard the LGBTQ community pushes are all influenced by the leadership of the Human Rights Campaign.

Methods

This analysis is based on a participant-observer viewpoint, but it also includes historical contexts and more recent episodes. For the data on 2019 merchandise, income, and 2019 lobbying expenses, Human Rights Campaign tax documents were reviewed. This data highlights patterns of activity and should not be extrapolated beyond this analysis.

There were varying expense amounts reported, which called into question the accuracy or reporting and the chances, particularly the potential for an undercount. For instance, it appears that in-house lobbying expenses are covered in public data as staff salaries and outside spending is covered by 990 reporting. To deal with this, the potential for an undercount four data points were used across the years. First, the highest lobbying expense number from any of the metrics was used over all four years. Then this number was doubled. Then this percentage (5.8%) was rounded up to 6%. In turn, for the price of merchandise, the number was reviewed and compared with the budget. Then the percentage (.458) was rounded up to 4.6 not 5%. This created one of the largest possible gaps to present a counter argument that these numbers were close to each other.

Under the Lobbying Disclosure Act, lobbying only needs to be reported if it is more than 20% of the salary of the employee. This will not account for federal lobbying under this cap. So, this is not a measure of lobbying, but rather only a measure of reported lobbying above this threshold.

LobbyView (lobbyview.org) is a lobbying tool run out of the Massachusetts Institute of Technology (MIT). The data on lobbying on LGBTQ issues has a number of limitations. The first is that numbers based on 990 forms may be an undercount. As noted, a comparison of three data points found LobbyView to be the most accurate, but there may be variations. Second, this analysis assumes all lobbying is specifically LGBTQ in nature. It does not take into account non-LGBTQ lobbying that an LGBTQ organization may make. For instance, lobbying for dolphins may be part of a grant and be included. This is likely not the case, but it is an important data distinction, nonetheless. Third, the LobbyView data only counts the spending on the highest seven political issues. As a result, there is an expected undercount.

Income

The HRC budget data comes from their 990 as approximately $48,000,000. For HRC lobbying expense in 2019, a review of Open Secrets by hand to include in-house and out-of-house lobbying spending came to $1,390,000 (Center for Responsive Politics, 2020). This was different from the LobbyView data for the top seven issues: $1,190,000. This was also different from the external spending reported on HRC's 990: $520,557. Finally, all of these were different from the Human Rights Campaign lobbying expense from Open Secrets: $890,000. As a result, the highest number was doubled to $2,780,000 and then 5.8% rounded up to 6%.

It is also useful to compare the lobbying efforts of the Human Rights Campaign with other organizations. There are a number of points from the Human Rights Campaign's lobbying profile. For instance, according to LobbyView data, the Human Rights Campaign has spent $34,438,115 between 1999 and 2020 on federal lobbying. The Human Rights Campaign also employs outside lobbyists. Of its 24 in-house lobbyists, 21 have worked for legislators.

One of the outside firms that the Human Rights Campaign has hired is Thorsen French Advocacy LLC, which states that it lobbied on the Equality Act and other legislative items. Specifically, Carlyle French conducted much of the lobbying. French was previously General Counsel for Republican Congressman Tom Delay of Texas. Since 2014 the Human Rights Campaign has spent over $600,000 hiring Thorsen French to lobby on its behalf since 2014, according to LobbyView (see Table 7.2).

Among Thorsen French Advocacy LLC's other clients is the Pharmaceutical Research and Manufacturers of America (PhRMA). According to data from the Center for Responsive Politics (2020), PhRMA has spent $260,000 on Republican campaigns in the 2020 cycle, $100,000 more than on Democratic races.

For other LGBTQ organizations, they are listed in order of total spending. This includes the Gay, Lesbian and Straight Education Network (GLSEN) which spent $3,002,036 between 2003 and 2020, mostly lobbying the Department of Education.

TABLE 7.2 Lobbying expenditures to Thorsen French Advocacy LLC

Firm	Expense	Year
Thorsen French Advocacy LLC	$20,000	2020
Thorsen French Advocacy LLC	$80,000	2019
Thorsen French Advocacy LLC	$80,000	2018
Thorsen French Advocacy LLC	$80,000	2017
Thorsen French Advocacy LLC	$110,000	2016
Thorsen French Advocacy LLC	$120,000	2015
Thorsen French Advocacy LLC	$120,000	2014
Total:	$610,000	

This total also includes outside lobbyists and six of eight lobbyists who worked for legislators. This suggests a sophisticated operation.

The next highest expenditure was $2,121,910 by Freedom to Marry between 2011 and 2015. There were no outside lobbyists. The Taskforce reports $1,343,987 between 2006 and 2020. SLDN (2003–2013): $853,419, with Jeff Trammell as outside lobbying. Log Cabin Republicans (2005–2018): $384,503. Mostly in-house, some outside lobbying. In addition, Immigration Equality only has no outside lobbying between 2019 and 2020, with $40,000 spent.

There was no reported outside lobbying at Task Force and Family Equality, and no data on NCTE, the National Transgender Advocacy Coalition (2001) or Transgender Human Rights Council (2006).

Data

Inequality index

On the Human Rights Campaign website, it announces the launch of the 2020 Corporate Equality Index (CEI). They note, "Human Rights Campaign Foundation's Corporate Equality Index is the national benchmarking tool on corporate policies, practices and benefits pertinent to lesbian, gay, bisexual, transgender and queer employees" (HRC, 2020a). The section below reviews businesses and corporations that have been awarded a score of 100 from the Human Rights Campaign Foundation. It notes a number of significant inconsistencies between the goals of the measurement and the actions of the recipient.

Central to any analysis of the CEI is to look at the fidelity of the corporations to the metrics (LGBTQ equality) established. An analysis to ensure the metrics suit the message. And a question of who gets power in the process. Who is the CEI for? These issues are raised in the analysis below:

In August 2015, the LGBTQ organization Pride at Work passed a resolution critical of the Human Rights Campaign because it felt the CEI did not capture the true nature of LGBTQ representation at the organization. *Advocate* magazine ran an article on this issue entitled, "Pride at Work Tells HRC: 'Enough is Enough'." The Pride at Work resolution stated, "Too often, HRC has catered to its big-moneyed donors at the expense of those who live on the margins" (Brydum, 2015). It adds, "These misguided priorities have disproportionately impacted the transgender community, people of color, and workers, … LGBT consumers look to the CEI when deciding how to spend their hard-earned money" (Brydum, 2015).

In 2008, a report from the Office of Senator Bernie Sanders (I-VT), entitled, "Top Corporate Tax Dodgers" states that in 2008 Goldman Sachs paid no federal income tax. Instead, "in 2008, Goldman Sachs received a $278 million refund from the IRS, even though it earned a profit of $2.3 billion that year" (Sanders, 2008). The report adds, "In 2010, Goldman Sachs operated 39 subsidiaries in offshore tax haven countries." This is important because according to Senator Sander's office, "in

2010, Goldman Sachs would have owed $2.7 billion in federal income taxes if its use of offshore tax avoidance was eliminated" (Sanders, 2008).

The Human Rights Campaign Foundation awarded Goldman Sachs with the 2011 "Workplace Equality Innovation Award" during the global financial crisis. On January 3, 2011, Goldman Sachs was worth $92.2 billion. Beaver (2016) notes that "HRC's willingness to whitewash the pasts of individuals and organizations in return for cold cash is nothing new." This gained the attention of Occupy Wallstreet's Queer Caucus. The Queer Caucus stated, "HRC honoring Goldman Sachs at this time reveals all one needs to know about the corporate LGBT lobby, and its disconnect from the 99% and the LGBT people it purports to represent" (Broverman, 2012).

Corporations that refuse to pay taxes are not supporting the LGBTQ community. They are structurally aligning themselves with existing power dynamics of white supremacy, sexism, transphobia, classism, homophobia, and ableism. Awarding powerful corporations with more power at the expense of marginalized communities is an example of the "heterosexual ask." There are additional examples.

Moreover, in 2019 Goldman Sachs paid nearly $10 million to approximately 600 workers; a report states that "the U.S. Department of Labor's Office of Federal Contract Compliance Programs (OFCCP) has entered into an early resolution conciliation agreement with Goldman Sachs & Co. LLC to resolve findings of race and gender-based compensation discrimination" (U.S. Department of Labor, 2019).

In addition, Facebook received a score of 100 from the Human Rights Campaign Foundation in 2020. Facebook is a sponsor of the 2020 Republican National Convention. The anti-LGBTQ platform adopted at the convention states: "We condemn the Supreme Court's ruling in United States v. Windsor, which wrongly removed the ability of Congress to define marriage policy in federal law" (Drabold, 2016).

Some would argue that the inauguration is nonpartisan. Pfizer has a 100 score from the Human Rights Campaign Foundation in 2020 and they donated $1 million to the Trump inauguration in 2016 (Balhaus, 2017). Microsoft/CDW has a 100 score from the Human Rights Campaign Foundation in 2020 and donated $500,000 to the Trump inauguration in 2016 (Romm, 2017). Dow Chemical also received a 100 score in 2020 and donated $1 million to the Trump inauguration in 2016 (Balhaus, 2017).

Pepsi (PepsiCo) received a 100 score from Human Rights Campaign Foundation in 2020. Pepsi has also been a corporate sponsor of Liberty University's "men's and women's hockey teams as well as various on-campus events and outdoor activities" (Brown, 2008).

Lockheed Martin has a 100 score from the Human Rights Campaign Foundation in 2020. The company has previously donated nearly $70,000 to Senator Ted Cruz (Center for Responsive Politics, 2020), who opposes LGBTQ rights. Cruz has stated that he opposes marriage equality, believes homosexuality is a choice, opposed the Dallas Mayor marching in a pride parade, and supported clerk Kim Davis refusing marriage certificates to LGBTQ couples.

Blackstone Group received a 100 score from the Human Rights Campaign Foundation in 2020. Their CEO donated more than $3 million to Trump-related campaign elements. CNBC has also reported that, "Blackstone's CEO is Steve Schwarzman, who recently gave $3 million to the pro-Trump super PAC America First Action and has been a close confidant of the President's since his inauguration" (Schwartz, 2020). In addition, Blackstone Group has donated $83,000 to Senator Marco Rubio. According to HRC (2016: 1), "Rubio has raised money in Florida for a key backer of conversion therapy."

Blackstone Group has also donated more than $93,000 to Senator Mitch McConnell who has a zero rating on the Human Rights Campaign congressional scorecard (Loftus, 2019). He voted in favor of a constitutional amendment to ban marriage equality and he was opposed to including sexual orientation as a hate crime category.

In short, there is an apparent discrepancy between the questions that the Human Rights Campaign Foundation uses to measure employment nondiscrimination in the CEI and the scope of additional funding or actions.

There are also intersectional considerations when looking at CEI measurements. For many in the queer and trans community the availability and access to HIV/AIDS drugs is essential. In 2017, Gilead put out a press release on their HRC score, stating, "Gilead Sciences today announced that it has received a top score of 100 percent on the Human Rights Campaign (HRC) 2018 Corporate Equality Index." Gilead has a 100 score from the Human Rights Campaign Foundation in 2020 even though there are concerns about the availability of the PrEP drugs they produce (Rowland, 2019).

According to National Public Radio, Truvada costs "$1,780 a month, or $21,360 per year—more than 350 times the cost of generic versions of the drug available in most other countries" (Simmons-Duffin, 2019). Groups like ACT UP and PrEP4All (2012) state, "If the federal government used its authority to push down drug prices, it would capture billions of dollars in Medicare and Medicaid savings, allowing them to scale up HIV prevention and treatment drugs to everyone who needs them across the country." In addition, there has been criticism regarding patent term extension. PrEP4All (2019) notes that, "When it appeared that Descovy may be safer, specifically for people living with HIV, Gilead intentionally delayed developing these drugs so they could maximize the profits of their existing regimens."

KPMG received a score of 100 on the Human Rights Campaign Foundation's CEI in 2020. In 2017, KPMG "agreed to pay out $420,000 to settle allegations that it discriminated against 60 Asian job applicants" (Mazzola, 2019). Morgan Stanley received a 100 score from the Human Rights Campaign. According to the *Washington Post*, in June 2020 the former head of diversity at Morgan Stanley "filed the lawsuit on behalf of Black female employees who are accusing the bank of systemic discrimination against Black financial advisers and trainees" (Jan & Merle, 2020). In 2020, Morgan Stanley received a score of 100 from the Human Rights Campaign Foundation.

The point is not that all of these businesses are guilty of disqualifying offences. The point is that there is hypocrisy by some of these businesses which should be considered in any measurement. This is certainly true if the CEI is to remain a respected tool of public education used by the Human Rights Campaign Foundation.

Wells Fargo received a 100 score from the Human Rights Campaign Foundation. In 2012, Reuters reported on Wells Fargo paying $175 million in response to racial discrimination claims. Reuters states, "A government investigation found 34,000 instances of Wells Fargo charging African Americans and Hispanics higher fees and rates on mortgages compared with white borrowers" (Rothacker & Ingram, 2012).

Walmart received a 100 score from the Human Rights Campaign Foundation. In 2009, Reuters reported that Walmart "had settled for $17.5 million a class action lawsuit in which plaintiffs claimed the retailer had discriminated against African Americans seeking jobs as truck drivers." In 2018, Walmart was accused of racial discrimination in the way it displayed beauty products; it was reported that hair products for Black customers were kept in a locked case (Vigidor & Brown, 2020).

Finally, in 2019, the Human Rights Campaign's President Chad Griffin noted the value of the Corporate Equality Index, stating, "Time and again, leading American businesses have shown that protecting their employees and customers from discrimination isn't just the right thing to do—it's also good for business" (Associated Press, 2019). Who is served by the Corporate Equality Index is a key question. Is it designed to return power to the powerful (i.e. corporations) or those disadvantaged by the system? I argue that the focus of the Human Rights Campaign's Corporate Equality Index is based on a model whose standards and marketing are designed to benefit powerful corporations. I suggest that several of its corporations have failed in their fidelity to the ideals of equality, and that the current metrics and measurements should be updated.

Opposing the formation of Q Street

In 2005, after the defeat of Democratic Presidential candidate, Senator John Kerry, I decided to form Q Street, an association for LGBTQ lobbyists and government affairs professionals. At the time, Republicans had won the White House, had 55 seats in the Senate, and a majority in the House with more than 225 members. Perhaps most importantly, 13 constitutional state amendments banned same-sex marriage in 2004, in Arkansas, Georgia, Kentucky, Michigan, Mississippi, Louisiana, Missouri, Montana, North Dakota, Ohio, Oklahoma, Oregon, and Utah.

This was one of the lowest political points for the LGBTQ community in modern times. However, the Senate LGBTQ staffers group had just formed and I thought it might be possible to leverage the power of LGBTQ lobbyists across D.C. to help smaller groups on more marginal issues. This also included breakfasts and meetings to have a space where LGBTQ lobbyists and government affairs professionals could collectively meet and work together. The first steering committee in 2005 included Mara Keisling, Dave Noble, and Kevin Cain.

However, the Human Rights Campaign took another view. I received a call when they got word that I was trying to start Q Street. I was told that it was "duplicative" of the work that the Human Rights Campaign was already doing. My response was that I was not aware that they were already happening. I was told that there were meetings from business groups that were happening, and that Q Street wasn't needed. I said I thought that it was important, I didn't see it as duplicating anything, and that I was going to move ahead. I hoped that they would participate. According to the current Board, there are more than 3,000 people on the Q Street mailing list in 2020.

Discussion

The Human Rights Campaign engages in gay mainstream lobbying. This can be seen by reviewing its "asks." The narratives and analysis below look at four "asks," including:

1. Ask for "don't ask, don't tell" repeal to be delayed;
2. Ask for support of non-inclusive ENDA;
3. Ask for "respectability"; and
4. Ask for a consumer business model of LGBTQ existence.

I have defined lobbying in two parts: (1) the negotiation of power in the executive and legislative branches in ways that returns power to the powerful; and (2) the use of the "heterosexual ask" to prioritize or avoid certain issues, set limits on the degree of change, and contain discomfort to the powerful. Here we examine these four situations.

Ask for "don't ask, don't tell" repeal to be delayed

In December 2009, there was a very important meeting on the future of DADT repeal at the Human Rights Campaign building. In the building, there is a long conference room able to fit a number of key stakeholders. Funders were there from the leading foundations across the country. Many of the leading LGBTQ organizations were there, including SLDN and myself. As a matter of fact, I had been working out of this building in the Raben Group's offices for the past month or so. The Raben Group were kind enough to put me up, and it was a cordial relationship.

The meeting was designed by the Human Rights Campaign to get a community buy-in around a tactical and strategic shift that had two key elements. First, "don't ask, don't tell" would not be considered in Congress until 2011. This would move it behind Employment Non-Discrimination Act (ENDA). Second, a new lobbying firm would head up the issue. The Human Rights Campaign was proposing to put millions of dollars behind what they called a new national campaign.

At the time "don't ask, don't tell" had a head of steam on it with a lot of public attention, but the Human Rights Campaign was making the argument that more work needed to be done on the Hill. As a result, they were going to manage the issue and move the consideration of repeal in Congress to 2011.

A leading consultant was seated across from me at the long table. The consultant laid out a national media, education, and lobbying plan for "don't ask, don't tell" with federal legislative introduction focusing on Senator Susan Collins of Maine and Senator Joe Lieberman of Connecticut because this would make the bill bipartisan. This appeared to be consistent with reports on February 2, 2010 when "Solmonese said his group has launched a campaign to bolster lawmakers who support repeal of the policy" (Roth, 2010). This was all work that Aubrey Sarvis at SLDN had been doing for the past two years, and that I'd been doing for the past five years. I spoke up.

I said that this plan would be good if it was 2006, but it wasn't. It was 2009. And repeal needed to happen in 2010. There was no guarantee Democrats would control the Senate after the 2010 election or that this issue would make it on the White House agenda as they readied for re-election. This work had been done, I stated, and it was important that "don't ask, don't tell" get repealed while we had the super majorities in the House and the Senate now. I said that the Hill was ready. We had managed the coalitions in the core offices, and we were ready to take on Republican opposition.

This fell like a lead balloon in the room. The consultant yelled at me. He said that I had been undermining the efforts by talking with House offices about other legislative options. He had heard from a congressional office that I was up on the Hill discussing options for repeal of "don't ask, don't tell," and that this was causing problems because we had a two-pager of legislative options that were different than the plans that he was laying out. I shot back that this was entirely appropriate, that we weren't hiding anything. The meeting ended, and we all retreated back to our organizations.

At that point I was approached by a colleague who worked at the Raben Group. I was told it was time for me to gather my things and leave the building. At first, I said, "Really? Why?" I was told that I had insulted their colleague, and this was the consequence. I was being thrown out of the building. As Nobel Prize winner and political scientist Dr. Elinor Ostrom notes, "repeated rule breakers are severely sanctioned and eventually excluded from the group" (Ostrom, 1998: 8).

Concern about Congress introducing the "don't ask, don't tell" repeal bill

2005

In 2005, we were on the verge of historic legislation to repeal "don't ask, don't tell." Personally, I had pushed myself harder than I ever had, with 100-hour weeks for the three months leading up to this legislative introduction to end the ban on gays, lesbians, and bisexuals in the military. This was not the end of the process; it was the start. I was working with congressional offices and co-sponsors finalizing legislation, while keeping an eye out for a Government Accountability Office (GAO) report that we were going to use as a tipping point for the need for the legislation. So, there were a lot of moving pieces, and this also included coordination with coalition allies like the Human Rights Campaign, Log Cabin Republicans, People for the American Way, NGLTF, and others.

I was surprised when I was called into a congressional meeting with a key office and told they had received a call from the Human Rights Campaign. Apparently, they had told the office that there was concern that introduction of the bill would be done poorly and that there would be a backlash. I was told there was specific concern about me, that I wasn't up to the job. This was giving the office pause about moving forward.

This meeting was the most disturbing of my entire lobbying career. Just days before the introduction of the bill to repeal DADT, there was an effort to stop the introduction of new legislation. However, I was able to mitigate any concerns. The legislation to repeal "don't ask, don't tell" was introduced with 57 co-sponsors. It was bipartisan, and there was no backlash.

2003

Around 2003, SLDN staffers and I went to the old Human Rights Campaign offices and sat down with their staff to talk about initial efforts to educate Congress about the need to repeal "Don't Ask, Don't Tell." It was a face-to-face meeting. They wanted a debrief on what we had been up to on Capitol Hill. We told the staff that a recent national story about gay and lesbian Arabic linguists in the military had provided an opportunity for meetings on the Hill. We had been getting calls from offices with questions and opportunities for face-to-face meetings. We were responding to that, and as a result our understanding of the potential for repeal had fundamentally been changed. The SLDN staff agreed that this moment was a turning point on "don't ask, don't tell." We could make some real headway for repeal and at least put forward an educational bill that had all the elements that we wanted; this would serve as a rallying point for organizing around the repeal of the policy.

The HRC staff were not impressed. They said that they thought this was a bad idea and that there was likely to be a backlash that would damage the LGBTQ community. I understood their concern and I shared it personally. We did not want this to go bad. However, I also got the impression that they did not like us working on the Hill, which was traditionally their territory.

I presented to them a reasonably comprehensive plan that there would be affirmative language to repeal "don't ask, don't tell," that there would be a non-discrimination policy forbidding treatment that discriminated against LGBTQ troops, and that this would be a bipartisan effort with 50 co-sponsors. They seemed to think this was far-fetched. They did not think we could get 50 co-sponsors, they did not think this would be bipartisan, and they thought that this could lead to the aforementioned backlash. The implication was that we were playing in their sandbox, we would make a mess of it, and they would be left to clean up. We were being told to back off repeal.

After the meeting, we were wandering through the building and we bumped into a Human Rights Campaign staffer who was an ally. She asked how the meeting had gone. We told her that it did not go well. She was incredulous. The question now was what to do. We certainly weren't going to stop having meetings with congressional offices on the Hill but knowing that offices were talking to the Human Rights Campaign about what we were doing, we had to make sure that our information was the best, and that we were providing a service to the offices that would mitigate any concern about this backfiring.

Ask for support of non-inclusive ENDA

Currah (2006: 21) states that the Human Rights Campaign "formally changed its federal legislative policy to be fully inclusive of transgender people in 2004." However, in September 2007 the Human Rights Campaign supported a non-inclusive ENDA bill. Stryker (2008: 152) notes that the Human Rights Campaign "lost what little credibility it had with the transgender community when it made an abrupt about-face and endorsed the sexual-orientation-only version of the bill." Human Rights Campaign Executive Director Joe Solmonese stated (Heywood, 2008),

> 'In that context, did I think then that it was best for the community that the bill pass? Yes,' Solmonese said. 'Do I still support that position? Yeah. What was best for our community was that the bill pass rather than fail. Sometimes it is hard for people to see the whole picture, but sometimes you are faced with choices.'

Signorile (2017) notes that "HRC, often in that '90s time warp, has worked against the best interests of the LGBT community as recently as 2014, when the group was still supporting the narrow Employment Non-Discrimination Act."

Concerns about the Human Rights Campaign continue to the present. In 2019, their President Alphonso David announced new initiatives aimed at transgender justice and impact litigation. In response, a letter written in October 2019 (Out. com, 2019a) from trans and non-binary leaders pointed to the Human Rights Campaign's recent trans initiative and stated:

> If HRC is truly committed to trans liberation, the organization's leadership must start with repairing, healing, and listening. They must start by addressing past harm, building genuine relationships, and demonstrating support for our leadership. They must bolster our work, not take credit for it. We invite a conversation with Alphonso David and other HRC leadership. We would welcome HRC's support—but we will not accept their cooptation of our movement.

These concerns point to a credit-claiming, top-down model where the hegemon establishes projects without incorporating or funding the same work that is already taking place, by community experts. Heteronormativity can be seen in the more conservative approaches. Spade (2009: 355) refers to the Human Rights Campaign as one of "the more conservative national gay and lesbian organization(s)." Heteronormativity preferences straight characteristics and the institution of het-erosexuality. This could be seen in 1984. Hindman (2019: 59) notes, "The Human Rights Campaign Fund (HRCF) stated in a flyer prepared for 1984's National Gay and Lesbian Lobby Day that lesbian and gay men should "present [themselves] and [their] views in a respectful, dignified manner. Dress appropriate to a business appointment."

Beam (2018: 82) recounts Violet Stanlet from the Center on Halsted in 2012, who stated, "'I can not be a part of putting money above principle. I can not be a part of enabling HRC's attempt to buy their way back into the Trans communities' good graces."

Riswold quotes a post on Tumblr (2013):

> HRC is an organization run by rich white men. They have consistently chosen not to support trans rights. They have consistently silenced POC organizations and organizers. They have accepted donations from, and even honored, multi-billionaire corporations who have done more than their fair share to contribute to the unequal distribution of wealth and to systematic racialized and gendered oppression in the US. Their vision of "equality"—as obviously signaled by their logo—is *not, and never has been*, equality *for all*. It is equality for those who can afford it. It's equality for those who can prove they are "just like everyone else," who respect and embody gender normativity, middle class sensibility, and white supremacy.

White, male, liberals present a chief obstacle to greater diversity. Gorski (2019:14) states, "Unlike the general frustration with non-activist 'white liberals,' this source of burnout was related to fellow activists, white activists, many of whom also adopted a white liberal stance and impeded movement progress." DeFilippis and Anderson-Nathe (2017) looked at queer liberation organizations. They add, "hooks argued that both groups have sought equality with White men, promoting their own interests in ways that perpetuate the exploitation and oppression of others" (DeFilippis & Anderson-Nathe, 2017: 112). White is treated as normative.

Gorski (2019: 13) adds that white activists can increase burnout in a community. He finds:

> several participants specified a particularly disappointing cause of their burnout as "white liberals." These were people—non-activists—participants identified as embracing a celebrating diversity orientation towards race, but who ultimately protected their privilege by balking at more serious con-siderations for racial justice. Vince (white man, thirties) explained, "The

people who have been most difficult to deal with are [white] people who say that they're liberal ..." Participants described "white liberals" derailing conversations about racism, lobbying activists to "soften" their anti-racism goals, and prioritizing their comfort over racial justice progress.

Ask for "respectability"

In both the issues selected (or not selected) and the "ask," power is returned to the powerful—heterosexual institutions.

Respectability politics can be seen in the issues that the Human Rights Campaign works on and the tactics that they employ. Respectability politics was embedded into the founding of the Human Rights Campaign. Endean (2006: 21) notes, "I have long thought the key to our success was to be seen not as a fringe, bizarre issue but as one that is respectable and mainstream."

The Human Rights Campaign symbolizes respectability politics in pursuing a mainstream agenda and narrative of LGBTQ life. Robinson (2012: 333), states that "in seeking to be normative gays and lesbians gender police their community, marginalizing and stigmatizing any difference and construing it as inferior." Robinson (2012: 328) adds that "Hekma (2006) asserts that the 'vices' within the community, like leather men and drag queens, must remain out of the public sphere, so that the mainstream LGBT community can maintain social acceptance."

The fight over respectability is a fight over who is normal and who is not, from inside the LGBTQ community. This policing defines who is human and who is not. Robinson (2012: 333) discusses Judith Butler (2004), who "argues that the struggle over norms is about who is human. Therefore, to achieve political legitimacy, those who assimilate regulate nonconformers and cast them as nonhuman—as other, unviable lives."

Narratives around diversity are one way to reassert normality and heterosexuality. Stone (2010: 467) argues, "diversity practices usually reinforce normativity by embracing racial and gender differences when they are visible and fundable, and suppressing differences when they are unpredictable, unprofessional, or messy." Therefore, heteronormative models are adopted. Robinson (2012: 329) notes the lies within heteronormativity: "Heteronormativity has implications for gender, as it constitutes feminine women and masculine men as the only viable options."

Respectability politics in regard to same-sex marriage is also an important consideration. Matsick and Conley (2015: 411) note, "With the legalization of same-sex marriage, we hope that researchers and gay rights activists need not be so entrenched in respectability politics when affirming same-sex relationships and instead can allow differences to prevail."

Gayness as a form of respectable LGBTQ person has been prioritized by the gay mainstream lobbying in ways that erase other identities. Murib (2017: 20–21) further states,

In many cases, the privileging of sexual orientation—namely, lesbian and gay political identities and political interests—entailed silencing the political agendas for transgender and bisexual-identified people, as well as butches, fairies, cross-dressers, queer people of color, and intersex-identified people, who also compromised the margins of the new "GLBT" identity.

Respectability politics is a process of internal erasure and sanitization of the community. Robinson (2012: 329) argues,

> there are rewards for being considered normal, so anyone who can pass as normal will do so. This yearning to pass as normal leads a stigmatized individual to be repelled by someone within one's own community who acts in stereotypical ways. This dislike of stereotypical people within one's own community leads to ingroup purification.

A key failure of respectability politics is that in self-regulating the LGBTQ community to appear to be perceived as a "normal" it also makes oneself invisible. There is a latent choice to be invisible and lose an identity by supporting heteronormativity and binary. Robinson (2012: 329) says that "through desiring recognition, certain stigmatized individuals internalize societal norms and self-regulate their behaviors in order to gain acceptance."

And it is no wonder. Robinson (2012: 328) states that "accordingly, Keuzenkamp et al. (2007) discovered that effeminate men who fit the gay stereotype are not taken seriously in certain service sectors of Dutch society." Gay, white, cis, masculine, able-bodied male identity is reproduced in organizations through hiring processes to satisfy the gay, white, cis, able-bodied male gaze.

> *This bias in favor organizing around the desires of the male gaze can lead to sexual harassment and assault of staff, interns, volunteers or members when not reviewed.*

The point of reproducing these stereotypes is to make people feel good in their elite status. Annual dinners, galas, and benefits serve as a benefit to the members. To make them feel good and to feel they are contributing to good work being done by the organization.

Respectability politics are ultimately about gatekeeping within the LGBTQ community. Normal customers become valid and valued members of society and achieve full humanhood. This conflict between normality and difference can be seen in the organization of both movements. It became a way of seeing the world and comported to respectability politics. Stone (2010: 469) looks at Ghaziani's work on the Marches on Washington and notes that in 2000, "Rather than a political venue to articulate widely supported LGBT movement demands, many queer activists argued that instead the march was just a celebration or party."

Infighting is a purification process between the two movements, and there is shame on the part of those who assimilate that plays a role in the process. Robinson (2012: 333) states, "to further the mitigation of one's own fear and shame, those who assimilate try to regulate the nonconformers through ingroup purification."

First, there are confidentiality or non-disclosure agreements (NDAs) made famous by the MeToo movement and seen in the case of Harvey Weinstein. Some social justice organizations use these NDAs to gag staff. Yet many organizations support legislation that was introduced in Congress in 2018 that, according to Vice News, "has a laundry list of goals, including regulating the use of non-disparagement and non-disclosure agreements, or NDAs. It would amend the tax code to make sure that harassment can't be written off as 'the cost of doing business'" (Sherman, 2018). However, this practice still takes place. One of the social justice coalitions standing up for this change to the law was the Economic Justice Project at Lawyers' Committee for Civil Rights Under Law. According to Vice, "The Committee is one of several humanitarian and civil rights groups that have endorsed the law, including the NAACP, the AARP, and the Human Rights Campaign" (Sherman, 2018). Clearly there is ideological support for the legislation, but the question arises about implementation.

For instance, in 2016, there were tensions on the Board of Christopher Street West (the non-profit that puts on L.A. Pride). According to *The Pride LA*,

> several board members complained publicly that the top-down management style of the board made their service useless. Among the complaints was the implementation of a non-disclosure agreement that prevented board members from discussing organizational matters outside the board. That apparently included discussions about CSW's position on transgender visibility.
>
> *(Masters, 2017)*

In addition, in a November 15, 2019 open letter in *Out Magazine*, former staff members in a dispute with the leadership of the National Center for Transgender Equality (NCTE) stated, "At least four people of color were told to sign nondisclosure agreements; no white former staff member of NCTE has reported doing the same" (Out.com, 2019b).

In addition, the National LGBTQ Task Force (2020) states on its website, "Interns may come into contact with sensitive information during their time here, so we need a signed confidentiality agreement before the beginning of work." Confidentiality agreements of this type appear commonplace.

Issue selection can also include the way political issues like endorsements are handled. For instance, the Human Rights Campaign endorsed Republican Senator Mark Kirk from Illinois for re-election in 2016. During a debate in October 2016, Kirk responded to then Democratic congresswoman Tammy Duckworth with a racist statement: "I had forgotten that your parents came all the way from Thailand to serve George Washington" (Jaffe & Lee, 2016). The Human Rights Campaign did not initially withdraw their endorsement based on his statement. Slate reported,

None of this, it seems, is especially troubling to the Human Rights Campaign, the world's biggest and most influential LGBTQ rights group. The HRC announced on Friday that it is maintaining its endorsement of Kirk over Duckworth, though it hopes Kirk will 'rescind his comments'—i.e., his racist jab.

(Stern, 2016)

Ask for a consumer business model of LGBTQ existence

There are several ways in which large hegemonic organizations advance the ideological vision. This can be seen when non-profits adopt governance elements built on neoliberalism like new public management (NPM). First, neoliberalism treats people like clients. People are paid members of an organization rather than free activist participants. Second, under this model, citizenship is not a set of rights that people are afforded under the U.S. Constitution, but rather citizenship is relative to the ability to purchase a series of products, which make you eligible for certain rights. You buy into health care and you buy a separate plan for pharmaceuticals. You pay tolls to go on certain roads. You pay for taxes for snow removal, water, and sewage. All of these represent products of the State that are not basic services. Third, consumerism influences the structure and management of non-profit organizations. The reliance on federal, state, and private grants shifts the focus and agenda of groups and forces them to prioritize the issues and metrics of funders. For instance, federal HIV grants often preference youth over elders, even though elders also represent a vulnerable community. But the elder lobby is not as appealing in the neoliberal model and sexual hierarchy as the youth model.

In all, neoliberalism is both a style of engagement and centered on free-market wealth creation, which returns wealth to the wealthy and power to the powerful. For our purposes, it is a commercial experience of being LGBTQ. The elements of NPM (Pollitt, 2013: 43) include a

> focus on outputs/deliverables, increased measurement/performance indicators, decentralized, leaner organizations, contractualization, increase in competition such as Market Type Mechanisms (MTMs), consumer treatment, Public-Private Partnerships (PPP's), shift in values toward efficiency (of inputs to outputs) and the individual customers, and professional management and accountability.

Many of these play out in the context of non-profit management.

However, there are serious problems with NPM. First, the implementation of a policy or program may not be fully implemented or fully measured. Second, rhetorical measurements are political tools because politicians can count on the limited memory of the public. For instance, governments or non-profits may say they will cut expenses by 25%, but no one is usually there to hold them accountable 12 months later. The output, therefore, may be the words. Fourth, NPM is based on assumptions about human behavior and utility maximization that may be wrong. People do not always choose the correct option, they make mistakes, forget things, and lack emotional capacity based on anxiety or other personal factors. Fifth, neoliberalism is an institution of heterosexuality. Heteronormative mainstream models are predicated on maintaining status quo power dynamics. Indeed, hegemonic heterosexuality is designed to reward the institutions of heterosexuality like NPM. Sixth, measurement of NPM is hard and has not happened in most cases (measurements measure indicators—not problems or people).

Treating people like consumers

The Human Rights Campaign's efforts are consistent with a corporate, consumerist, neoliberal image. One way to look at the consumerist approach of the Human Rights Campaign is through their levels of membership (HRC, n.d.):

- General Membership: begins "with a gift of $35 or more annually."
- HRC Partner: "support equality each month with contributions of $5 or more."
- The Federal Club: "annual contribution of $1,200 to $4,999."
- The Federal Club Council: "annual gift of $5,000 or more."

Each level of membership confers benefits and status. The NPM principle of consumerism is the epitome of the gay mainstream lobbying and the opposite of the LGBTQ lobbying, which relies on intersectionality. Intersectionality believes people are heterogeneous because we function at the intersection of multiple identities. Stone reviews Ward's book *Respectably Queer*, which notes that "queer intersectionality is an approach that strives for racial, gender, socioeconomic, and sexual diversity but also resists the institutional forces that seek to contain and normalize differences, or reduce them to their use value" (Ward, 2008: 19). This is the business model that can reproduce oppression.

Intersectionality speaks to the way in which people are heterogeneous and cannot be reduced to an essentialist, one-dimensional character of themselves for the benefit of those in power. Pepin-Neff and Caporale (2018: 555) note the importance of intersectionality

> because of the way it informs the way political actors articulate problems and solutions and the way power dynamics are considered. It is a theory that responds to the way fluid, heterogeneous identities are made hierarchical and stand-alone elements by the powerful in society to return power to themselves. Intersectionality acknowledges that because we have simultaneous and heterogeneous identities, these identities interact and cross in ways that amplify multiple oppressions .... It challenges the notion that a person's multifaceted identity can be reduced and prioritized by society, law, policy, and the

media to a single identity that best suits the way those in power would like to address oppression as a means to remain in power.

Another key principle of neoliberalism is competition between non-profits. The idea is that this is better for the consumer because it makes groups professionalize their services and provide better products. This also means that citizens who are now consumer clients are placed in the position to choose between one group and another. Groups have to design strategies to attract enough people to donate to their issues.

Neoliberalism in the non-profit context also means that there are metrics and it is results oriented. The Human Rights Campaign has four documents that exemplify metrics and measurements for equality: the annual Corporate Equality Index (CEI), Healthcare Equality Index (HEI), Municipal Equality Index (MWI), and State Equality Index (SEI). These embody a neoliberal new public management form of non-profit governance where report cards of this type provide public education to consumers, influence policies adopted by corporations and set precedents for local and state public policies. However, the key to any analysis is what exactly is being measured.

The questions are what do members of the organization receive and in what order? Who gets what first? Do the poor get equality before the rich get their benefits, their social status? It does not appear that the Human Rights Campaign's dinners are aimed at the poor. The Human Rights Campaign's retail stores are selling a retail brand identity to those who can afford it. A system of affordable equality deceives both the buyer and the seller. Attempting to market and "supersize" queerness rewards neither the vendor nor the client because queerness is not a hamburger with fries. It can be neither bought nor sold. Equality as a consumer-friendly commodity reproduces racism, sexism, classism, ableism, homophobia, and transphobia. Equality as a consumer-friendly commodity privileges white, gay, cis, men.

Citizenship as the purchase of a series of products

The Human Rights Campaign's budget boomed in the 1990s, quadrupling in size under the leadership of Elizabeth Birch from 1995 to 2004. During this period, the Human Rights Campaign often treated people like customers in the way it set itself up as a membership organization. Stone (2010: 466) notes that "the LGBT movement has grown into a national movement with large, formal, professional organizations staffed by predominantly white, middle-class professionals." Building on this, DeFilippis and Anderson-Nathe (2017: 129) note that:

> The mainstream groups' focus on issues of concern to White, middle-class gay and lesbian American citizens has failed because the solutions that benefit the most privileged segment of a marginalized group often end up not helping

those below them. Worse, these solutions frequently stigmatize further those people on the bottom.

Issues are packaged as purchasable commodities. These are the issues that motivate donations. How issues are discussed informs who they are meant to appeal to and how they are funded. Beam (2018: 2) looks at the way non-profit narratives are class specific; he uses the example of homeless queer youth and notes that "the family rejection narrative is important insofar as it is a compelling story for Ali Forney's prime donor base: middle and upper income white gay and lesbian couples." Beam (2018: 2) adds:

> It constructs *queer* youth homelessness as exceptional, separate from the figure of the *undeserving* poor so readily at hand. In other words, like so many organizations across the LGBT movement, Ali Forney's approach to an issue it wants to address is driven by what wealthy donors need to hear in order to motivate them to give money.

Issues are designed to be cared about by many people.

Donors become commodities. Beam (2018: 6) says, "These privileged members of the community are the 'major donors' that LGBT nonprofits court, appeal to as 'leaders,' and to whom they are therefore beholden." This means organizations that adopt non-profit models may feel forced to focus on single issues not simply because that is part of the neoliberal model, or because people are boundedly rational (i.e. have a limited cognitive architecture that means that our memories are bound by time) and not always able to deal with the overwhelming nature of systems of oppression as a fundraising narrative, but because donors care about one issue more than another, so chasing the issues the donor cares about pins organizations into a single-issue model. Beam (2018: 5) further states, "But those select few wield incredible power to determine the agenda of the movement with their money, through donations to the nonprofit organizations through which the LGBT movement largely operates."

Yet intersectionality and diversity can also be falsely made into a purchasable item. Stone (2010: 470) writes that

> radicalism has been somewhat integrated into formal LGBT organizations but oftentimes in conventional ways, such as changing a mission statement to reflect bisexual and transgender inclusion rather than embracing multi-issue politics that would include the full range of potential transgender issues such as poverty, homelessness, and health care.

Indeed, tokenism can turn issues and staff around "diversity and inclusion" into commodities that help organizations appear more sensitive to racism and sexism, in particular, than they may otherwise be.

Non-profit structure

The non-profit industrial complex is a large part of neoliberal movement building. Beam (2018: 6) notes that the non-profit structure pushes organizations into single-issue politics that reinforce the neoliberal capitalist model: "That the issues deemed most important by those most privileged within the LGBT community have come to be so exclusively dominant is, I argue, a function of the structure of the movement itself, the nonprofit system." This stands apart from the LGBTQ lobbying that puts those most marginalized at the center of the decision-making process.

Beam (2018: 11) says:

> I locate LGBT nonprofits: an apparatus that produces, disciplines, and regulates particular queer subjects. Nonprofits, then, operate as a form of hybrid statecraft, a critical relay in circuits of governance that knit the disciplinary technologies of the welfare state to the biopolitical scope of the neoliberal security state.

Stone (2010: 466) adds to this by arguing that part of this push toward neoliberalism is the emphasis on professionalism in the non-profit space. She adds, "Professionalization suppresses dissent and radicalism, encouraging organizations to engage in single-issue politics. Rather than realize the vision of queer intersectionality, professionalization promotes diversity in narrow and predictable ways, reflecting the class biases of the corporate culture from which it came."

Murib (2017: 17) argues that coalitions were formed to mitigate competition and based on broader patterns of the policy process that were becoming decentralized. For example, when the fight with the Clinton Administration over LGBTQ in the military first began in 1993, a group called the Campaign for Military Service was formed to fight back. Murib (2017: 19) adds that coalitions were used to defend against opponents from the far-right:

> These assaults from the Conservative Right compelled leaders of various gay, lesbian, bisexual and transgender interest groups and organizations to establish a working coalition to engage in political actions like lobbying and conduct events like parades to bring people together to present a unified front and project critical mass.

This is echoed by Stone (2010: 468), who notes that

> this professionalization streamlined decision making and facilitated the sharing of resources to combat the religious Right. Becoming corporate-like and professional also became a way to increase the legitimacy of the LGBT movement in the eyes of the public and politicians alike.

This is particularly important in more complex conversations about public administration and the shift from NPM to "joined up governance" that relies on civil society organizations to provide safety net functions. As the welfare state is eroded, non-profits pick up the pieces and the services and become part of the neoliberal model, part of the private non-profit governance structure within a defined process. They also rely on government grants that support this decentralized model, further tying non-profits to the government and to government priorities that determine what "benchmarks" are met and how. This creates a process where a non-profit's mission may be compromised by the need to chase grant funding and divergent grant priorities.

Conclusion

Businesses may support Pride but when they dodge paying taxes, they undermine the social safety net for all queer and trans people, particularly the most marginalized.

This chapter has argued that the Human Rights Campaign supports the gay mainstream lobbying that advantages heterosexual institutions. The Human Rights Campaign is one of the leading hegemons within the LGBTQ advocacy community in the United States. Like many other large organizations within a policy domain, it has built this leadership through a neoliberal mainstream approach to politics. Neoliberal market approaches can be seen in a model of professionalism, financing through large galas from major donors, and attention to quantitative indexes that highlight measurable effects of their work.

The Human Rights Campaign employs the "heterosexual ask" and equality governance. This means that their requests on political issues return power to the powerful and seek equality only in so much as it does not disrupt those in authority. Together these tactics reproduce oppressions. The Human Rights Campaign also appears to be a political marketing company that builds this brand and fundraises by engaging gay mainstream lobbying issues.

The Human Rights Campaign establishes which issues should be on the agenda and who should benefit. Issues are often prioritized for the benefit of mainstream allies over more radical constituencies. This is equality governance. Within this process, the implications suggest that this protects some politicians more than those being discriminated against. Therefore, equality governance produces inequality because the tactics that are used to engage the House, Senate, White House and the organization itself return power back to these heteronormative institutions rather than redistributing power.

The implication of the Human Rights Campaign's use of equality governance while a large organization in the LGBTQ community, or hegemon, is that it provides political cover for politicians or companies to be both pro-gay and anti-intersectional. This is more than picking one identity over another (i.e. white and cis over Black and trans) or any number of lived experiences. It involves using at least one identity to erase another and keep it invisible. The celebration of whiteness harms Black communities in the same way the celebration of the moneyed class perpetuates biases and renders poor people, and poverty, and homelessness hidden features of society.

As noted, the Human Rights Campaign's business model is rooted in this repro-duction because it privileges white, gay, male major donors. The result, in part, is an approach to lobbying on LGBTQ issues that uses heteronormative tactics.

Here we see the impact of gay mainstream lobbying in a way that is funded and perpetuates a consumer vision of LGBTQ life that reproduces oppressions. This view advocates for respectability politics, which has broad powers to regulate norms. This includes reinforcing sexual hierarchies, the shape of coalitions, and who will be labelled outsiders.

The approach of the Human Rights Campaign is contested by the idealized task of large organizations to design structures and systems that disrupt the benefits of intersectional oppressions. This includes standing up to those with power, centering those on the margins, and embracing the non-mainstream issues that hurt the LGBTQ community. All organizations face a choice, to look at the issues they work on and the tactics they employ. Hegemons feel this responsibility more than most organizations because they have the potential to leverage their influence and redistribute power. This puts added pressure on groups like the Human Rights Campaign.

References

Associated Press (2019, April 12). *First Data earns top marks in 2019 Corporate Equality Index*. https://apnews.com/press-release/pr-businesswire/7de0ead4e8b24dcb9825cb0503b34348

Balhaus, R. (2017, January 31). Donald Trump inauguration drew more than 18 corporate donors. *Wall Street Journal*. www.wsj.com/articles/donald-trump-inauguration-drew-more-than-18-corporate-donors-1485924877

Beam, M. (2018). *Gay, Inc.: The Non-Profitization of Queer Politics*. University of Minnesota Press.

Beaver, A. (2016, February 2). Why is the Human Rights Campaign honoring Goldman Sachs? *Huffington Post*. www.huffpost.com/entry/hrc-goldman-sachs_b_1257465

Bibi, E. (2020, June 1). Human Rights Campaign president Alphonso David on the launch of pride month and anti-racism. Human Rights Campaign. www.hrc.org/news/hrc-president-alphonso-david-on-the-launch-of-pride-month-and-anti-racism

Bendery, J. (2009, December 18). Immigration bill leaves out gays: Move fuels friction among Democrats. Roll Call. www.rollcall.com/2009/12/18/immigration-bill-leaves-out-gays/

Broverman, N. (2012, February 1). Queer Group to protest HRC gala honoring Goldman Sachs. Advocate. www.advocate.com/news/daily-news/2012/02/01/queer-group-protest-hrc-dinner-honoring-goldman-sachs

Brown, E. (2008, December 18). Pepsi becomes first corporate sponsor of Ultimate LU. Liberty University. www.liberty.edu/index.cfm?PID=18495&MID=5741

Brydum, S. (2015, August 30). Pride at work tells HRC: "Enough Is enough." *Advocate*. www.advocate.com/business/2015/08/30/pride-work-tells-human-rights-campaign-enough-enough

Butler, J. (2004). *Undoing Gender*. Routledge.

Center for Responsive Politics (2020). Lobbying data summary. www.opensecrets.org/federal-lobbying/

CNN (2009, October 28). Obama signs hate crimes bill into law. www.cnn.com/2009/POLITICS/10/28/hate.crimes/

Crenshaw, K. (1989). Demarginalizing the intersection of race and sex: A black feminist critique of antidiscrimination doctrine, feminist theory and antiracist politics. *University of Chicago Legal Forum*, (1), 139–167. https://chicagounbound.uchicago.edu/uclf/vol1989/iss1/8

Crenshaw, K. [@sandylocks] (2020, June 26). Intersectionality is not additive. It's fundamentally reconstructive. Pass it on [Tweet]. https://twitter.com/sandylocks/status/1276571389911154688

Currah, P. (2006). Gender pluralisms under the transgender umbrella. In P. Currah, R.M. Juang, & S.P. Minter (Eds.), *Transgender Rights* (pp. 3–31). University of Minnesota Press.

DeFilippis, J.N., & Anderson-Nathe, B. (2017). Embodying margin to center: Intersectional activism among queer liberation organizations. In M. Brettschneider, S. Burgess, & C. Keating (Eds.), *LGBTQ Politics: A Critical Reader* (pp. 110–133). New York University Press.

Drabold, W. (2016, July 18). Read the Republican platform on same-sex marriage, guns and Wall Street. *TIME*. https://time.com/4411842/republican-platform-same-sex-marriage-abortion-guns-wall-street/

Duberman, M. (2018). *Has the Gay Movement Failed?* University of California Press.

Endean, S. (2006). *Bringing Lesbian and Gay Rights into the Mainstream: Twenty Years of Progress* (V.L. Eaklor, Ed.). Routledge.

Evans, B., Richmond, T., & Shields, J. (2005). Structuring neoliberal governance: The nonprofit sector, emerging new modes of control and the marketisation of service delivery. *Policy and Society*, *24*(1), 73–97. https://doi.org/10.1016/S1449-4035(05)70050-3

Faderman, L. (2015). *The Gay Revolution: The Story of the Struggle*. Simon & Schuster.

Flores, R. (2016, January 22). Bernie Sanders backpedals on "establishment" charges. *CBS News*. www.cbsnews.com/news/bernie-sanders-backpedals-on-establishment-charges

Gamson, J. (2000, March 30). Whose millennium march? The Nation. www.thenation.com/article/archive/whose-millennium-march/

Geidner, C. (2015, June 3). Internal report: Major diversity, organizational problems at Human Rights Campaign. BuzzFeed. www.buzzfeednews.com/article/chrisgeidner/internal-report-major-diversity-organizational-problems-at-h

Ghaziani, A. (2008). *The Dividends of Dissent: How Conflict and Culture Work in Lesbian and Gay Marches on Washington*. University of Chicago Press.

Gilead Sciences (2017, November 9). Gilead Sciences announces 100 percent score on 2018 Human Rights Campaign Corporate Equality Index [Press release]. www.gilead.com/news-and-press/company-statements/100-corporate-equality-score

Gorski, P.C. (2019). Fighting racism, battling burnout: Causes of activist burnout in US racial justice activists. *Ethnic and Racial Studies*, *42*(5), 1–21. https://doi.org/10.1080/01419870.2018.1439981

Heywood, T. (2008). HRC leader stands by non-inclusive ENDA decision. Pride Source. https://pridesource.com/article/29930

Hindman, M.D. (2019). Promiscuity of the past: Neoliberalism and gay sexuality pre- and post-AIDS. *Politics, Groups, and Identities*, *7*(1), 52–70. https://doi.org/10.1080/21565503.2017.1310117

Human Rights Campaign (n.d.). Become a member. www.hrc.org/get-involved/memberships

Human Rights Campaign (2016). 2016: Republican facts: Marco Rubio. https://assets2.hrc.org/files/assets/resources/GOP_Site-Rubio.pdf?_ga=2.29429689.706608427.1604087712-265044273.1602613123

Human Rights Campaign (2020a). Corporate Equality Index: 2020. www.hrc.org/resources/corporate-equality-index

Human Rights Campaign (2020b). Form 990: Return of organization exempt from income tax. https://hrc-prod-requests.s3-us-west-2.amazonaws.com/HRC-990-FY20.pdf

Human Rights Campaign Foundation (2020). Corporate Equality Index 2020: Rating workplaces on lesbian, gay, bisexual, transgender and queer equality. https://hrc-prod-requests.s3-us-west-2.amazonaws.com/files/assets/resources/CEI-2020.pdf?mtime=20200713132437&focal=none

InfluenceWatch (2020). Human Rights Campaign. www.influencewatch.org/non-profit/human-rights-campaign/

Jaffe, A., & Lee, T.G. (2016, October 28). Illinois senator draws fire for racially charged attack on opponent's family. CBS News. www.nbcnews.com/news/asian-america/mark-kirk-questions-tammy-duckworth-s-family-s-service-heritage-n674331

Jan, T., & Merle, R. (2020, June 16). She was Morgan Stanley's first diversity officer. Now she's suing the bank for racial bias. *Washington Post*. www.washingtonpost.com/business/2020/06/16/she-was-morgan-stanleys-first-diversity-officer-now-shes-suing-bank-racial-bias/

Loftus, T. (2019, July 17). Wall Street firms, not Kentuckians, are leading Mitch McConnell's campaign donations. *Courier Journal*. www.courier-journal.com/story/news/politics/2019/07/17/mitch-mcconnell-reelection-campaign-wall-street-firms-donate-money/1745611001/

Masters, T. (2017, January 12). LA Pride board members resist non-disclosure agreements, resign. *The Pride LA*. https://thepridela.com/2017/01/la-pride-board-members-resist-non-disclosure-agreements-resign/

Matsick, J.L., & Conley, T.D. (2015). Maybe "I do," maybe I don't: Respectability politics in the same-sex marriage ruling. *Analyses of Social Issues and Public Policy*, *15*(1), 409–413. https://doi.org/10.1111/asap.12085

Mazzola, J. (2019, January 16). KPMG pays $420K to settle Asian discrimination allegations. NJ.com. www.nj.com/essex/2017/06/kpmg_pays_420k_to_settle_asian_discrimination_alle.html

Murib, Z. (2017). Rethinking GLBT as a political category in U.S. politics. In M. Brettschneider, S. Burgess, & C. Keating (Eds.), *LGBTQ Politics: A Critical Reader* (pp. 14–33). New York University Press.

National LGBTQ Task Force (2020). About: Interns & fellows. www.thetaskforce.org/about/interns-fellows.html

Ostrom, E. (1998). A behavioral approach to the rational choice theory of collective action: Presidential address, American Political Science Association, 1997. *American Political Science Review*, *92*(1), 1–22. https://doi.org/10.2307/2585925

Out.com (2019a, October 1). An open letter to HRC from trans community leaders. www.out.com/activism/2019/10/01/open-letter-hrc-trans-community-leaders

Out.com (2019b, November 15). This is why we left the National Center for Trans Equality. www.out.com/transgender/2019/11/15/why-we-left-americas-largest-trans-advocacy-organization

Pepin-Neff, C., & Caporale, K. (2018). Funny evidence: Female comics are the new policy entrepreneurs. *Australian Journal of Public Administration*, 77(4), 554–567. https://doi.org/10.1111/1467-8500.12280

Pollitt, C. (2013). *The Essential Public Manager*. Open University Press/McGraw-Hill.

PrEP4All (2012). National HIV prevention program. www.prep4all.org/hivprogram

PrEP4All (2019). Patent term extension reform. www.prep4all.org/pte-reform

Ramirez, G. (2015). The queer roots of the Esperanza Peace and Justice Center in San Antonio, Texas. In U. Quesada, L. Gomez, & S. Vidal-Ortiz (Eds.), *Queer Brown Voices: Personal Narratives of Latina/o LGBT Activism* (pp. 151–170). University of Texas Press.

Reuters (2009, February 20). UPDATE 1-Wal-Mart settles trucker discrimination lawsuit. https://fr.reuters.com/article/idUSN2030481320090220

Riley, J. (2019, May 14). HRC is "disgusted" that President Trump opposes the Equality Act. *Metro Weekly*. www.metroweekly.com/2019/05/hrc-says-its-disgusted-that-president-trump-opposes-the-equality-act/

Ring, T. (2020, May 6). Nation's largest LGBTQ organization endorses Joe Biden for president. Advocate. www.advocate.com/election/2020/5/06/nations-largest-lgbtq-organization-endorses-joe-biden-president

Robinson, B. (2012). Is this what equality looks like? How assimilation marginalizes the Dutch LGBT community. *Sexuality Research and Social Policy*, *9*(4), 327–336. https://doi.org/10.1007/s13178-012-0084-3

Romm, T. (2017, February 7). Before immigration furor, tech giants donated to Trump inauguration. *Politico*. www.politico.com/story/2017/02/tech-giants-trump-inauguration-234776

Roth, B. (2010, February 2). "Don't Ask" ignites policy war. Roll Call. www.rollcall.com/2010/02/02/%C2%91dont-ask-ignites-policy-war/

Rothacker, R., & Ingram, D. (2012, July 12). Wells Fargo to pay $175 million in race discrimination probe. *Reuters*. www.reuters.com/article/us-wells-lending-settlement/wells-fargo-to-pay-175-million-in-race-discrimination-probe-idUSBRE86B0V220120712

Rowland, C. (2019, March 16). An HIV treatment cost taxpayers millions. The government patented it. But a pharma giant is making billions. *Washington Post*. www.washingtonpost.com/business/economy/pharma-giant-profits-from-hiv-treatment-funded-by-taxpayers-and-patented-by-the-government/2019/03/26/cee5afb4-40fc-11e9-9361-301ffb5bd5e6_story.html

Sanders, B. (2008). Top corporate tax dodgers. www.sanders.senate.gov/imo/media/doc/102512%20-%20JobDestroyers3.pdf

Schwartz, B. (2020, August 17). Private equity giant Blackstone hires pro-Trump lobbyist David Urban to target Pentagon, State Department. CNBC. www.cnbc.com/2020/08/17/blackstone-hires-pro-trump-lobbyist-to-target-pentagon-state-department.html

Sherman, C. (2018, July 18). #MeToo prompted lawmakers to come for those non-disclosure agreements. Vice News. www.vice.com/en/article/vbjd98/metoo-prompted-lawmakers-to-come-for-those-non-disclosure-agreements

Signorile, M. (2017, March 26). How the Human Rights Campaign is helping the GOP to retain the Senate. *Huffington Post*. www.huffpost.com/entry/how-human-rights-campaign-helping-the-gop_b_9545778

Simmons-Duffin, S. (2019, May 30). AIDS activists take aim at Gilead to lower price Of HIV drug PrEP. NPR. www.npr.org/sections/health-shots/2019/05/30/727731380/old-fight-new-front-aids-activists-want-lower-drug-prices-now

Spade, D. (2009). Trans politics on a neoliberal landscape. *Temple Political & Civil Rights Law Review*, *18*(2), 353–373. https://digitalcommons.law.seattleu.edu/faculty/161

Spade, D., & Willse, G. (2013, September 6). Marriage will never set us free. Organizing Upgrade. https://archive.organizingupgrade.com/index.php/modules-menu/beyond-capitalism/item/1002-marriage-will-never-set-us-free

Stern, M.J. (2016, October 28). Human rights campaign maintains endorsement of Sen. Mark Kirk after racist comment. Slate. https://slate.com/human-interest/2016/10/human-rights-campaign-maintains-mark-kirk-endorsement-after-racist-comment.html

Stone, A.L. (2010). Diversity, dissent, and decision making: The challenge to LGBT politics. *A Journal of Lesbian and Gay Studies, 16*(3), 465–472. https://doi.org/10.1215/10642684-2009-040

Stryker, S. (2008). *Transgender History*. Seal Press.

Tumblr (2013). Queer insurrection. https://queerinsurrection.tumblr.com/post/46926274808/clever-title-tba

U.S. Department of Labor (2019, September 30). U.S. Department of Labor reaches conciliation agreement for $9,995,000 in back pay and interest [News release]. www.dol.gov/newsroom/releases/ofccp/ofccp20190930

Vaid, U. (1995). *Virtual Equality: The Mainstreaming of Gay and Lesbian Liberation*. Anchor Books.

Vigidor, N., & Brown, E. (2020, September 1). Walmart says it will no longer lock up African-American beauty products. *New York Times*. www.nytimes.com/2020/06/10/business/walmart-black-hair-beauty-products.html

Ward, J. (2008). *Respectably Queer: Diversity Culture in LGBT Activist Organizations*. Vanderbilt University Press.

8

CONCLUSION
The future of LGBTQ lobbying

Introduction

The future of LGBTQ lobbying is trans.

Lobbying is an important aspect of the agenda-setting and policy implementation process. But lobbying, government relations, and public policy are transphobic.

Transgender people have been denied representation and access to government resources and civility. They have experienced police brutality, murder, rape, and child theft. This violence against trans people creates a relationship between them and the State that subordinates the trans lived experience. Moreover, they have been fired from jobs in government relations, communications, fundraising, or lobbying. This has limited their ability to be heard. It would therefore be reasonable that the trans community would look for representation and advocacy elsewhere. However, in the United States, a survey by the author found that transgender people make up 21 percent of LGBTQ activists (Pepin-Neff & Wynter, 2020). This is higher than the average of all survey respondents who identified as trans, which was 16 percent. Therefore, transgender lobbying takes place in the face of transphobic, cisgender political institutions. Trans lobbyists are often those who identify openly as transgender or nonbinary in an act of political resistance when the government is working to erase those identities. In short, trans people face discrimination from the government *and* LGBTQ organizations and still make up one in five activists. This helps teach us that trans lobbying and LGBTQ lobbying are important because marginalized issues are different.

Trans lobbying has been going on for decades by grassroots activists, elected officials, academics, and professional lobbyists. For instance, Monica Helms created the Transgender Pride Flag in 1999 and also co-founded the American Veterans for Equal Rights (AVER) in 2003. The first trans activist on the stage at the DNC convention was Mara Keisling in 2004, who also founded the National Center for

Transgender Equality. One of the first federally funded non-binary programs was "Gendertopia," which was launched at Outright Vermont in 2009. The push for federal policy change for trans in the military took off in 2012, including Spart★a. The National Center for Transgender Equality's trans survey began in 2015. The largest federal trans rights victory was litigated by trans lawyer and lobbyist Chase Strangio in 2020.

In addition, trans lobbyists include: Brenda Churchill, Harper Jean Tobin, Paula Neira, Diego Sanchez, Earline Budd, Carter Brown, Rodrigo Heng-Lehtinen, Shannon Minter, Masen Davis, Pauline Park, Kasey Suffredini, Jennicet Gutiérrez, Riki Wikchins, Melissa Sklarz, TS Candii, Eloise Brook, Kylar Broadus, Dana Kaplan, Teddy Cook, Norrie, Dana Beyer, Tre'Andre Valentine, Emmett Schelling, Andrea Nicolette Segovia, Gunner Scott, Christiana Hammond, Dean Spade, Chelsea Manning, India Moore, Dru Levasseur, and Raffi Freedman-Gurspan.

Two standouts are Harper Jean Tobin at the federal level, who is one of the most successful federal policy experts for trans issues in American history. And Brenda Churchill, a state lobbyist in Vermont. Brenda was the first transgender campaign aide for the first trans major party nominee for governor, Christine Hallquist.

The potential for trans lobbying builds off the most exciting move in LGBTQ politics this decade, which is the leadership, campaigns, and election of trans candidates like Andrea Jenkins and Phillipe Cunningham in Minnesota, Sarah McBride in Delaware, Taylor Small in Vermont, and Danica Roem in Virginia. As well as the race of Christine Hallquist for Governor in Vermont. Here, trans candidates broke new ground that fundamentally changed the trajectory of American politics.

The future of LGBTQ lobbying is to address other issues, which, like trans rights, receive the least attention and whose groups are afforded the least power. Marginalized issues like poverty, white supremacy, homelessness, sex work decriminalization, prison reform, trans murder rates, and HIV criminalization will all come into focus more in the 2020s. At the core of *marginalized lobbying* are the values and action that come from queerness.

I argue that queerness redeems the practice of lobbying. Queerness and transness function in the way that Kimberlé Crenshaw talks about intersectionality, as "reconstitutive." This alters lobbying from its capitalist, homophobic, racist, sexist past to something new. This repurposed form of lobbying highlights the benefits of queerness and transness to the political process.

Queerness and transness are particularly important to this story because they note that the systems that make marginalized populations vulnerable also make them disruptive, and this can be powerful. For instance, within a system of structural white supremacy and hegemonic heterosexuality, white heterosexuals are more than the norm, they are viewed (and political institutions are meant to protect) these groups in such ways that they are are socially superior. Therefore, queer and trans people of color are always viewed as a disruption to the established

system. The default status as disruptive can either be furthered by celebrating difference or it can be subordinated by assimilationist strategies that reify entrenched
heteronormativity.

Literature review

To recap, there are two types of lobbying: LGBTQ lobbying and gay mainstream
lobbying. LGBTQ lobbying is intersectional and centers the priorities, actions, and
agenda of the public policy process on those most marginalized: the poor, the
homeless, disabled, and migrants. The work of gay mainstream lobbying has led to
historic progress for the institution of heterosexuality.

The struggle for the future of lobbying is toward an approach that restructures
organizing, lobbying, and fundraising into an intersectional approach so the process of functioning demonstrates a change to the underlying power dynamics. At
issue is who gets power. For instance, abandoning the power and benefits that come
from hegemonic heterosexuality is hard, but necessary, if the LGBTQ community
is going to be anti-racist and pro-Black.

Restructuring the future of LGBTQ lobbying involves creating LGBTQ
organizations that change the power dynamics. One opportunity comes in the
form of an association for LGBTQ lobbying.

I founded Q Street in 2005. Q Street is the LGBTQ lobbyist and Government
Affairs Association in Washington, D.C. The first steering committee comprised
myself; Mara Keisling, who had founded the National Center for Transgender
Equality in 2003; Dave Noble, who was the Executive Director of Stonewall
Democrats; and Kevin Cain, who was the lead lobbyist for the American Diabetes
Association. I pitched the idea to them at the old X and O on Connecticut Avenue
in Dupont Circle (which became our organizing and meeting spot) and they were
all incredibly supportive, but curious to see how it would go. Figure 8.1 was the
first logo.

The original goals of Q Street were to create a network that allowed lobbyists to:

1. Connect all LGBTQ lobbyists with the LGBTQ legislative issues that the
    LGBTQ groups were working on;
2. Provide a way for corporate lobbyists to help LGBTQ groups gain access to
    Congressional members they wouldn't otherwise be able to; and
3. To build a community among the LGBTQ lobbyists so we had an identity
    in D.C.

Q was designed as a tool for maximizing the capacity of the LGBTQ lobbying
community around LGBT legislative issues. But there were major flaws. I was trying
to impress colleagues, so the first breakfasts took place at the expensive Mayflower
Hotel. This is both racist and classist.

The reason Q worked was that people showed up from the start. With support
from Mara, Dave, and Kevin, I said that I would put together a list of people and we

FIGURE 8.1 First Q Street logo

would start by having a launch event. The founding event was a reception at DDB Issues and Advocacy where I worked on New York Avenue.

We started with a list of about 50 people and I think there were 30 people at the launch. This was supported by my colleagues Joanne Howes (a co-founder of EMILY's list) and Adam Smith (now famous from his Texts with Hillary).

Following this, the breakfasts took off because people stepped up and came. For example, heavyweights like Trevor Potter and Jeff Trammel were willing to come and this lent Q credibility. From the start, Q was nonpartisan, and we all worked hard to make sure this was a safe space for lobbyists from every company or organization and every political party.

Q Street was able to leverage the power of many lobbyists to provide a service to those serving vulnerable populations during a very difficult time. It has continued to this day with an email list of 3,000 and has worked that delicate balance between corporate influence and non-profit organizing.

Methods

This study has highlighted the usefulness of participant-observation lobbying, providing narratives as data for LGBTQ studies and lobbying studies. The research has also addressed LGBTQ lobbying, the "ask," loser issues, the "heterosexual ask" as agenda-setting items, equality governance, and equality permanence.

The "heterosexual ask" and lobbying operate within the broader heterosexual public policy. In response, LGBTQ lobbying is one element of "marginalized lobbying," which focuses on intersectional issues and populations that are marginalized by systems and structures in society.

There are several areas of research that could also be expounded upon in the future. Most of these are related to media. For instance, there has been no main work to follow "The Celluloid Closet" by Russo (1981) which looked at the representation of LGBTQ people in film. *Acts of Gaiety* by Warner (2012) looks at performance art, *Queer Popular Culture* by Peele (2007) examines queer and trans moments in literature and media. Media also examines the role of newspapers in "Gay Press, Gay Power" by Baim (2012) and online communities (Wexelbaum, 2015).

Studies on international cases will also benefit the queer and trans communities. Current literature includes Namibia and South Africa (Currier, 2012), Somalia (Jama, 2015), global LGBTQ policies (Thoreson, 2014), and Australia (Willett, 2000).

The study of LGBTQ organizations could be of large benefit to LGBTQ studies as well as the organizations themselves. Groups like the Equality Federation, Equality Florida, Q Street, Silvia Rivera Law Project, National LGBTQ Chamber of Commerce, and Transgender Law Center could all be provided research information that they incorporate into their work. This would also build "LGBTQ lobbying" as an area of study and concept in the political science sub-field, within lobbying studies.

Data

The future of LGBTQ lobbying is open to change because of a flaw in the system.

In the absence of understanding and the presence of ambiguity, lobbyists can run their own show. They make the deals that they want and report back on what they want. For instance, I was once in a meeting where I was offered a job by a Congressman and never reported it; where I was told my boss was crazy and never reported it; got screamed at by a committee staffer, and never reported it; salvaged our issue from being abandoned by our lead office and never reported it. In each case I solved the problem, and in each case my boss would not have understood.

Again, it is unclear to most people what lobbyists do. This is on purpose. Lobbying as a profession is designed as a mostly self-regulating system in order to maximize ambiguity. A cloudy process is useful when dealing with academics, special interest groups, coalitions, and especially bosses. This makes lobbying powerful. Lobbying is seen as a "dark art" in the underbelly of politics. Something that happens in the shadows and hallways after hours. And yes, bluntly, it is all of these things. It is affirmatively ethically dubious at times. Yet, somehow produces results in the form of important federal legislation, illegal tickets to the ballet, or a well-deserved appointment to a commission, all in the same day.

But lobbying is something else. Lobbying is the third major political party. The one that is occasionally on the people's side and which operates in surprisingly open view and transparency. Corporations will always have both access and more access. It is for the marginalized populations that lobbying is so important. For these groups, their votes do not translate into representation. They are deviants and queers in a system based around white, male, English-speaking, cisgender, masculine, heterosexual, Christian, middle-class, able-bodied identities from the Global North.

This ambiguity serves the process of constructing hierarchies of identity. If people do not know where an identity came from, how it is reduced to one dimension and where power goes as a result of the hierarchy, then organizations are in a better position to invent characters.

Discussion

This book began with an intersectionally sensitive paradigm about shifting the underlying power dynamics between the privileged and the marginalized. Denying the benefits of racism to white people, the benefit of sexism to men, the benefits of homophobia to straight people, the benefits of transphobia to cisgender people, and the benefits of ableism to those without a disability. To conclude this book, I note four important takeaways:

1. Lobbying is the choice of the priority of the issue and the nature of the ask. This redefines what lobbying is. To advocate on behalf of an issue or cause to pass legislation;
2. The pressures and costs that define lobbying are about power and discomfort;
3. Heteronormative institutions are manipulating gay mainstream lobbying into reproducing oppression; and
4. Pride allows for a lens into the future of delegated recognition in the LGBTQ community.

Lobbying is the choice of the priority of the issue and the nature of the ask

I have argued that lobbying is the negotiation of power with the executive and legislative branches in ways that return power to the powerful; and the achievement of "the ask" through the imposition of political penalties. These elements reconsider lobbying.

Under this analysis, lobbying is not the advocacy of an issue to achieve policy change. Rather, it is the strategic choice of a political issue that may disrupt power and the ask, which may discomfort the powerful. It is power that achieves policy change, not "good" lobbying, therefore the focus of analysis should be on the direction of power.

The pressures and costs that define lobbying are about power and discomfort

Second, the research question posed at the start of this book was: Under what pressures and at what costs does LGBTQ lobbying occur?

The answers are centered around these six choices:

1. Power disrupted or power returned?
2. The "LGBTQ ask" or the "heterosexual ask"?
3. Equality permanence of equality governance?
4. Discomforting LGBTQ tactics or comforting gay mainstream tactics?
5. Loser issues or loser issues
6. The male gaze or intersectionality?

These are the pressures and costs that this book has outlined. These note the direction of power or the disruption of power.

Heteronormative institutions are manipulating gay mainstream lobbying into reproducing oppression

And third, heteronormative institutions find in lobbying a new way to oppress the LGBTQ community. They do so by manipulating the gay mainstream lobbying community into adopting heteronormative issues and tactics into seeking power for themselves, when the real benefit is the return of power to the powerful.

When gay mainstream lobbyists employ heteronormative issues and tactics this model reproduces racism, sexism, classism, ableism, transphobia, and homophobia that privileges the white, cis, male, religious, heterosexual society. In this we see heterosexuality gain an ally in spreading oppression. This includes the structural repetition of the heterosexual male gaze, sexual hierarchy, respectability politics, and norm setting for the emotional habitus and political trajectory of the community.

In addition, there is an opportunity cost to LGBTQ rights. The resources and time used to achieve gay mainstream victories aimed at assimilation and liberation have occurred in tandem with the hollowing out of the LGBTQ community, making the community more susceptible to legislative defeats.

Our own enemy: LGBTQ Pride

An analysis of Pride also illustrates the circumstances and future of LGBTQ lobbying. This is a critique of delegated recognition from the State and the other side of the institution of "Pride." This is not a judgement about the individual motivations of Pride. Institutionally, this includes two main points. First, the way heteronormative oppression can be reproduced in the decisions and priorities around the structures and systems that influence Pride. Second, how losing can look like winning for the LGBTQ community. This is not a dialectical approach. While I understand that Pride can be an enjoyable experience for some, the point of this analysis is to note the way Pride can harm others. It can represent corporate exploitation of the LGBTQ community to the benefit of heterosexual institutions. Pride can be assimilated into a collective narrative rather than the celebration of different types of individuals. Indeed, one example that helps illustrate how power is negotiated in the interests of the powerful is the concept of Pride.

I argue that Pride has a noble past as protest but that there are theoretical considerations of the way Pride is interpreted as vanity exercise and status-building routine. In addition, there are practical problems to the way Pride is implemented with a business model and as a corporate event. The Pride of today centers sexism, homophobia, racism, ableism, transphobia, serophobia, classism, and heteronormativity as dictated by the assimilation and respectability politics of the modern mainstream gay movement. It also centers the feelings of white, male, cis gays over the emotions of others. Pride as an emotional celebration privileges the emotions of those in the majority over those in the minority.

One important example of recognizing the different contexts of Pride as an individual event is the way Pride was a sign of life and "Pride in life," not just a lifestyle in the mid-1980s through the mid-1990s. I would argue that Pride was still much more consistent with a protest, but that may well have been at the individual level. Peterson, Wahlström, & Wennerhag (2018: 2) note:

> Since the first Pride demonstrations in 1970 in New York, Los Angeles and Chicago the tradition has travelled globally. Despite its origins in the US, the tradition has become translated into new contexts to suit different national and local settings. Pride parades today provide sites of tension and ambivalence—between commercialization and politicization, festivity and protest, normalization and contention.

Institutionally, in the Western colonized context, the feeling of Pride means you need to prove something to someone. To seek validation of the straight world or the gay world (the gay, white, cis world) rather than an acceptance of identity on the basis of identity, of doing absolutely nothing. Liberation is not seeking validation for doing something. Crawford and Ostrom (1995) note this component of Pride by stating that someone may gain pride for following a prescription or a set of social norms. In addition, Nathanson (1992: 83) defines pride in a clinical sense around three conditions, including

> (1) a purposeful, goal-directed, intentional activity is undertaken while under the influence of the affect interest–excitement; (2) this activity must be successful in achieving its goal; following which (3) the achievement of the goal suddenly releases the individual from the preceding effort and the affect that accompanies and amplifies it, thus triggering enjoyment-joy.

Therefore, Pride as a feeling that embodies an event also means to have achieved something. To be someone. To have done the prescribed task, bought the consumer good at the commensurate price. However, identity is still valid without the acceptance of others. Several concepts help articulate this.

If something does not affirmatively engender change then it comes at a cost. An opportunity cost. An opportunity cost is defined as the same expenditure of energy, money, time, or resources on the *next most* viable task or event. For instance, if the 50 states were not working on Pride events in June, what could they accomplish? This begs the question of what change does Pride produce? Visibility, yes. Sexual freedom, yes. Collective self-acceptance, maybe. But is this the end in itself? Is this as far as we need to go? Pride has become less about creating change for those who desperately need it, helping the helpless in our community. Yet change is the responsibility at hand. As uncomfortable or difficult a conversation as it is, let's take a moment and call out Pride for what it is, who it represents, and who it does not.

Latent power

I argue that Pride is perceived as "good" based on the norms of heteronormative society. This is a dynamic of power that is put on the LGBTQ community based on what political science literature refers to as "latent" power. This is about manipulating people's preferences to get them to willfully choose options that will ultimately harm them (Lukes, 1974). Lukes (1974: 24) characterizes latent power by saying:

> Is it not the supreme and most insidious use of power to prevent people, to whatever degree, from having grievances by shaping their perceptions, cognitions, and preferences in such a way that they accept their role in the existing order of things, either because they can see or imagine no alternative to it, or because they see it as natural and unchangeable, or because they value it as divinely ordained and beneficial?

In other words, Pride is a social construct that LGBTQ people believe gives them a degree of recognition and acceptance, but this recognition comes through a heteronormative lens that may only give us what we perceive to be individual freedom. We may be willfully embracing a liberal, heteronormative picture of limited Pride and acceptance.

Indigenous colonialization theory

Pride is a form of delegated recognition that ultimately oppresses the LGBTQ community. To make this argument, I review indigenous colonialization theory and argue that decolonization is an important lens through which to consider queer liberation from heteronormative oppression. In Glen Sean Coulthard's (2014) book *Red Skin, White Masks*, he addresses the way recognition of a community comes about. He states,

> First, I claimed that Fanon's critique of Hegel's theory of recognition convincingly unpacks the ways in which delegated exchanges of political

recognition from the colonizer to the colonized usually ends up being structurally determined by and in the interests of the colonizer.

(Coulthard, 2014: 152)

In other words, the oppressor writes the rules for allowable, tolerated, delegated recognition (Pride) in a way that preferences heterosexual institutions, not LGBTQ society. We are starting to see the limits of that oppressor toleration in some of the Pride celebrations across the country, including the Black Pride in D.C. and the Reclaim Pride Coalition.

Underlying this delegated recognition of Pride is the reality that the State is designed to return power to itself. However, Pride also returns power to heteronormative society when it reproduces systems of oppression that are consistent with the straight world, like racism, sexism, transphobia, and ableism, that can be seen in the way different groups are included or excluded from Pride events. For instance, not all events at Pride are wheelchair accessible, not all spaces consider neuroatypical people, and not all spaces are welcoming to women.

Assimilation is an important concept here because it is the process by which power exerts itself in the face of a threat. For instance, the State and its institutions see a threat from the LGBTQ community because the State is hetero-patriarchal and bounded by the fragility of white, male, masculinity. In response, the goal of the State is to erase a feeling of discomfort and disgust for the majority of the citizenry. So, erasure, assimilation of the different in the name of heteronormative masculinity, is the structural design of the State, and its institutional products (such as delegated recognition) work to preserve its interests.

In short, the oppressed should not accept anything from the oppressor. This specifically includes delegated recognition. The power dynamic at hand reinforces oppression. The oppressor cannot and does not give true freedom to the oppressed. Pride, as a form of delegated recognition, currently exists in the oppressor's world, not the LGBTQ world. Heteronormative institutions allow LGBTQ people to celebrate and march as guests in the hetero-cis world. As a result, Pride is designed to benefit the oppressor. This is why oppressor-based ideologies like racism, sexism, ableism, and classism are reproduced so easily in Pride parades and festivals, because they return power to the oppressor. In addition, this is why institutions like neo-liberalism and capitalism find a path to dominance in oppressor-based models.

There is also an emotional element to assimilation. Coulthard (2014: 152) adds, "Fanon also identifies the subtle ways in which colonized populations often come to develop what he called 'psycho-affective' attachments to these circumscribed, master-sanctioned forms of delegated recognition." In other words, a group can come to desire and emotionally benefit from the delegated recognition it receives from an oppressor. I believe this is where we have arrived at today. Pride provides an emotional high during the month of June or through parades and festivals, but ultimately leaves us all with painful after-effects.

The LGBTQ community pays three prices for the right to party. The first is assimilation to heteronormativity, which comes with the reproduction of oppressions. The second is the abidance to respectability norms in order to facilitate assimilation. In other words, dominant power dynamics will allow us to replicate their oppression if we demonstrate the commensurate amount of respectability to their norms. And the third price is the belief that in the face of assimilation we no longer need LGBTQ spaces for ourselves. Under a false sense of progress, we eliminate many of our spaces of difference that defined us as a people. This narrative often says, "I guess this is the natural trend of things." So, rather than seeing this as cultural erasure and heteronormative neo-imperialism, we welcome it as success and a natural state of affairs.

This is consistent with Coulthard (2014: 156), who notes, "According to this view, contemporary colonialism works *through* rather than entirely *against* freedom." What seems like true freedom is a version of freedom sold by the powerful to those without power as a way to gain the approval of people in power. As a result, the LGBTQ community feels like it owns Pride, when really this delegated recognition and freedom is a trap. Understanding this argument is helped by looking at Michel Foucault's understanding of power. Koopman (2017) notes that Foucault would say: "Power is all the more cunning because its basic forms can change in response to our efforts to free ourselves from its grip." Again, the sad reality is that there are different versions of freedom that are sold to different groups as a way of gaining their support.

To end this point, Coulthard (2014: 153) notes, "Fanon viewed these practices of Indigenous cultural self-empowerment, or *self-recognition*, as insufficient for decolonization." I would echo these sentiments. Pride (and the reproduction of oppression) does not solve the problem of a discriminatory society. It is also insufficient as an end point for reclaiming LGBTQ identity. As Simpson (2011: 17) notes, decolonization must happen "on our own terms, without the sanction, permission or engagement of the state."

Emotional oppression

Pride elicits some specific feelings and disregards others. This is a form of emotional oppression that we often overlook. Emotional oppression is under-critiqued in academia and in LGBTQ politics. Emotional oppression is based on two fundamental elements: people are oppressed for having certain emotions, and people are rewarded for certain emotional expressions.

This is seen often with LGBTQ people who are expected to have a prescribed emotion—"happy pride"—about the month of June. This includes the expectation to be "gay" or "proud." This produces emotionally exclusionary consequences. First, there is a hierarchy of emotions where some are accepted, and others denied. Being sad, depressed, or angry about "Pride" is not welcomed. Tweeting about how sad Pride makes you because you have depression is not seen as cool or in keeping with the context. In short, a person's full humanity is denied through emotional oppression. You are accepted only on the terms of expected emotional presentation.

Literal "Pride" has been proclaimed as the validated and correct emotion for LGBTQ people in acknowledgement of their gender identity and sexuality. This has been agreed upon by certain LGBTQ people (i.e. white, gay, cis men) and the majority of straight people. This is a form of emotional oppression that both oppresses other emotions and rewards "Pride" as an emotion by LGBTQ and straight people. Indeed, Pride is a distributive mechanism that does not allow for dangerous, radical emotions like outrage and depression, and instead is designed to be fun and happy.

Furthermore, there is a spatial and temporal element. Pride is often not seen as the right time for certain emotions, nor is it seen as the correct space for different emotions. The way in which emotions are delegated to space and time can be seen in other LGBTQ events. Transgender Day of Remembrance (TDOR) is seen as a moment for annual communal sadness. This is similar to previous attention toward World AIDS Day. However, today we hear more about transgender murders and less about AIDS deaths than we did 20 years ago, so there has been a shift in the sentimentality around the two events.

The question that I raise in this book relates to "why" again. Why are we celebrating while other people are experiencing trauma? Celebrations of self have their place, but they are not a means in and of itself. What has Pride accomplished? In many ways, it is designed to not work toward change. You don't change underlying power dynamics from a place of being happy. If you are proud and happy it is an unfortunate situation that change is less likely to happen. In all, there are emotional consequences to Pride in terms of how/if people are included and on what terms.

Governmentality

Pride is a self-governed concept by LGBTQ people. This collective consciousness raises a final element, which comes from what Foucault called "governmentality." Governmentality is the way people self-govern themselves by abiding by collective rules and norms. Coulthard (2014: 156) defines it in the Indigenous context as "a relatively diffuse set of governing relations that operate through a circumscribed mode of recognition that structurally ensures continued access to Indigenous peoples' lands and resources by producing neocolonial subjectivities that coopt Indigenous people into becoming instruments of their own dispossession." This point about "becoming instruments of their own dispossession" is important. Essentially, the argument is that by collectively agreeing to norms, emotions, and to reproduce oppressions, we are active participants in our own erasure and oppression. So, rather than Pride being an event that showcases sexuality and gender identity, it is a group exercise in self-erasure.

What does the State get when we believe that Pride is in our own best interests?

The State gets complicity from the LGBTQ community when we believe that Pride is in our own best interests. First, complicity means self-regulation (i.e. governmentality) and collective regulation of each other on the basis of the rules of the heteronormative social order. This is physical compliance and includes acceptance of the definitions of liberal freedom under these rules. Second, complicity is emotional compliance and submission. A feeling that translates into LGBTQ affection for a system of oppression that is built to subjugate the LGBTQ community. Actively believing in the best interests and continuation of Pride even when it provides select rewards to some but reproduces systems of oppression toward others. In short, all are ultimately punished by this system. Third, complicity is the belief that Pride is the only path to self-recognition. This is the liberal definition of freedom and delegated way toward an LGBTQ identity. The only way to move forward is to work within the prescribed system. Fourth, the path for de-marginalization currently asks LGBTQ people to comply with the system rather than change the system. Indeed, Pride puts the onus on us to change and be accepted.

In all, I have reviewed the theoretical objections to Pride. Here, we see the liberal heteronormative version of freedom on display for LGBTQ people. This definition and understanding of freedom as something given by the State creates the foundation for how LGBTQ people navigate the transition from the closet to being out. Pride is a key piece of this. Straight people allow us to have Pride events because they think they are getting the better deal. It is ultimately an event that returns power (in this case enjoyment without any challenge to power dynamics) back to themselves.

However, the recognition of the State is immaterial to the dignity of the individual. Reclaiming dignity from the State is not possible because the State cannot and does not provide dignity to LGBTQ people. It is not designed to do so. The State is designed to assimilate differences in order to maintain power for those in power, heterosexuals. Pride convinces the LGBTQ community that we seek assimilation, creating erasure from within our communities and facilitating our own eradication. To be clear, Pride serves the interests of straight people by allowing LGBTQ people a degree of delegated symbolic recognition while delivering no real action. I would like now to move beyond the theoretical and look at the practical implementation of Pride as a series of events across the United States.

Pride events

Pride has not always been bad or performatively self-obsessed. Yet today, Pride obscures our power and our oppression. Imagine if you will, the largest series of events for a community in every major city, with presidential candidates marching, support from the public, and the attention of the whole world. And what do you get for this visibility? What tangible achievement is met by such monumental collective action, annually? For a month of festivities? You might think this was the most well-funded, legislatively successful, publicly supported movement in America. That would be the expectation for such a given set of statistics (see Table 8.1). What if there was a month-long public demonstration of 12 million attendees across the entire country, annually, with virtually no opposition, with no federal laws passed, few state laws passed, few city council ordinances passed, and that instead

TABLE 8.1 Leading Annual Pride attendance by city

City	Attendees	State
Anchorage	8,000	AK
Fayetteville	16,000	AR
Little Rock	3,000	AR
Conway	500	AR
Huntsville	300	AL
Birmingham	20,000	AL
Phoenix	37,000	AZ
Flagstaff	6,000	AZ
Tucson	6,000	AZ
Los Angeles	170,000	CA
Anaheim (Gay Days, Disneyland)	30,000	CA
Chula Vista	7,000	CA
Pasadena	1,000	CA
Davis	4,000	CA
San Diego	360,000	CA
Oceanside	7,000	CA
Santa Rosa	5,000	CA
Sacramento	18,000	CA
Palm Springs	125,000	CA
Orange County	25,000	CA
San Francisco	1,000,000	CA
Fresno	3,000	CA
San Jose	10,000	CA
Long Beach	80,000	CA
Oakland	42,000	CA
Durango	1,000	CO
Colorado Springs	50,000	CO
Denver	425,000	CO
Longmont	3,000.00	CO
New London	1,000	CT
Norwalk	3,000	CT
District of Columbia	400,000	D.C.
Dover	3,500	DE
Bradenton	4,000	FL
Miami Beach	145,000	FL
St. Petersburg	200,000	FL
Fort Lauderdale	120,000	FL
Jacksonville	20,000	FL
Tampa	50,000	FL
Melbourne	10,000	FL
Pensacola	40,000	FL
Lake Worth	25,000	FL
Wilton Manors	40,000	FL
Tallahassee	3,500	FL

(*continued*)

TABLE 8.1 Cont.

City	Attendees	State
Palm Beach	20,000	FL
Orlando	150,000	FL
Augusta	14,000	GA
Savannah	15,000	GA
Atlanta	300,000	GA
Honolulu	30,000	HI
Boise	60,000	ID
Des Moines	25,000	IA
Chicago	1,000,000	IL
Bloomington	15,000	IN
Indianapolis	50,000	IN
Kansas City	33,000	KS
Wichita	2,000	KS
Lexington	30,000	KY
Covington	2,000	KY
Louisville	15,000	KY
West Hollywood	170,000	CA
Baton Rouge	14,000	LA
New Orleans	82,000	LA
Worcester	20,000	MA
Boston	750,000	MA
Baltimore	30,000	MD
Portland	10,000	ME
Bangor	2,500	ME
Lansing	6,000	MI
Ferndale	20,000	MI
Detroit	25,000	MI
Pine City	400	MN
Minneapolis	400,000	MN
St. Louis	300,000	MO
Kansas City	33,000	MO
Biloxi	800	MS
Starkville	2,500	MS
Helena	5,000	MT
Charlotte	165,000	NC
Asheville	10,000	NC
Greensboro	15,000	NC
Winston-Salem	29,000	NC
Fayetteville	3,000	NC
Raleigh	62,000	NC
Omaha	5,000	NE
Rochester	3,000	NH
Portsmouth	4,000	NH
Deming	8,000	NM
Santa Fe	3,000	NM
Albuquerque	14,000	NM

TABLE 8.1 Cont.

City	Attendees	State
Ashbury Park	25,000	NJ
Reno	10,000	NV
Las Vegas	10,000	NV
Albany	30,000	NY
Long Island	10,000	NY
Brooklyn	40,000	NY
Harlem	15,000	NY
Queens	40,000	NY
White Plains	1,000	NY
Syracuse	5,000	NY
Buffalo	20,000	NY
New York City	2,000,000	NY
Cincinnati	100,000	OH
Dayton	5,000	OH
Toledo	10,000	OH
Cleveland	6,500	OH
Sandusky	150	OH
Columbus	500,000	OH
Oklahoma City	85,000	OK
Tulsa	30,000	OK
Eugene	5,000	OR
Lincoln City	1,000	OR
Portland	60,000	OR
Bend	5,000	OR
Philadelphia	25,000	PA
Lancaster	7,000	PA
Phoenixville	1,000	PA
Providence	100,000	RI
Harrisburg	1,000	PA
New Hope	15,000	PA
Pittsburgh	95,000	PA
Columbia	85,000	SC
Charleston	5,000	SC
Nashville	75,000	TN
Knoxville	6,000	TN
Memphis	15,000	TN
Houston	500,000	TX
Austin	400,000	TX
Dallas	50,000	TX
Beaumont	2,500	TX
San Antonio	10,000	TX
Fort Worth	5,000	TX
El Paso	12,000	TX
Salt Lake City	60,000	UT

(*continued*)

TABLE 8.1 Cont.

City	Attendees	State
Bellingham	10,000	WA
Tacoma	15,000	WA
Spokane	24,000	WA
Bremerton	2,000	WA
Olympia	15,000	WA
Seattle	400,000	WA
Milwaukee	45,787	WI
Green Bay	10,000	WI
Madison	2,000	WI
Cheyenne	120	WY
Centreville	4,000	VA
Richmond	15,000	VA
Hampton Roads	30,000	VA
Burlington	3,000	VT
Total:	**12,449,257**	

featured high rates of transgender murder, high rates of youth suicide, bullying in school, high rates of LGBTQ youth homelessness, almost no fundraising for state-wide LGBTQ organizations, little federal infrastructure, and more LGBTQ spaces going out of business? You would say I was mad. That, nationally, Pride surely must produce more. That at the very least the goodwill from thousands of events should count for something.

It would be a scandal. The voices would be calling for restructuring, not that we continue to leave out real change until people lose interest and the funding dries up. Surely, it would be hubris to believe the party or parade never ends. Indeed, this would mean we are left with a further weakened LGBTQ social infrastructure.

I argue that the current conception of Pride is not a series of events about difference, but rather performances of curated consumer capitalism about sameness, to show each other how to behave the same in keeping with heteronormative institutions and perceptions. Heterosexuality is the big winner from Pride. Currently, the emotions around Pride connect LGBTQ people to a consumer identity. The definition of consumerized is "to make (goods or a product) suitable or available for mass consumption" (Dictionary.com, 2020). Pride is therefore a form of mass assimilation. While some would argue that the rate of equality for the LGBTQ community has been historically fast, I would argue that instead what we are seeing is a fast rate of LGBTQ assimilation.

Pride is consumerized when organizations attach Pride to their brand identity and the brand is designed for mass consumption. Pride is connected to their version of a specific LGBTQ identity. This is a white, male, masculine, cis, gay, thin, able-bodied, young, sexualized brand. In addition, when certain items are constructed to be imbued with Pride, such as putting a rainbow on a product, it is a retail identity. Items instilling Pride can be bought or sold. The items of identity are transferable. They can be passed from one person to another. Finally, consumerization occurs when certain items are saturated with Pride, meaning that something is known to produce Pride in someone relative to other groups of people, and this is replicated to produce Pride in masses of people. This includes the possession of money relative to the poor, being a happy gay person relative to being sinful, being in a couple relative to being single. So, this produces an individual experience of being "better" than others in order to counteract anti-LGBTQ discrimination that says someone is worse than others.

This effort to consumerize LGBTQ culture can be seen in comments about "rainbow capitalism." Maine Ethics (2018) notes that:

> Rainbow capitalism is when businesses incorporate queerness and the LGBTQ+ rights movement into their marketing, products, etc. in order to capitalize off of the purchasing power that queer people have. Rainbow capitalism was a move by companies to market themselves as queer friendly to get LGBTQ+ consumers to buy their products. Rainbow capitalism was also designed to take advantage of the new wave of allyship for queer people. It thrives in part because of the acceptance of white, gay, cisgender people, while erasing queer POC, because in our society those people aren't as "socially accepted" in terms of consumption.

To be clear, I have no objection to parties, parades, festivals, 5k runs, dog shows, flamboyance, breasts, dicks, super camp, dancing, consensual sex in public, leather, bears, furries, plushies, drag culture, gender play, spanking, orgies, polyamory, reproductive sexuality, bath houses, or communes.

The issue for me, as an academic and lobbyist, is the discrepancy between the focus of the LGBTQ community on parties and our responsibilities to help those in need. This is a choice, the same choice as in lobbying where one issue is prioritized and another one disappears.

I argue that Pride is not appropriate if our community's suicide rate, homelessness rate, homicide rate, arrest rate, and incarceration rate have not been addressed. The combination of poverty, unemployment, and discrimination toward transgender people of color, which has exacerbated arrests for sex work and incarceration of transgender people, are issues that go to the heart of how Pride is conceptualized, who it is for, and who it is not for. For instance, below is a list of problems in the LGBTQ community while Pride is being celebrated.

Problems in the LGBTQ community while Pride is being celebrated

There are ongoing critical problems in the LGBTQ community. For instance, systematic neglect is killing queer youth and lesbians. This reminds me of what Bobby Kennedy said, "For there is another kind of violence, slower but just as deadly, destructive as the shot or the bomb in the night. This is the violence of institutions; indifference and inaction and slow decay" (Kennedy, 1968). Indeed, the state of the

LGBTQ community in the United States includes a number of considerations, including the annual U.S. suicide rate, which increased 24% between 1999 and 2014, from 10.5 to 13.0 suicides per 100,000 people, the highest rate recorded in 28 years. According to Reuters, "24 percent of the suicide deaths in the 12 to 14 age group were among LGBT youth in 2013–2015" (Rapaport, 2019). LGBTQ people made up 8% of suicides among young adults 25 to 29 years old. LGB adults are more than twice as likely as heterosexual adults to experience a mental health condition. According to the Williams Institute, 40% of the homeless youth served by agencies identify as LGBTQ (Durso & Gates, 2012). There are no laws banning conversion therapy in 32 states.

There were also more than 37 murders of trans and gender non-conforming people in 2020, and 26 in 2019. In 2018, gay and bisexual men accounted for 26,197 new HIV diagnoses in the United States (Centers for Disease Control, 2018). Twenty-four percent of lesbians and bisexual women are poor, compared with only 19% of heterosexual women. African American same-sex couples are significantly more likely to be poor than African American married heterosexual counterparts and are roughly three times more likely to live in poverty than white same-sex couples. In addition, President Trump has banned transgender military service. Twenty-nine states have laws on the books that criminalize HIV transmission. We also see raids and police harassment that still occur at LGBTQ cruising spots. There are continued transgender arrests, transgender imprisonment, and transgender convictions for sex work. Only 20 states and the District of Columbia have anti-discrimination or anti-bullying laws that explicitly protect LGBTQ students. Thirty states do not collect data on sexual orientation. Senior care discrimination and elder abuse against LGBTQ people is rampant. LGBTQ domestic violence goes on without attention or funding. Finally, lesbian cancer is barely a thought outside of lesbian circles.

On this last point, it is alarming to read from the National LGBT Cancer Network (2019):

> So far, the information we have on breast cancer in lesbians has been both limited and contradictory. The large national cancer registries and surveys *do not collect data about sexual orientation*, leaving lesbians embedded and invisible among this vast wealth of information.

This is criminal. And it is an affirmatively political decision to avoid collecting this lifesaving data. The LGBTQ community as a whole should be outraged. The items above point to a set of community challenges that are not priorities for the vast majority of the community, even as we celebrate Pride.

Conclusion

This book has contributed to the literature which states that queerness and transness is important because they challenge other social constructions and break down norms and oppressions that can free the gay mainstream lobbying and heterosexual community of their homophobia, transphobia, racism, sexism, classism, and ableism. Put another way, this book is challenging the status queer.

Indeed, we should have narrative tactics that do not appeal to the whitest middle-class donor base, but rather centers marginalized identities, people of color, the poor, those living in precarity, poverty and income insecurity, and on the margins. This is an opportunity for learning for the advantaged who are engaged in gay mainstream lobbying.

In this book, I have argued for a new conception of lobbying, LGBTQ lobbying. This falls under an umbrella of marginalized lobbying. Here, the argument being made is that there are many different ways to approach lobbying. This is no one shape or type of lobbying, but like all mixtures of art and science, there are elements and versions that suit distinctive lobbyists on different issues, at various times.

Reconsidering advocacy discourse in the LGBTQ community is not new. For instance, the "GLBT" initials and acronym came out of defensiveness. Murib (2017: 19) notes that the formation of the GLBT identity was part of frame or stigma transformation, which "describes a process through which political actors modify existing framings of group identity and associated political interests to generate new understandings of the group that will attract more participants and garner broad support." Therefore, GLBT was more than an acronym but a framing device to introduce a unified coalition to the public and push back against far-right opponents. This linkage of four identities meant something more as a collective than any consideration of singular gay rights previously. It suggested a new marginalized identity, a unified agenda and collective force that was now politically legitimate across the advocacy community.

Finally, this chapter critiqued Pride as a flawed priority in the LGBTQ community. I note that Pride celebrations differ from Pride protests of the past. Current Pride celebrations come in the form of delegated recognition from an oppressor, which places the LGBTQ community in a weakened position. In addition, Pride is prioritized by the community but achieves little in the face of other real challenges. These challenges—like women's health—are instead made invisible.

The end.

References

Baim, T. (Ed.). (2012). *Gay Press, Gay Power: The Growth of LGBT Community Newspapers in America*. Prairie Avenue Productions and Windy City Media Group.

Centers for Disease Control (2018). HIV and gay and bisexual men. www.cdc.gov/hiv/group/msm/index.html

Coulthard, G.S. (2014). *Red Skin, White Masks: Rejecting the Colonial Politics of Recognition*. University of Minnesota Press.

Crawford, S.E.S., & Ostrom, E. (1995). A grammar of institutions. *The American Political Science Review, 89*(3), 582–600.

Currier, A. (2012). The aftermath of decolonization: Gender and sexual dissidence in postindependence Namibia. *Signs, 37*(2), 441–467. https://doi.org/10.1086/661715

Dictionary.com (2020). *Consumerize.* www.dictionary.com/

Durso, L.E., & Gates, G. J. (2012). *Serving our youth: Findings from a national survey of services providers working with lesbian, gay, bisexual and transgender youth who are homeless or at risk of becoming homeless.* Williams Institute. https://escholarship.org/uc/item/80x75033

Jama, A. (2015). *Being Queer and Somali: LGBT Somalis at Home and Abroad.* Oracle Releasing.

Kennedy, R. (1968). Remarks to the Cleveland City Club, April 5, 1968. John F. Kennedy Presidential Library. www.jfklibrary.org/learn/about-jfk/the-kennedy-family/robert-f-kennedy/robert-f-kennedy-speeches/remarks-to-the-cleveland-city-club-april-5-1968

Koopman, C. (2017, March 15). Why Foucault's work on power is more important than ever. Aeon. https://aeon.co/essays/why-foucaults-work-on-power-is-more-important-than-ever

Lukes, S. (1974). *Power: A Radical View.* Macmillan Press.

Maine Ethics (2018). What is rainbow capitalism? Main Ethics. https://maineethics.com/mainemusings/whatisrainbowcapitalism

Murib, Z. (2017). Rethinking GLBT as a political category in U.S. politics. In M. Brettschneider, S. Burgess, & C. Keating (Eds.), *LGBTQ Politics: A Critical Reader* (pp. 14–33). New York University Press.

Nathanson, D.L. (1992). *Shame and Pride: Affect, Sex, and the Birth of the Self.* W.W. Norton.

National LGBT Cancer Network (2019). *Lesbians and breast cancer risk.* https://cancer-network.org/cancer-information/lesbians-and-cancer/lesbians-and-breast-cancer-risk

Peele, T. (Ed.). (2007). *Queer Popular Culture: Literature, Media, Film, and Television.* Palgrave Macmillan.

Pepin-Neff, C., & Wynter, T. (2020). The costs of pride: Survey results from LGBTQI activists in the United States, United Kingdom, South Africa, and Australia. *Politics & Gender, 16*(2), 1–27. https://doi.org/10.1017/S1743923X19000205

Peterson, A., Wahlström, M., & Wennerhag, M. (2018). *Pride Parades and LGBT Movements: Political Participation in an International Comparative Perspective.* Routledge.

Rapaport, L. (2019, February 21). One in four pre-teen suicides may be LGBT youth. *Reuters.* https://in.reuters.com/article/instant-article/idUSKCN1QA2JQ

Russo, V. (1981). *The Celluloid Closet: Homosexuality in the Movies.* Harper & Row.

Simpson, L.B. (2011). *Dancing on Our Turtle's Back: Stories of Nishnaabeg Re-Creation, Resurgence, and a New Emergence.* Arbeiter Ring Publishing.

Thoreson, R.R. (2014). *Transnational LGBT Activism: Working for Sexual Rights Worldwide.* University of Minnesota Press.

Warner, S. (2012). *Acts of Gaiety: LGBT Performance and the Politics of Pleasure.* University of Michigan.

Wexelbaum, R. (Ed.). (2015). *Queers Online: LGBT Digital Practices in Libraries, Archives, and Museums.* Litwin Books.

Willett, G. (2000). *Living Out Loud: A History of Gay and Lesbian Activism in Australia.* Allen & Unwin.

INDEX

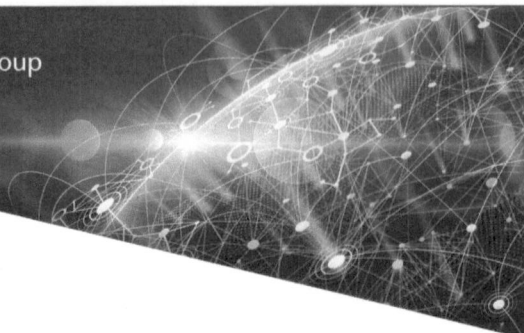